ADVANCE PRAISE FOR

THE PROBLEM SOLVING JOURNEY

"Hoenig's unblinking curiosity about the thinking process has produced one of the most original and useful business books of the year. What keeps us coming back to this serious and analytical work is his uncanny gift of making a quote or a vignette into a window—with something always happening on the other side that makes the elusive magic of problem solving a grand and systematic process."

—*Naomi Seligman, Founder, The Research Board*

"Chris Hoenig has cracked the code on how professionals can solve problems faster, cheaper and better, using technology as an ally rather than a crutch. This book not only changes the way we navigate complex problems, it changes how we think about navigating those problems."

—*Tim McClure, Co-founder, GSD&M Advertising*

"One doesn't usually describe a professional book as a 'page-turner,' but that fittingly describes Chris Hoenig's *The Problem Solving Journey*. The adventure of reading it is as rewarding as the ultimate destination, a comprehensive insight into and understanding of what it takes to optimize your problem-solving skills. It's as much a guide book for life as it is an instruction manual for professional success."

—*Dr. Alan B. Salisbury, former Chairman of Learning Tree International USA, Inc, and COO of the Microelectronics and Computer Technology Corp. (MCC)*

"Problem solving is the key to managing in the information age yet, until this book, no one had provided the roadmap to becoming a world class problem solver. Hoenig's book maps out this route and offers numerous valuable tools in a lively and engaging format that draws the reader into the minds of great problem solvers—revealing what you can learn from them and apply in your own work. This book is indispensable to anyone who aspires to be a leader in the new economy."

—*Donald Gips, Group Vice-President, Global Marketing & Sales, Level 3 Communications*

"*The Problem Solving Journey* combines the best from the fields of leadership, managerial decision making, problem solving, and knowledge management. Hoenig's six problem solving 'personalities' will frame these fields and the very nature of professional work for years to come."
> —*Guilbert Hentschke, Professor of Education and Management, Rossier School of Education, University of Southern California*

"From the challenge to the complete solution, this seminal work on problem solving is a 'must- read' for all senior executives *and* those aspiring to be. Certain to become a graduate level text/reference book, it should also be every project manager's bible. Chris Hoenig has captured and blended the art, science, discipline and psychology of problem solving in a unique and thoroughly credible, and easily understood guide, applicable to any-sized problem—the bigger the better. Breaking the process into six basic and logical elements, he beautifully defines and explains them using highly topical, interesting and relevant real cases, leaving little or nothing to the imagination. If I were a CEO, I would have a copy in the hands of all my senior staff!"
> —*Major General Don Lasher (ret), and former Chief Information Officer, USAA*

"For journalists, executives, teachers and all professionals, this book is an entertaining and accessible guide to problem solving. Chris Hoenig outlines six essential 'skills,' mapping a clear path through the process. The book offers the reader both inspirational and practical tools to achieve personal and professional goals."
> —*Roberta Oster Sachs, Emmy award-winning network news producer*

"This is the best business book since *In Search of Excellence*. Instead of telling the 'what' stories of great companies, Hoenig explains the 'how' behind great problem solvers. The result is a timeless recipe for business success that is a must-read for everyone from Fortune 100 CEOs to Web entrepreneurs."
> —*Tom Melcher, former Executive Vice-President for Strategic Development at CNET and currently CEO of There, Inc.*

"Having the right knowledge is vital to survival in the age of information overload. Hoenig provides the precisely tailored, high value knowledge we all need to get ahead and stay ahead."
> —*James Adams, CEO of IDefense, Inc.*

THE
PROBLEM
SOLVING
JOURNEY

The
PROBLEM
SOLVING
JOURNEY

Your Guide to
Making Decisions
and Getting Results

CHRISTOPHER HOENIG

PERSEUS PUBLISHING
Cambridge, Massachusetts

Author photo by Linda Creighton.

A CIP catalog record for this book is available from the Library of Congress.

ISBN 0-7382-0280-0

Perseus Publishing is a member of the Perseus Books Group.

Text design by Jeff Williams
Set in 10-point New Caledonia by Perseus Publishing Services

Perseus Publishing titles are available at special discounts for bulk purchases in the U.S. by corporations, institutions, and other organizations. For more information, please contact the Special Markets Department at HarperCollins Publishers, 10 East 53rd Street, New York, NY 10022, or call 212-207-7528.

Find us on the World Wide Web at http://www.perseuspublishing

First printing, October 2000
1 2 3 4 5 6 7 8 9 10—02 01 00

To the love of my life—Susan.

Your patience has humbled me. Your life force has inspired me.
Your dedication has enabled me. Your beauty has moved me.
Your spirit has sustained me, and your love has surrounded me.
May our own adventures continue to grow in splendor,
and may the sound of our footsteps on the road together echo softly
forever.

To my daughter, Sophia.
The princess of our hearts and the queen of your destiny;
What a miracle you have brought to our journey through life
with your priceless lessons and purest of joy.

The problems that exist in the world cannot be solved by the level of thinking that created them.

ALBERT EINSTEIN (1879–1955)

It is not the strongest of the species that survives, nor the most intelligent;
It is the one that is most adaptable to change.

CHARLES DARWIN (1809–1882)

Our problems are man-made; therefore, they can be solved by man.
And man can be as big as he wants.
No problem of human destiny is beyond human beings.

PRESIDENT JOHN F. KENNEDY (1917–1963)

CONTENTS

1   Generate the Mindset

Develop Potent Ideas and Attitudes   *1*

The Innovator: Examples from Visa International (Former
President Dee Hock), the consumer safety movement
(Ralph Nader), Amazon.com (CEO Jeff Bezos), literature
and the arts (Toni Morrison), Prudential Life Insurance
(Former President Ron Barbaro), and the U.S. Marine
Corps (Commandant Charles Krulak (ret.))

2   Know the Territory

Ask the Right Questions and Get Good Information   *37*

The Discoverer: Examples from Monsanto Chemical (CEO
Robert Shapiro), Celera Corporation (Dr. Craig Venter),
Human Genome Sciences (Dr. William Haseltine), weather
prediction (NOAA, Dr. Ants Leetmaa, Dr. D. James Baker),

6 Deliver the Results

Practice Intuitive, Disciplined Execution 203

The Performer: Examples from around the world solo sailboat racing (Isabelle Autissier), Federal Express (Former CIO Ron Ponder), IBM (CEO Lou Gerstner), Stanford Law School (Dean Kathleen Sullivan), Enron Energy (President Jeff Skilling), Skyscraper Construction (Dominic Fonti), and the Department of Defense Stealth Program (Paul Kaminski)

PREFACE

Knowing how simple elements generate complex results is the ultimate source of power.

Three primary colors blend to make up the paintings and films that capture our imagination. Twelve notes underlie the beautiful music that lifts our hearts and spirits. Five fundamental forces are at the heart of how the physical universe works. Four amino acids code the instructions for creating every form of life on Earth. Two binary states are the foundation of the digital processing that underpins the information age.

In each of these cases, a journey of mastery began by isolating a few basic elements and continued by acquiring the deep knowledge of how they interact—whether it is to produce art, the cosmos, life, or the Web. Each time such knowledge is developed, vast amounts of human potential are unleashed.

In the same way, there are six essential skills involved in human problem solving—generating mindset, acquiring knowledge, building relationships, managing problems, creating solutions, and delivering results. This book defines those six essentials, explains them, helps you assess the nature of your ability, and shows how the essentials can be applied to any problem or opportunity you're trying to solve. The tougher, larger, and more demanding a problem or opportunity is, the faster and more competitive your environment is, the more important these six essential skills become.

I don't mean the "old" problem solving—traditional cookbook approaches that are small-scale, linear, deficiency-oriented, and tactical. I do mean a "new" and rapidly evolving definition of problem solving that encompasses large scale, nonlinear, opportunity-oriented, and strategic work. This is problem solving in the age of biotech, the Web, smart materials, and the global economy.

We live in an era where technology is our primary tool, knowledge the strategic asset, and problem solving the paramount skill. Problem solving ability is now the most sought-after trait in up-and-coming executives, according to a recent survey of 1,000 executives by Caliper Associates, reported in the *Wall Street Journal* by Hal Lancaster, "Managing Your Career." In an economy where knowledge is power and professionals face tougher, more complex issues and possibilities at an accelerating rate, no one can expect to succeed without knowing how to solve problems—how to gather information, weigh options, make decisions, and take effective action. To put it bluntly, if you're not a problem solver, your career potential is limited.

Nevertheless, in every sector of our economy, thousands of projects and initiatives are started every day, in processes involving people, technology, and knowledge assets, that waste resources and/or fail to deliver. The reason is a capability gap, rooted in mismanaged knowledge, hard-to-control technology, and inadequate problem solving skills.

What is at the root of this problem solving gap? Common knowledge. Common knowledge of these six essentials and how they interact.

When groups of professionals share knowledge and vocabulary, their efficiency and effectiveness skyrocket. Yet in a world where ever more opportunities cut across the lines of disciplines, professions, or industries, most of us are entrenched in specialties and stovepipes, often divided and conquered by experts. We look at parts, not parts and wholes. We focus on tasks instead of problems, problems instead of opportunities, and opportunities instead of adventures. We are still drowning in information overload, still reinventing wheels too often, mesmerized by technologies that don't always match real problems, and dazzled by promoters who lack enduring fundamentals or essential values.

The common knowledge that underlies problem solving excellence is timeless; it has been trapped, fragmented, and confused for too long. Why is this? Many great problem solvers are simply unaware of how they do it. Others know, but only pass the knowledge on in a few carefully chosen mentoring relationships. Once a portion is uncovered, it goes to serve a new consulting firm that meters it out at thousands per day. And few of the resources available today—management books, training programs, consulting services, or even websites—adequately address this gap. What is needed is a clear outline of the universal knowledge that underpins excellence in problem solving, making it widely accessible.

This book distills the essence of that common knowledge, gleaned from two decades of research and practice in this field. To illustrate the six essential skills, I've carefully chosen nearly forty intriguing case study vignettes that show how the knowledge is applied in a multitude of fields—including medicine, engineering, science, business, art, law, and government. The problem solvers themselves range from Nobel laureates and CEOs, social workers and investigators, to coaches and artists. Inside these covers you can identify your own problem solving profile and navigate the six essentials of a problem solving journey, from how to generate the mindset to what's necessary to deliver results.

The book also explains that much of this essential knowledge already resides in each of us. It is waiting to be discovered, shared, and exploited to create and realize untapped individual and collective potential.

Some have already started the problem solving journey. They include individuals and organizations that have arrived at a new level of performance. They are a new generation of problem solvers, who have speed, efficiency, maneuverability, high thrust, and sophisticated levels of control. They form and reform organizations and alliances with great fluidity to match progressions of problems and opportunities. They achieve high rates of innovation and evolve rapidly to meet changing market demands and possibilities. They are determining the future of their professions, their communities, their nations, and our world. Above all, they are thinking on a new level.

I invite you to join them and encourage you to read about these six essentials, understand them, disagree about them, apply them, test them, and teach them. You will find that they represent a source of general knowledge that is powerful but often hidden from view. Bringing it out into the open can help you and your organization go places you've never been before.

ACKNOWLEDGEMENTS

This work has germinated and blossomed over more than ten years. It could never have been successful without loved ones who encouraged, friends who advised, professional colleagues who assisted, and readers who critiqued, as well as the great and generous men and women from whom I learned so much by working with them, questioning them, observing them, or reading about them. Nevertheless, in the end, I am the only one responsible for any errors that remain.

I owe an incalculable debt of gratitude to these people who helped, assisted, supported, reviewed, edited, researched, believed in, and comforted me over the years: Susan Riker, who endured the trials and tribulations only the wife of an author can know; Dick Bennett, Ed Brush, Larry Gruver, Gaston De Gara, and Ed Bettendorf, who all saw the man within the boy; Richard Langhorne, who nurtured the first seed of inspiration fifteen years ago; James Adams, who kicked me out the door and got me on the road; Wayne Kabak, who met me there and took me the first great distance; Scott Gould, Michele Flournoy, John and Betsy Neiva, Roberta Oster, Clarence and Pat Hoenig, Harland and Ann Riker, Gretchen Hoenig, Don Gips, Liz Berry, David Riker, and Liz Hoenig, who cheered, encouraged, supported, and believed in me from the start; Marv Langston, a peerless intellect, valued friend, and early patron saint who helped bring the idea to life; Jack Harris, Gail Polsby, and Beth Naftalin, who provided wise counsel all along the way; Karen Ball, an author's ideal companion, who researched so professionally and wrote the case study foundations with energy and insight; Greg Lichtenberg, who helped edit the manuscript in its final stages, working closely with me to turn a very rough diamond into something approaching a gemstone; Erik Calonius, David Whitman and Lynn Rosellini, Mavis Schelly, David Cole, Bart van Dissel, Bill Roege, Richard Weatherly, Rob Leland, John Britti, Bruce McConnell, Kim Corthell, Jim Whittaker and Steve Ritterbush, who all critiqued and/or edited portions of the manuscript at various stages along the way and invariably told me what I needed to hear; James Hritz, who contributed important research; Scott Gould, Andrea Weiss, and Lauren Fox, my partners, who stuck by me as I struggled to balance the challenges of being an author and a CEO; Tom Melcher and John Driscoll, my devoted friends, who always told me the right direction to go in, even if I wasn't ready to hear it yet (Tom, one of the best problem solvers I know, also contributed deeply to the design and essence of the book); Margot Singer, Karl Keller, John Koskinen, Michael Doyle, David McClure, Tim McClure, Gene Dodaro, Ona Noble, Edith Pyles, Vincent Sweeney, and Helen Ward, who all, in their various ways, contributed to my inspiration, confidence, and determination to complete this project; Rockwell Kent, whose graphic art in that jewel of a book, *N by E,* captured my imagination by evoking the pathos of the journey; the Rockwell Kent Legacies and the University Press of New England, who gave me permission to use Kent's graphics; all the participants in the interviews and case studies, who gave their valuable time in the interest of a greater good; my board members, who offered both helpful insights and unflinching support; Marco Pavia, who expertly guided the manuscript to publication; Silvine Marbury Farnell, who brilliantly and professionally found the flaws and provided the fine grit to polish the final version; and especially to Nick Philipson, my editor at Perseus Books, who was an unfailing champion through the entire process, and who with insight, professionalism, camaraderie, and the highest degree of civility, made the best possible traveling companion for this problem solving journey. Finally, for anyone I have inadvertantly missed, please forgive my oversight and accept my humblest apology.

INTRODUCTION:
THE SPIRIT OF THE JOURNEY

Men go out into the void spaces of the world for various reasons.
Some are actuated simply by a love of adventure, some have the keen
thirst for scientific knowledge, and others again are drawn away from
the trodden path by the "lure of little voices," the mysterious fascination
of the unknown.

—SIR ERNEST SHACKLETON (1874–1922)

Take a moment and ask yourself this—what are the two or three toughest problems or opportunities you've ever solved? A daunting project? A difficult working relationship? A threatening situation? A complex question or decision? When you have the images of your experiences in mind, then consider—what were the lessons you learned from them? What were the things in each case that really made a difference and that could continue to make a difference in future situations? You've now taken the first step on the problem solving journey, thinking on a higher level, and if you read ahead, you'll never look back.

At 6:45 P.M., on October 24, 1915, Sir Ernest Shackleton was, however, starting to look back. He had begun an ocean voyage from England six months ago, and was now more than 10,000 miles from home and hundreds of miles from land on a frozen Arctic sea, in a single wooden ship with twenty-three men. Shackleton had made two previous attempts to be the first to reach the South Pole. Both times he had failed, although on one trip he came within 100 miles of his goal. He was eventually beaten to this historic discovery, yet he did not give up, but merely changed his objective. His problem that October night was how to cross the Antarctic continent, a journey of thousands of miles, first by sea and then over land by dogsled. The opportunity was to gather scientific knowledge and become the first in history to accomplish this feat. The temperature was as low as minus 100 degrees Fahrenheit, with winds up to 200 miles per hour. The ice pack was so tight, he must have begun to doubt whether he'd ever reach land.

At that moment, his worst fears were realized. The ship, *Endurance*, was trapped in ice, stranded, with no means of communication, thousands of miles from rescue across the worst ocean in the world. Worse still, the ice pressure gripped, squeezed, and then slowly crushed the boat. It rapidly sank, leaving him and his men stranded, with winter coming on and little hope of ever being rescued or returning alive.

In Shackleton's now famous adventure, the irony is that he never reached his destination. Once his ship was gone, he spent the next two years battling the drifting ice floes and Arctic winter, in unimaginable conditions. And in an end to a story that is so extraordinary it pushes the limits of believability, he succeeded in escaping with his small band by sailing thousands of miles through towering waves in a spare lifeboat to Georgia Island, which enabled the entire expedition to be rescued.

Most of us will never attempt the likes of what Sir Ernest Shackleton attempted early last century. His quest has become a celebrated human adventure, a legend in the annals of exploration. It fits in that small class of great journeys people have made from the known into the unknown: Marco Polo's from Europe to Asia: Columbus's journey from the Old World to the New; Burton and Speke's journey from the outer edge of the African continent to the source of the Nile; Lewis and Clark's from the Atlantic to the Pacific; America's from the Earth to the Moon.

So why does a book about problem solving begin with the story of a great journey? The mixture of problem solving and adventure blends two rich sources of knowledge into one. And the blend is a natural one. After all, every problem is an adventure, involving a movement from situation A to situation B, and every adventure is a problem to be solved, involving a movement from point A to point B. Exactly like an adventure, problem solving is a journey from a starting point to some distant destination. It is a journey through fear and exhilaration, confidence and disappointment, into the unknown.

By the way, you may have noticed by now that I sometimes speak of "solving" both problems and opportunities. The fact is, solving a problem and "solving" an opportunity involve exactly the same process of moving from one state to another. The difference lies only in the point of view: When we fear change, we call what demands it a problem; when we welcome change, we call what invites it an opportunity.

Thinking of the solution of problems (or opportunities) as journeys brings the topic alive. Professional knowledge about problem solving is by definition abstract. But the language, images, ideas, and principles of adventure and exploration make it accessible and invest it with the drama that real problem solvers experience: the disciplined planning, the long waits, the moments of crisis and celebration. Moreover, since we have all traveled, the metaphor helps us tap into personal and collective sources of wisdom about the principles and practices of problem solving journeys.

In fact, not since the age of exploration several centuries ago has the image of travel carried such power and relevance. The wide frontiers of a new knowledge-based, technology-driven, global village stretch out before us—wide open with possibility. For this reason, leaders in business and society frequently use the metaphor of adventure to express themselves. It has also become a fixture of how the new technology elites communicate.

It would be easy for a problem solver to view Shackleton's trip as a failure. He suffered from poor planning, ineffective weather-forecasting skills, insufficient knowledge of polar ice patterns, and inadequate equipment. What should we think of someone who dreams up a new adventure, spends two years attempting it, never even gets close to the destination (in fact, never even gets to the starting point!), and barely makes it back home alive? What executive or project leader, in today's results-oriented professional world, would be considered successful with that track record?

On the other hand, why has he become such a legend? Why has his adventure been told and retold generation after generation? Why has his experience been studied and dissected so comprehensively, treated in everything from art exhibits and TV specials to courses and management books? The truth is, many view it as a success. He tackled impossible odds and made it out alive. He demonstrated a supremely positive and constructive mindset, showed a dedication and loyalty to his crew that has been unparalleled, devised many innovations to survive, and showed a dogged perseverance in solving the problem of how to escape alive.

Beyond the debate over success or failure, anyone who hears his story feels a rush of admiration for the sheer human achievement. Shackleton and his men symbolize something special about the spirit of a journey, something that Teddy Roosevelt captured in these words:

It is not the critic who counts, nor the man who points out how the strong man stumbles, or where the doer of deeds could have done them better. The credit belongs to the man who is actually in the arena, whose face is marred by dust and sweat and blood, who strives valiantly, who errs, and comes short again and again, because there is no effort without error and shortcoming; but who does actually strive to do the deeds; who knows the great enthusiasms, the great devotions; who spends himself in a worthy cause; who at the best knows in the end the triumph of high achievement, and who at the worst, if he fails, at least fails while daring greatly; so that his place shall never be with those cold and timid souls who know neither victory or defeat.

Success in life is not guaranteed, whether we are following our personal dreams or trying to solve the world's problems. But the highest honors go to those who embrace the spirit of human adventure, whether in the pursuit of knowledge, or the service of one's fellow man, or merely the fulfillment of personal goals. Moreover, although the spirit of exploration is often equated with rugged individualism, adventures are not usually singular efforts. A society encourages or discourages the spirit of adventure, as do families, communities, and businesses.

This book is about the knowledge and skills of great problem solvers and adventurers: the mindset, the wisdom, the loyalty, the vision, the tools, and the discipline. By focusing on the timeless six essentials that drive success in problem solving, it is intended as a practical guide on one's professional travels. But between the lines you will find the same spirit that arises from Ernest Shackleton's story, one which transcends success and failure and simply embraces the wholly unique journey of our own development—struggling, creating, and fulfilling our potential.

In the pages ahead are collected the best knowledge I have found in twenty years of practicing in this field. Behind it is a decade of research on hundreds of case studies, a review of the literature on problem solving, as well as interviews with leading problem solvers of today. There is also my personal experience as an entrepreneur, government executive, inventor, and investigator.

The illustrations presented here are not complete case studies but something more akin to highlights. Each one has been chosen to show one facet of a journey—a best practice, principle, or technique that shows up repeatedly in great problem solving. Furthermore, many examples of advanced problem solving in science, mathematics, engineering, or medicine have been purposely left out. Too often in the past this field has been either oversimplified or overcomplicated. I have chosen a mix of examples that combine a genuine sophistication with accessibility that puts them within nearly anyone's reach.

This book has one central idea:

There are six essential problem solving skills that apply to any type of problem or opportunity. (See Figure I.1.) The difference between the best and the worst problem solvers is how many of these six skills they can marshal (by themselves or with others) and how deeply the skills are understood, individually and collectively. Poor problem solvers understand them incompletely and therefore cannot marshal a complete capability. Great problem solvers know them well enough to pull together and manage all six or exhibit one in great depth as part of a team.

The journey from novice to world-class expert—in any field—begins by understanding these essentials, practicing them, mastering them at one level, and then moving on towards the limits of your potential.

The Six Essentials of Problem Solving   FIG. I.1

I - Generate the Mindset
Develop potent ideas and attitudes

Creating teams and organizations
that are innovative and decisive

II - Know the Territory
Ask the right questions and get good
information

Acquiring and absorbing strategic
knowledge on a continuous basis

III - Build the Relationships
Cultivate quality communication and
interaction

Building trust and loyalty by
exchanging and delivering value

IV - Manage the Journeys
Choose destinations, and set directions

Working on the right projects for
the right reasons at the right time

V - Create the Solutions
Design, build, and maintain optimal
solution

Designing the best end-to-end,
complete, and well-supported
solutions

VI - Deliver the Results
Practice intuitive, disciplined execution

Implementing solutions effectively
in complex, competitive situations

At some point in this process, the best problem solvers rise above their profession in a multidisciplinary fashion. Each of the six essentials represents a bundle of habits, skills, and knowledge that come together in problem solving "personalities." Each personality draws its strength from a variety of specialties. A select few of these have been identified and mapped against the six essentials as a rough guide to the nature of this interdisciplinary knowledge. (See Figure I.2.)

The six personalities serve as a convenient way to assess yourself and others you work with, so that you can determine what your own personal mixture of strengths and weaknesses is and how you can put together a complete problem solving capability. They should be considered a guide, not a formula. Every individual has a unique mixture of the personalities. Some are intensively focused on one or two, others have a broader blend. What is important is that in every problem solving effort, the more personalities present, the higher the probability of success. And, as with any personality, the better you get to know them and how they work together, the better a problem solver you will be. Great problem solvers know their strengths and weaknesses, and they build teams to compensate for them—creating wholes that are equal to or greater than the sum of their parts.

Each of the book's parts is devoted to explaining one of the six essentials and its corresponding personality. At the end, there's a "Guide to the Guide," which shows in more detail how they all work together. At any time, feel free to skip to

The Six Problem Solving Personalities   FIG. I.2

Problem Solving Essential	"Personalities" (likely professional source of knowledge and skill)
Mindset	**The Innovator** (artist, entrepreneur, visionary, designer, counselor, poet, spiritual leader)
Territory	**The Discoverer** (scientist, historian, researcher, investigator, journalist, teacher, accountant)
Relationships	**The Communicator** (politician, civic leader or civil servant, social worker, legislator, publicist, agent, salesperson)
Journeys	**The Playmaker** (commander, executive, physician, judge, consultant, coach)
Solutions	**The Creator** (architect, builder, engineer, inventor, investor, trader, author)
Execution	**The Performer** (athlete, attorney, entertainer, nurse, musician, customer representative)

the back (p. 245) and look at all the pieces of the puzzle, or simply relax and take the guided tour, which will get you there in good time.

Starting with Part 1 ("Generate the Mindset"), each essential advances from the previous one to arrive, by Part 6 ("Deliver the Results"), at a complete problem solving thought process. With each new essential in turn, start by asking questions and stimulating your intuition about what you already know. This approach, in combination with the stories and lessons, leads to a deeper level of understanding, better decisions, and ultimately better results.

Part 1—"Generate the Mindset" (the Innovator)—focuses on progressing from self-doubt to innovation by developing potent ideas and attitudes, above all through seeking out alternative points of view. It improves your effectiveness in moving creatively through a problem solving effort. An Innovator asks:

- Seems like a conventional approach; aren't there other ways of looking at this problem?
- We've seen and solved this type of problem many times; what's the opportunity here to change the way we do business?

An Innovator's potent mindset sets the stage for discovery, because the combination of commitment and open-mindedness generates the widest possible field of possibilities and opportunities to consider. Without this essential, the range of potential issues and scope of knowledge is limited from the start.

Part 2—"Know the Territory" (the Discoverer)—concentrates on moving from innovation to insight by asking the right questions and getting good, timely information. Better knowledge helps you define problems more effectively, choose the best routes, and identify what's at stake. A Discoverer asks:

- We simply don't know enough to define this problem well; why don't we step back and answer some key unknowns before we go any further?
- That's a well-structured proposal, but have we really learned from our past mistakes in that area?

A Discoverer's knowledge of a territory brings understanding and insight, which reveal the most likely problems and opportunities in higher relief. With more investigation, their causes and implications become more apparent as a foundation for action. Without this essential, a problem solver may choose an unworkable journey or one that creates unnecessary risk.

Part 3—"Build the Relationships" (the Communicator)—covers how to move from insight to community by cultivating quality communication and interaction and so creating an ever expanding circle of relationships based on service, loyalty, and identity. It gives you the support and human context needed to effectively create and implement change. A Communicator asks:

- This may make a lot of money, but it's going to threaten some of our best business relationships in the process. Is it really worth it?
- What do our customers and stakeholders think about this? Will our solution add value and build loyalty?

Through their mastery of relationship-building, Communicators connect potential journeys to their actual implications for real people. Communicators help determine whether a problem solving effort is worthwhile, for whom and why. Then they generate a core group that will tackle the journey and a network that will support the effort. Without this essential, there may be no reason to solve the problem at all. Or there may be a reason, but no one convinced enough to take part.

Part 4—"Manage the Journeys" (the Playmaker)—focuses on moving from building a community to giving that community a sense of direction and clear priorities by choosing destinations and strategies. By fostering the understanding of the stages of any problem solving journey, it helps you set goals, define success, and develop effective plans. A Playmaker asks:

- Interesting idea, but are we reaching high enough here? What's our real purpose?

- That's a neat tool/technology, but are we solving the right problem? What are our priorities?

A Playmaker takes the attitude, knowledge, and people brought into play by Innovators, Discoverers, and Communicators and shapes the destination, direction to be taken, and strategies to be followed to make the journey a reality. Without the Playmaker, Creators waste time and effort trying to create solutions before the problems are clearly defined.

Part 5—"Create the Solutions" (the Creator)—shows how to move from leadership to power by designing, building, and maintaining optimal solutions. It helps you learn to bring the best technology, people, and tools together in complete, flexible solutions that will fit the problem you're trying to solve. A Creator asks:

- Great idea, but do we really have the right people and capability behind it? What is the purpose of our design?
- Sure that's the right problem to tackle, but are we willing to invest in the technology it will take to actually solve it? Are the economics viable?

A Creator takes the requirements and goals of a Playmaker, which define the journey, and figures out what it will take to get the group where they want to go. When there is more innovation, better knowledge, richer relationships, and better defined problems, solution design and construction are more focused and efficient. Without the Creator's well-designed solution, problem solvers cannot get where they need to go—or they may be stranded part way there when a poorly designed solution breaks down.

Part 6—"Deliver the Results" (the Performer)—concentrates on moving from power to sustainable advantage through intuitive and disciplined implementation, which allows you to continually exceed expectations. It will help you conquer complexity, friction and scale with simplicity, discipline, and a competitive edge. A Performer asks:

- That's a brilliant strategy, but can we execute it?
- Those time frames and resources are unrealistic; what are our biggest risks and how can we manage them up front?

Performers take the goals and strategies of the Playmaker and the solutions of the Creator, and work to achieve full resolution of the problem. Innovation, knowledge, and well-developed relationships aid in their efforts. When all the other roles are done well, the performer is able to focus completely on achieving full resolution and not on redesign, unplanned maintenance, or changing requirements. Without the Performer's experienced execution, the best solutions and the best plans can still fall prey to unanticipated factors or lose out to a more effective competitor.

Becoming a Good Problem Solver

Once you've understood the six essentials at the highest level, the next question is, how good are you at problem solving and how good can you become?

Let's start by defining what it means to be good. Simply put, the best problem solvers are the ones who create and realize the most potential. They tackle large-scale problems or those with a high degree of difficulty. They are especially innovative. Or they may be very efficient and effective, able to solve a particular problem repeatedly and better than any of their competitors.

The difference between being one of the best problem solvers and one of the worst comes down to how many essentials you can bring to bear, how well they are working together, and how deeply they are understood. (See Figure I.3.) The worst problem solvers are unaware of their own potential and that of others, and actually destroy it, whereas the best not only realize their own potential but create new potential as well.

The difference between the best and the worst is more starkly revealed the tougher, bigger and more challenging a problem or opportunity is. If you're tackling something that feels overwhelming or that is stretching your capabilities, the

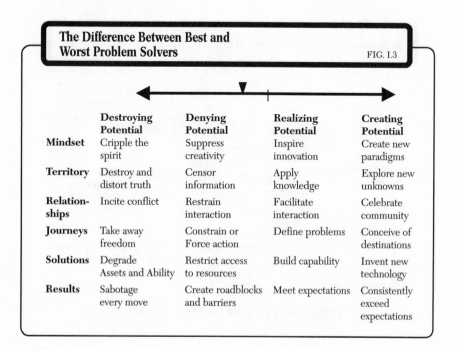

The Difference Between Best and Worst Problem Solvers   FIG. I.3

	Destroying Potential	**Denying Potential**	**Realizing Potential**	**Creating Potential**
Mindset	Cripple the spirit	Suppress creativity	Inspire innovation	Create new paradigms
Territory	Destroy and distort truth	Censor information	Apply knowledge	Explore new unknowns
Relationships	Incite conflict	Restrain interaction	Facilitate interaction	Celebrate community
Journeys	Take away freedom	Constrain or Force action	Define problems	Conceive of destinations
Solutions	Degrade Assets and Ability	Restrict access to resources	Build capability	Invent new technology
Results	Sabotage every move	Create roadblocks and barriers	Meet expectations	Consistently exceed expectations

lessons in this book are ones you ignore at your peril. True professionals are always rooted in the essentials of problem solving and critical thinking. Deepening their knowledge of these essentials over time, they get better and better at more complex variations and dynamics. But they never just assume the essentials will take care of themselves. As soon as they do, they get into trouble. Instead, they constantly practice and refine them.

The bottom line is, problem solving at the world class level is a hard thing to do. There are no silver bullets or magic elixirs that will produce it, in spite of what many self-improvement gurus would have you believe. People devote themselves to it over long periods of time in their careers. The good news is that the six essentials are accessible to anyone. If they are applied diligently, you can enhance your capability and influence. The bad news is, professionals spend billions of dollars every year on knowledge, technology, and training around the world, and not nearly enough of it emphasizes good problem solving essentials. You might ask yourself, whether you're buying a book, taking a course, going to a conference, or getting a degree, how well does the knowledge help you to solve problems effectively and improve your problem solving capability in a measurable fashion? If you can't answer this question directly, you're either on vacation or your time and money could be better spent somewhere else.

Getting the six essentials working together takes effort. The pieces have to be put together in your own mind, then assembled and exercised in concert until

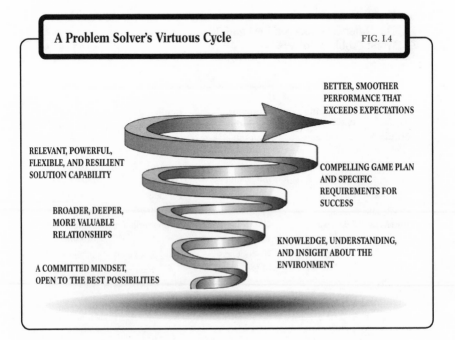

A Problem Solver's Virtuous Cycle　　　　　　　　　FIG. I.4

BETTER, SMOOTHER PERFORMANCE THAT EXCEEDS EXPECTATIONS

RELEVANT, POWERFUL, FLEXIBLE, AND RESILIENT SOLUTION CAPABILITY

COMPELLING GAME PLAN AND SPECIFIC REQUIREMENTS FOR SUCCESS

BROADER, DEEPER, MORE VALUABLE RELATIONSHIPS

KNOWLEDGE, UNDERSTANDING, AND INSIGHT ABOUT THE ENVIRONMENT

A COMMITTED MINDSET, OPEN TO THE BEST POSSIBILITIES

you get a working system of thinking, questioning, communicating, decisionmaking, and problem solving. Getting them working in harmony allows you to create a "virtuous cycle" of problem solving effectiveness. (See Figure I.4.) The more of the six essentials of problem solving you can bring to bear, and the better you can perform them in concert, the more likely you will be to get a virtuous cycle started. Conversely, if few of them are utilized, and utilized ineffectively, you will confront the exact opposite of the virtuous cycle, a vicious one. (See Figure I.5.)

The most frequent mistake made by problem solvers is to jump too quickly to solutions, without following a process. Creating a virtuous cycle appears to start far from a solution. But the time spent up front thinking through alternatives, building knowledge, getting the right people involved, and defining the issue clearly is earned back in the end. Furthermore, the investment is multiplied many fold in the handling of subsequent problems, as the virtuous cycle builds on itself.

Conversely, as the vicious cycle illustrates, a weak effort in any one of the six essentials can inhibit a problem solving effort or bring it down, following patterns familiar to many professionals: Closed minds limit what is considered possible from the beginning; inadequate knowledge leads to a major oversight; poor planning wastes resources in design and construction; problem employees or political conflicts constrain achievement; badly designed solutions soak up time and money in execution.

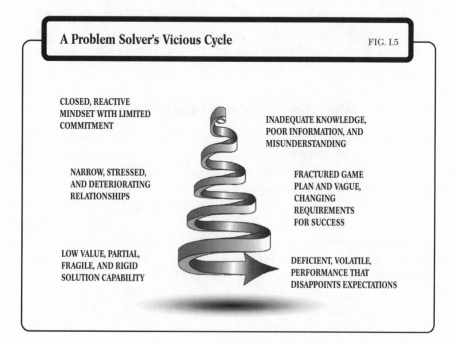

A Problem Solver's Vicious Cycle   FIG. I.5

CLOSED, REACTIVE
MINDSET WITH LIMITED
COMMITMENT

INADEQUATE KNOWLEDGE,
POOR INFORMATION, AND
MISUNDERSTANDING

NARROW, STRESSED,
AND DETERIORATING
RELATIONSHIPS

FRACTURED GAME
PLAN AND VAGUE,
CHANGING
REQUIREMENTS
FOR SUCCESS

LOW VALUE, PARTIAL,
FRAGILE, AND RIGID
SOLUTION CAPABILITY

DEFICIENT, VOLATILE,
PERFORMANCE THAT
DISAPPOINTS EXPECTATIONS

For those who want more detail on how the six essentials work together and on the virtuous and vicious cycles, the "Guide to the Guide" goes into more depth—and of course the discussion will mean more after you've studied each essential separately.

So was a problem solver like Sir Ernest Shackleton one of the best or one of the worst? Once you've completed The Problem Solving Journey, you'll decide for yourself. In my view, he became a legend because he was a courageous and effective problem solver. But above all, he represents the spirit of the problem solving journey. He set out on a bold adventure, persevered against all odds by changing his perspective, reframed goals for his men, and developed new capabilities in response to new demands. He demonstrated efficiency, effectiveness, innovation, and adaptability. But it was his spirit in the face of massive forces impossible to control that elevated Shackleton. Paradoxically, it was "failure" that took him down roads of endurance, resourcefulness, and sheer human will that few had taken before. It made his story a heroic one and ultimately a story of success.

The new professional economy places an increasing premium on individuals with the mind, body, and soul of the adventurer—the problem solver—on people who can conceive, organize, and lead expeditions that add value to society, business, and humanity. They have an adventurer's blend of innocence and wisdom, self-reliance and a willingness to collaborate, professional competence and the capacity to scale new peaks, as well as the resilience to persevere through uncharted waters and dark, unmapped forests.

And just as in the old economy or the next economy after this one, no amount of buzz, momentum, or technology will cover the lack of problem solving essentials for long. True problem solving capability is what drives enduring advantage in any field, at any time, in any place.

What This Book Has to Offer in Practice

Because this book applies in any field, it can be used by many different types of individuals pursuing different purposes. An employee may use it to improve job performance. A team leader might apply lessons to troubleshoot project issues. The leader of an organization may seek new competitive advantage by bringing this thinking deep into the company's culture, strategy, and operations. A community leader might use the essentials to create a more focused and successful neighborhood improvement campaign. Or a teacher might use the framework to construct lessons around problems and opportunities rather than merely topics.

Readers will have widely varying reactions to what follows. This is natural. No one book can make every reader comfortable. Those with a more conceptual bent may want to see more theory, explanation and direction, while more concrete types may want deeper examples and richer stories. Those who prefer straightforward, linear thinking might wish the framework were more structured, with a step-by-step recipe for solving problems, while those who tend toward more nonlinear thought patterns could find the structure too limiting. Just be aware, this book takes a deep stab at pulling together and simplifying a complex, challenging field. More could obviously be done on any of the topics, but the goal here is to create a new, more focused starting point so that many more people can begin to understand a vast territory. This is a first step, not the end of the journey.

This first step, however, has the potential to take you a long distance. The trick is to take an evolutionary, not a revolutionary, approach to learning and absorbing the knowledge that follows. There are no quick fixes here. Trying to master all the skills at once won't work as well as becoming familiar with them gradually and as you try them out over time. Look for the areas that seem to be most relevant for a current problem or opportunity, and begin there. Follow your instincts. Skip around. Take your time getting comfortable with the ideas. Let them sink in slowly.

They have a quiet way of working themselves into your problem solving approach, sometimes without your even knowing it. Over time, you'll begin seeing the connections, the interrelationships, how the different personalities affect one another. You'll feel a virtuous cycle begin. The sense of progress, forward movement, and momentum will become tangible.

More concretely, expect the initial impact to come with increased awareness, as your critical thinking faculties are challenged, enhanced, and reinforced. The next level of benefit will come with better, more incisive questions about the work you're involved in and the other problem solvers you work with. After better questions will come better problem solving. By this time, you'll be able to see speed, efficiency, and quality all increase. If your progress continues, it will have an impact on your career as a whole, by allowing you to move into higher-level positions, with more responsibility, or to take on tougher, more challenging and interesting issues. Finally, you'll be able to lead, coach, and teach others, helping them to become better problem solvers—the ultimate destination in any problem solving journey.

Part One

⇜Generate the Mindset⇝

The Innovator

Develop Potent Ideas and Attitudes

Life is either a daring adventure or nothing. To keep our faces toward change and behave like free spirits in the presence of fate is strength undefeatable.

—HELEN KELLER (1880–1968)

Generating the right mindset is the most intangible, and yet in some ways the most important, influence on how well we solve problems. A problem solver with the wrong mindset will miss the rich opportunities hidden in crises, turn back when persistence might win the day, fall victim to vulnerabilities, accept unnecessary sacrifices, and never discover what can be accomplished by pushing one's own limits. The wrong mindset can undermine almost any advantage, whereas the right mindset, generated and re-generated in the face of setbacks and doubts, makes a problem solver an Innovator, one who finds unrecognized possibilities and sees them realized in ways others barely dream of.

An innovative mindset combines spirit, creativity, and the will to move beyond self-doubt to determination and innovation. Above all, Innovators view the world in a special way. They see potential where others see only pain. They envision the mountain top, even when they're in the valley. Innovators have a state of mind, whether individually or collectively, that combines relentless focus and an ability to manage tension and ambiguity with perceptual flexibility and openness. This combination allows them to uncover new areas for exploration while maintaining resilience and balance in trying circumstances.

1

Christopher Columbus's First Voyage
Across the Atlantic, Aug. 3–Oct. 11, 1492

Put yourself in the shoes of Christopher Columbus—the ultimate Innovator—five centuries ago before he took his first journey westward into the Atlantic, when no one had ever sailed more than four or five days away from shore. What no one could imagine was getting beyond the barrier of fear—the vast unknown ocean.

And yet Columbus had a vision, he saw the possibility of treasure and commerce where others saw only danger. He committed so wholeheartedly to that vision that not even dozens of rejections and ongoing penury could dissuade him from pursuing a journey to Asia via the West. He built on his technical strengths as a seaman to plan a viable journey and eventually marshal an expedition. And during the journey, when his men felt the constant tension of choosing between their safety and the riches ahead, Columbus knew that he could deliver both. He not only pushed the limits of what people believed was possible, he broke through them completely and opened up a new world, one so vast that even he could not comprehend the full significance of what he had done.

Innovators like Columbus break through fear, ignorance, and misperception to create possibility. They conceive of new journeys that have never been thought of before or stumble on them through a combination of restlessness, resilience, and desire. They summon the courage to pursue dreams. Even though things may not turn out as planned, they change the landscape of their world and open up possibilities for others to follow in their footsteps. Innovators today in the field of health are exploring immortality, while others in business are creating the global village. Innovators in the military are building foundations for peace, while civic Innovators envision a world without poverty or hunger. The pursuit of these visions means long, punishing, and heroic efforts with uncertain outcomes.

Both at the start and throughout a long adventure, it is mindset that makes the difference. At the beginning, the right mindset helps overcome fears of venturing into the unknown. It aids in establishing the morale and commitment of everyone in the supporting crew. In the midst of the trials and tribulations, it keeps you going, generating the faith and courage to press on. When impossible unknowns and impenetrable problems present themselves, the right mindset guides you in searching for creative approaches.

The Innovator's Central Idea: The Best Innovation Comes
from Taking Alternative Points of View

Mindset is powerful, because attitudes, emotions and beliefs drive our perceptions of the world. How we see the world determines whether and how we want to change it, as well as how we feel about our situation on the road and the prospects for a journey ahead.

We all perceive the world differently—whether it is because of our experience, culture, profession or personality. In the realm of science, it appears that the real world corresponds to the way it is measured and independently observed. Not so in the realm of mindset. In this arena the world is real only to the degree we can see it and absorb it, which is a function of our mental models, assumptions and biases, strengths and weaknesses. Where some people see structures, others see voids. Where some see threats, others see opportunities. These discrepancies are often caused by nothing more than the differences in their perceptual lenses, created by their belief systems and personal histories. Everyone has a different way of seeing.

Innovators have a unique and flexible way of seeing and thus the ability both to develop original points of view and then to incorporate those of many others. Albert Einstein tells the story about the origin of his innovations being in his ability to adopt a particular point of view—God's. He simply asked himself, how would God create the universe? This starting point eventually led him to his breakthrough in the theory of relativity.

Developing alternative points of view and seeing the points of view of others are the roots of both creativity and objectivity. Pain can be either something to work through or information to respond to. Joy can mean either celebration, or impaired judgment that should inspire caution. Risk can mean either a threat or an opportunity. A victim can either be in need of sympathy, or in need of challenge.

A problem solving journey is the sum of many different points of view. (See Figure 1.1.) How we view the world, our journeys through it, and our personal

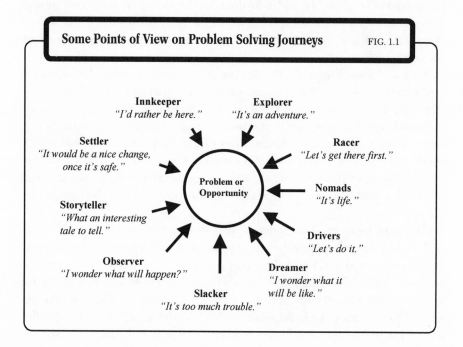

Some Points of View on Problem Solving Journeys FIG. 1.1

Innkeeper
"I'd rather be here."

Explorer
"It's an adventure."

Settler
"It would be a nice change, once it's safe."

Racer
"Let's get there first."

Problem or Opportunity

Nomads
"It's life."

Storyteller
"What an interesting tale to tell."

Drivers
"Let's do it."

Observer
"I wonder what will happen?"

Dreamer
"I wonder what it will be like."

Slacker
"It's too much trouble."

or organizational destinies varies widely from pessimism to optimism, hope to fear, depression to enthusiasm. All the elements of character, clear reason and deep passion, humor and sincerity, independence and commitment, are necessary to be the best possible Innovator. Innovators cultivate the ability to see themselves and their challenges through others' eyes and to experiment with holding many different perspectives on a person, problem, question, event, or situation.

Tapping into these alternative perspectives of ourselves and others, testing them, choosing the most valuable, sustaining a flexible point of view through further inquiry, and then integrating the perspectives in new ways—all these together constitute the powerful mindset of the Innovator.

Innovators in Action: Visa International and the Global Payments System

If the Innovator's central idea is taking alternative points of view, then how does that apply in practice? The following story of Dee Hock, Visa International, and the creation of a global payments system shows how an Innovator in action opens up fields of potential rather than limiting them.

Dee Hock, the man who turned Visa into a $1 trillion-plus corporation, has advice for professionals around the world on the issue of mindset. Lighten up. "I often say to people that the only serious work that ever occurs is with an incredible amount of laughter," he said as he discussed his thoughts on problem solving. "You can count on it. It's as close to a law of the universe as you can get. Where there are a group of people assembled in serious, somber, ponderous conduct, nothing is happening."

Hock was a small-time Seattle banker thirty years ago when he began the credit card revolution. People were paying with cash or checks then. Today, electronic transactions pound out a constant rhythm in every country around the world. Visa has grown by 10,000 percent and still expands at about 20 percent per year. In nearly all the countries of the world, with over 500 million clients, and sales over $1 trillion, Visa is ubiquitous. Hock has been inducted into the Business Hall of Fame and was named by *Money* magazine as one of eight individuals who have most altered the way people live in the past quarter century.

Like many Innovators, Hock doesn't believe in conventional problem solving. It's based on deficit language, he says. Too linear. It robs a person of the ability to think in new concepts. Problem solving needs to be looked at as opportunity-oriented, strategic, and nonlinear to be effective. Pressed to better define the way he tackles difficult endeavors, he's stumped for a minute. Play and opportunity? "That's a factor. A playful mind. A child doesn't approach anything with a fixed set of parameters. Playfulness is an essential part of the universe. My god, even evolution is playful. All it does is experiment. It observes the marvelous things that occur from time to time and protects and replicates them."

The Visa story began when there was no Visa. By the late 1960s, the infant credit card industry was out of control. Banks were losing tens of millions of dollars to fraud and technical glitches. *Life Magazine* ran a cover depicting the banks as Icarus flying to the sun on wings of plastic. Underneath, there was a red sea (for losses) into which the banks were soon to plunge with melted wings. Bank of America called a meeting of its licensees in Columbus, Ohio, to sift through their problems with interchange and authorization of payments. Over a hundred bankers crammed into a hotel conference room. There was acrimony and finger pointing. They finally broke for lunch, and when they returned, Hock was standing at the front of the room. He turned the bankers' problems into an opportunity.

Hock suggested a permanent panel of seven that would advise the Bank of America on how to fix its problems. His point of view was, working together could work. It was hardly a novel brainstorm—the idea of a committee—but after a morning of infighting, the bankers were so happy to have a proposal they stood up and applauded Hock. Then they elected him chairman of the committee.

In observing the chaos of the time, Hock recognized that it was just that apparent problem that created the opportunity at hand. He used the fact that all these people were in the same room, with a common frustration, to keep them working together. He saw an opportunity to create a new order and took the initiative. In doing so, he accepted the personal risk and the responsibility for an outcome. Hock had a simple vision of a universal currency that drove him forward, and he committed to achieving it. He would need to go back to that vision, that insight, again and again. When colleagues saw Hock and his staff coming to a negotiating session with Bank of America officials, they used to crack, "Here come the revolutionaries."

Over the coming weeks, Hock learned that losses were not in the tens of millions, but in the hundreds of millions—the problem was even worse than he had imagined. "And suddenly," he says, "like a diamond in the dirt, there it lay. The need for a new concept of organization and a precarious toehold from which to make it happen."

Many of the personal strengths that underlie Hock's growing success emerged out of what one might think is a vulnerability, an almost complete lack of higher education. He is largely a self-educated mountain boy, a loner, an iconoclast—painfully shy. By turning this trait into an introspective, thoughtful quality of mind, he takes an Innovator's view of the world. Because his education was not dominated by courses in traditional disciplines, he became a generalist. He absorbed and learned from many different fields, history, economics, politics, science, philosophy, without paying any attention to disciplinary boundaries. This approach allowed him to combine and recombine knowledge in new and creative ways throughout his career.

To devise the new organization, Hock formed another panel. He and three handpicked allies checked into a hotel in Sausalito, California, for a week to hunker down and figure it out. Hock had a rule for the week's pow-wow. No problems were going to be discussed, only design principles. In this way, he guaranteed that his panel could only discuss vulnerabilities as if they were strengths. If the principles were sound in the context of the vision they were trying to achieve, he theorized, the answers to their problems would show themselves.

About a dozen principles emerged. They included the concept of equitable ownership by all participants and the ideas that power had to be distributed "to the maximum degree" and must be "infinitely malleable yet extremely durable." The panel created the new National Bank-Americard Inc., known as Visa today. Hock was hired as president, and he is largely credited with making credit card use as everyday and normal as apple pie.

To reconceive the concepts of bank, money, and credit cards, Hock had to push the limits of the banking culture. He came to believe that money had become "nothing more than guaranteed, alphanumeric data recorded on valueless paper and metal. It would become data in the form of arranged electrons and photons, which would move around the world at the speed of light, at minuscule cost." He believed that credit card was a misnomer, that a credit card transaction was rather an "exchange of value in the form of arranged electronic particles."

And he believed that whatever organization could best globally guarantee and exchange that data would have a market so big it "beggared the imagination." Again, he had to push the limits of the existing banking community and its hierarchical structure. Hock recalled, "It became clear that no hierarchical corporation could do it, . . . no existing form of organization could do it. On a hunch, I made a calculation of the resources of banks worldwide. The total dwarfed the resources of most nations. Jointly they could do it, but how?"

Power resided with the board, made up of top executives from licensee banks. Hock set up a voting system to prevent one type of bank from dominating. Big banks couldn't gang up on small ones; banks on one coast couldn't turn against those on the other. The old vague wording of BankAmericard's interchange payment system was replaced with a new setup based on a sliding scale of fees, paid to the new organization. Rather than make an either/or choice between competition and cooperation, he seamlessly blended the two. Banks could still try to steal one another's customers, but they had to agree on certain standards for issuing cards that merchants could accept.

Visa has now evolved so far that in 1999 nearly $1.7 trillion in products and services were purchased using Visa cards. Visa's market share was 55 percent, more than all its competitors combined. More than 800 versions of the Visa card were being used at more than 16 million locations in 300 countries and territories.

Long retired from Visa, Hock is still innovating. He has written a book, *Birth of the Chaordic Age*, about his concepts for chaordic institutions (i.e., institutions that combine chaos and order) and has now taken on projects to create them in agriculture, health care, fisheries in the northwestern Atlantic, and world religions. "I'm doing it for the pure joy of it, because I think we have no future as a species if we don't get on with it," said Hock. And it's clear he's still proud of his first "chaord" and the men and women who helped make it happen. "Given the right circumstances, from no more than dreams, determination, and the liberty to try, quite ordinary people consistently do extraordinary things."

In summary, the starting point for good problem solving is a combination of mental attitude and emotional fortitude. It is about the spirit, drive, and energy that make people proactive, creative, and willing to make a personal commitment and take responsibility for resolving a problem.

Innovators summon a combination of willpower, faith, devotion, resilience, and flexibility to conceive of something new and commit to making it happen. Ultimately, it is the combination of playfulness and purposefulness that distinguishes the mindset of innovative problem solvers from others.

The rest of this part covers in more detail how the best Innovators think and attack problem solving. If you'd like to learn more about the other five essentials before going deeper into this one, the book is designed so that you can skip directly to the next part, "Know the Territory," on page 37. If you choose to read on, the following chapters will show more thoroughly how Innovators start with a basic optimism and eventually progress to more profound levels of creativity.

- "Turn Problems into Opportunities: From Doubt to Possibility" shows how skepticism and optimism move an Innovator from negativity to seeing larger fields of possibilities for positive change. Ralph Nader's role in the genesis of the consumer safety movement illustrates how such an approach can shape a career, a generation, and an entire economy.
- "Commit to the Summit: From Possibility to Commitment" pinpoints how moving from a sense of possibility to a visceral personal choice to strike out on a new journey causes the world to change as we do. The story of Jeff Bezos and Amazon.com illustrates how such a mindset can make commercial history.
- "Create Strength out of Vulnerability: From Commitment to Confidence" looks at how an Innovator creates new strengths by seeing and acknowledging vulnerabilities yet overcoming them. Nobel laureate Toni Morrison's powerful literary work chronicling the African-American experience reveals the power of shared awareness, knowledge, struggle.
- "Have It Both Ways: From Confidence to Determination" defines what it takes to move from confident pursuit of an opportunity to a stubborn

refusal to settle for half measures or compromises that is often at the root of dramatic innovations. This story tells how Ron Barbaro, former president of Prudential Insurance in Canada, broke through barriers of perception with his living death benefits for suffering AIDS patients.

• "Transcend Limits: From Determination to Innovation" explains how reconceptualizing limits can create breakthrough solutions that lay the path for an organization's future. In this case, former Commandant Charles Krulak describes how the Marine Corps designed a crucible to forge its next generation of soldiers.

TURN PROBLEMS INTO OPPORTUNITIES

From Doubt to Possibility

A wise man will make more opportunities than he finds.
—SIR FRANCIS BACON (1561–1626)

In today's competitive world, the game most often goes to those who can turn problems into opportunities. This kind of transformation is easier said than done. The initial analysis of a problem situation is often negatively tinged and colored by biases, feelings, and misperceptions that must be recognized and appropriately discounted. Only by seeing past such distortions can an Innovator focus both on what needs to be fixed and on new opportunities hidden beneath the surface.

Opportunities often come disguised as problems or paradoxes. Apparently insignificant difficulties can mushroom quickly into disasters. Problems that appear similar to ones solved before may actually harbor new potential. The difference between the way something first appears and its true potential for good or harm is often difficult to assess. This difficulty comes up because problems and opportunities are two sides of the same coin. Problems are deviations from a desired state. They often progress in an unwelcome direction. The challenge is to stop their momentum. An opportunity, on the other hand, is perceived as something favorable, and its direction is welcome. Increasing the momentum of an opportunity is the real challenge.

In times of change, problems and opportunities arise at a heightened rate. And the time, when it is ripe, often does not last for long. When you are faced with a problem, find opportunities to roll it in a favorable direction. When you find an opportunity, look for the problems that surround it, so that they can be rolled into opportunities too.

Few men have demonstrated the capacity for turning problems into opportunities more than Ralph Nader, famous for his crusade confronting companies that disregard the safety of consumers. The way that Nader turned the problems of the GM Corvair into the modern consumer safety movement is one of the great stories of American society in the twentieth century. It places him alongside reformers such as Ida Tarbell and Upton Sinclair—both of them problem solvers who turned the bright light of public scrutiny onto the corruption and abuse of power in their times.

Ralph Nader and the Consumer Safety Movement

From the beginning, Ralph Nader saw the problem of large, corrupt, and often uncaring corporate giants ignoring dangerous threats to public safety. After these behemoths had lined the pockets of elected officials, the government was unable to exert the necessary influence to even identify problems, much less solve them. In this massive problem, Nader saw the opportunity to permanently raise consumer awareness of both safety issues and their representatives' apathy, to create a movement outside government that would bring the voice of consumers into the democratic process.

These days, after decades of vigorous battles and hard-won victories, Nader could easily become dejected by the hurdles facing his various crusades—the media gone soft, Congress still beholden to special interests, the nation lulled into a false sense of well-being. But he just doesn't have time for it. "Back in college I researched all the philosophic literature on pessimism, and I found that no one could show me it has any function other than a self-indulgent one," Nader says from his shabbily outfitted conference room at the Center for the Study of Responsive Law. "Every defeat leads to a higher level of creativity," he likes to say. "You're never depressed. In the citizen movement, you've got to be in a mode where you're never defeated."

He has been called the "national nag" and "St. Ralph," but Nader has some impressive victories from his more than thirty years of fighting injustice. As a hungry new graduate from the Harvard Law School, he almost single-handedly started the auto safety movement with his 1965 book *Unsafe at Any Speed.* That book accused General Motors of ignoring defects in its Chevrolet Corvair. GM hired a private eye to snoop into his personal life, digging for scandal to discredit him. A Senate subcommittee investigated GM's activities, and Nader was launched as an American hero.

His success, Nader says, has required walking a fine line between doubting and believing, between acknowledging reality and bursting with the optimism that he could do something to improve it. "There are two ways to go through life," he says, "One is to believe everything. The other is to disbelieve everything. Both avoid thinking. I've met people who believe to the point of gullibility, and then I've met people who constantly disbelieve. Those are traps that people set for themselves. Sometimes, they never get out of them. People who succeed share the same characteristics: optimism, persistence, resilience, level-headedness, and controlled indignation."

"One has to be skeptical, but not cynical," he says. "Skepticism allows you to both doubt *and* believe, and not get trapped with either one. There's a distinction between being cynical and being skeptical. If you're cynical, you tend to withdraw with curled lip, drop out, and say 'A pox on both your houses.' If you're skeptical, you have a similar appraisal of the situation—but you engage." You have to avoid becoming jaded, like the newspaper editor he came across years ago. The man had his feet up on his desk, a cigarette glued to his lips, as Nader outlined auto safety problems. "So what else is new?" the newspaperman said. Nader reflects on that now. "Part of being jaded is having a low level of curiosity," he says.

Cynicism tricks you into thinking you know everything about a particular situation. Innovators cultivate the ability to be absolutely objective and intellectually honest. They look behind the disguises, under the camouflage, and through the disinformation. They look beyond the prejudices and misconceptions. They know it's important to drill beneath the surface of a problem and walk around it a bit to make a complete assessment. Every situational assessment depends on one's point of view. By cultivating the mental ability to "drill down" into something at various depths and "walk around" it from various points of view, we begin to see things differently—even to see them as others may.

Walking around and drilling down into a problem—that's how you get a complete field of view. But eventually it comes down to a focused assessment. Making such an assessment requires judging what true harm or benefit could accrue to whom and what to do about it. The right mindset is crucial. Because at this point—when it comes to real threats and windfalls—strong emotions, misperceptions, and unexamined assumptions often take over. Critical thinking can take a back seat. An Innovator's mindset, then, is much more than simply a "positive attitude." It requires rigorous, tough-minded, practical thinking if true opportunities, not pipe dreams, are to be seen in problems. And it requires the ability to bring that vision to others in order to jump-start any process of change. Nader excels at both.

One of his missions is to convince people that progress is not what they perceive it to be—to see the true potential for harm or benefit in things most of us take for granted. "Everyone used to see a factory smokestack billowing fumes and think progress," he explains. It took a while to for the public to understand pollution. To get his points across, Nader has to be persuasive. He doesn't have a massive political action committee, which can dole out big money to lawmakers. He can't warn a corporate leader that his plants will be shut down or moved overseas unless things change. Or promise a Congressman a nice Wall Street job if he votes the right way. He doesn't have that kind of power. At least not yet.

Part of Nader's persuasive ability lies in his genuineness and passion for correcting wrongs—the clarity of his vision of what is wrong and how right could be achieved. Nader's vision of justice, he says, came from his parents and their dinnertime conversations. He read the great "muckrakers"—such writers and crusaders as Ida Tarbell and Upton Sinclair—at age twelve or thirteen and says he found himself trembling with excitement. He considers himself a muckraker in that tradition, with one exception: "We don't just write about it. We take it the next step, we try to make it happen."

"If you don't think you can do anything about problems, which is what most people feel, then you just turn away," he says. "People who think they're powerless tend to let it go, but because I feel I can do something about them, the injustice becomes an irritation to me. The other side of apathy is powerlessness."

He lists among his heroes Lou Gehrig, who played 2,130 consecutive baseball games, often in pain from injuries. "He wasn't a natural athlete, you know," Nader explains, adding, "It's important to be able to stand tall, to have the courage of your convictions, believe in yourself, and have resilience if you are up against a disappointment or a temporary defeat. These are some of the qualities of great athletes in the arena of sports—on the basketball court, baseball diamond, or football field. You never give up, keep bouncing back, and hold your head high when you walk off the field. Those are the characteristics young people should emulate in a much more important place—the citizen arena."

Nader says American history taught him that just one person, or a mere handful, can change things for the better. Just look at the abolitionist crusade, or the six women in an upstate New York farmhouse who started the suffragette movement. The list goes on: civil rights, the environment, the labor movement. They were all started by people with the mindset that they personally could turn a problem into an opportunity by serving others. Service is the core of his public philosophy as a citizen. As he puts it, "It's like the ancient Athenian code of citizenship, which could be paraphrased as, 'I pledge to leave Athens better off than when I found it.'"

Innovation in Action: The Doubting and Believing Game

First choose a problem or opportunity that you or your colleagues are either having an especially tough time defining or that is causing a great deal of controversy. Take five minutes, and play the doubting game. Write down or discuss everything you can that expresses skepticism about the issue: Can you really do anything about it? Is it really a problem? Why should you care? Even if it is a problem, is the effort worth it? Next, take another five minutes and play the believing game. "We can do something about it. It is not just a problem but an opportunity. This is something worth caring about and acting on. We'll be able to succeed if we try." When you finish, take note of whether and how the exercise has changed anyone's point of view or raised any new information or considerations. Keep cycling through doubting and believing points of view until a collective point of view emerges.

COMMIT TO THE SUMMIT
From Possibility to Commitment

Obstacles cannot crush me. Every obstacle yields to stern resolve.
He who is fixed to a star does not change his mind.

–LEONARDO DA VINCI (1452–1519)

Seeing problems and opportunities clearly is only a beginning. Innovators must commit to realizing the potential in a situation—to resolution. They commit to reaching the summit no matter what it takes. Merely being proactive and responsible won't bring you to the heights. Checking off activities accomplished on a to-do list is satisfying. The difficulty is that you can be busy but never really achieve anything. For an innovative problem solver, what counts is not the number of things you've done, but how many resolutions you've delivered with the most impact for the least energy and effort.

You must develop a personal commitment so strong that it overcomes all obstacles. Otherwise, inevitably, you fall prey to technical distractions, become mired in complexity, or simply get tired, and the once promising opportunity is lost. The intermediate goals may alter, or the path may involve detours, but Innovators will still make something happen that matters. If something really does prove to be impossible, then they won't waste any time in moving to a new arena or project—where once again they will demonstrate their commitment to making a difference.

As a modern day adventurer into the new territories of cyberspace, Jeff Bezos, founder of Amazon.com and *Time*'s Man of the Year, is the epitome of an innovative mindset. Far beyond the technical sophistication of Amazon and its e-business strategy, his journey stands out for an underlying commitment in the face of serious unknowns, consistent skepticism, and overwhelming odds.

Jeff Bezos and the Creation of Amazon.com

In the beginning, when Bezos ran his on-line bookstore out of the garage of his rented suburban house, he would load his cyber customers' packages in the back of his Chevy Blazer and drive them to the post office himself. Now the post office sends eighteen-wheel trucks with forty-foot containers to Bezos's warehouse every day. "Anybody who had predicted what has happened would have been committed to an institution immediately!" Bezos said, uttering his trademark burst of laughter.

Because of Amazon.com's failure to turn a profit in more than four years of doing business, Wall Street has become deeply split over the company—valuing it at one point in 1999 at more than $30 billion, then the next year at a fraction of that amount. However, as market forces relentlessly reveal the true, and often lackluster, economics behind many of the dot.com miracles, Bezos and his financial team have to work ever harder to persuade dubious investors that many years of high investment rates are really anything more than a pyramid scheme in sophisticated disguise or simply a tough, low margin retail business.

Nevertheless, Bezos persists with his vision. He has been busy extending Amazon.com's tentacles into other retail industries—from music and videos to gifts and pharmaceuticals. He sees an America in twenty years where nearly everything you could want to buy will be available on line. Fun-filled shopping districts will thrive, Bezos thinks, but lousy stores will be squeezed out of business. "Strip malls," Bezos predicts, "are history."

It is a cliché—but success really does begin in your mind. If you can conceive of something, you can do it. It can start with a wild dream, righteous anger, restlessness, a sense of discomfort, or pure inspiration. Take that impulse, process it, weigh its risks and returns. Finally, make a decision—take the first step forward on your journey. Once you do, the world will start to change with you.

In 1994, Bezos read that the Web was growing astronomically and began scheming to find an opportunity, an enterprise that would succeed. "The wake-up call," according to Bezos, "was reading that Web use was growing 2,300 percent a year." He brainstormed a list of twenty products that he thought might sell well through on-line commerce. There were two criteria: The product had to be something with real customer value, and it had to be something that couldn't be sold as efficiently without the Internet. His list included books, music, magazines, clothing, computers, and software. He whittled the list down to books and music, and eventually pared it down to just books—with rigorous thinking and detailed competitive and market analysis.

Bezos knew he was on to something. Then he made the commitment. This was not just any decision to change jobs. He and his wife packed their belongings and told the movers they were headed west. They'd let them know where as soon as they knew. His boss had taken Bezos on a stroll through Central Park. He tried to talk Bezos out of leaving, reminding him of the financial risks and the fierce competition he would face—maybe even from his old friends at work. Bezos was willing to take the risk.

Once you have made the commitment to solve a problem, you will hear a quiet voice of determination guiding you. You'll recognize it by its tone of genuineness and authority. Everyone else will see it in your facial expression and the tone in your voice. Its authenticity will be beyond question. When you face setbacks and failures along the way—which you will—you will be prepared to pick yourself up again and again, persist in spite of the naysayers, overcome the competition, and win.

You'll need to cultivate the mental toughness to reject rejection, accept self-doubt, allow yourself rest, and keep putting one foot in front of the other. (See Figure 1.2.) As Bezos got started on his own journey, he dialed up would-be investors on his cell phone. Three people in the publishing industry immediately told him he'd never make it. They marked his business plan as a loser, saying it wasn't worth betting on. His commitment carried him forward despite the skepticism.

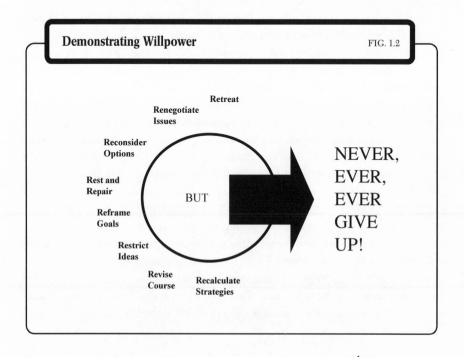

Bezos persevered—and raised several million dollars from venture capitalists. He originally named his enterprise "Cadabra," but discarded it because it sounded too much like "cadaver." So he settled on Amazon, drawing inspiration from the world's largest river. Though his business wasn't even a trickle yet, he remained committed to his vision of the summit, a virtual bookstore that would be the biggest river of books flowing on the planet. With just four employees, Bezos set up shop in the garage of the house he and his wife MacKenzie had rented in the Seattle suburbs. Extension cords snaked throughout the cramped space; a potbellied stove sat in the middle of the room. They wrote the software before the furniture even arrived.

Bezos reminds me of a memorable story about commitment, perhaps apocryphal, that I once heard about Winston Churchill. He was invited to give a commencement address to a graduating college class—in the years after the Second World War and his legendary leadership through such dark times. He got up in front of the young audience and looked out at them with wise, deep eyes and a heavily scarred soul. There was silence. He scanned the crowd knowingly and said, slowly and with a deliberate, rising cadence, "Never, . . . ever, ... ever, . . . ever, . . . give up." At which point he sat down. It was a six-word commencement address—one that the students would never forget.

In that spirit, Bezos still keeps his eye on the big prize. Stock price gyrations are just one of the many things he shrugs off. "I ask people around here, think about how do we create real value five years from now, because we can actually affect the stock price five years from now, whereas none of us has any control over what the stock price is tomorrow," Bezos has said. Though he has been under pressure to start turning a profit, he remains resolute that his strategy of aggressive advertising and internal investments is what really counts.

"Some people could say, 'I'd be more comfortable if you rejiggered your business plan so you could make money now and grow from profits,'" Bezos says. "We believe that would be shortsighted strategy. People who don't believe that, I'd say don't invest in our stock." Whether he can create a lasting brand across dozens of product categories and manage the inventory and distribution economics of such a massive retail operation are the ultimate questions. Or will the whole scheme simply collapse of its own increasing weight?

Bezos tries to stay clear-eyed and focused. "We hold ourselves to a very high standard in terms of customer experience," Bezos has said, "and we're growing faster than almost any other company has ever grown. So that takes a huge effort, and of course we wouldn't have it any other way, because we're trying to change the world and improve it in a small way, and maybe even a little more than a small way. And that's not supposed to be easy. It's supposed to be hard."

Commenting further, he emphasizes the aspect of innovation so few appreciate. The inspiration is often the easy part; the hard part is the discipline of working through many ideas to find the few best ones: "Ideas are important, but they are relatively easy. What's hard is taking that list of a hundred ideas and ranking them and picking the three that we're actually gonna do."

It's hard work. But echoing Dee Hock's insight, Bezos manages to keep on laughing much of the way. Amazon.com's motto—"Work Hard, Have Fun and Make History"—reveals the very personal passion and commitment that dreamed up the adventure, got it started, and keeps it going every day, no matter where it eventually ends up.

Innovation in Action: Finding the Quiet Voice

Take a moment to listen to your own quiet voice. Find a place where you can be alone, settle yourself, and if you've made a commitment to something already and are keeping it—celebrate. If you've lapsed in your commitment, renew it. If you've not made a commitment, explore the possibility of making one. And when you've finished, write down in a few sentences, for yourself and no one else, what that quiet voice believes, and carry it with you in your wallet or purse, as a reminder when things get tough.

CREATE STRENGTH OUT OF VULNERABILITY

From Commitment to Confidence

*He who, conscious of being strong, is content to be weak,
shall be the paragon of all mankind.*

–LAO-TZU (C. 600–550 B.C.)

The mental and emotional commitment that seems certain when we are strong may come apart when we feel weak. Innovators should learn their strengths, of course, but it's equally important to know one's vulnerabilities, the weaknesses and fears that drain the life from even the strongest commitments. To acknowledge inner and outer vulnerability requires moving beyond denial and defensiveness to the core of what it means to be human. By openly pinpointing, embracing, and learning to compensate for vulnerabilities—and to laugh at ourselves—we can turn apparent weaknesses into strengths and move from commitment to a deeper confidence.

Such transformation requires courage and self-understanding. Those who openly admit and even explore vulnerabilities are often the most beloved. Such an attitude can turn a healthy sense of inadequacy into the buoyant enthusiasm for struggle which is so essential to mindset. To be human is to be vulnerable. Problem solvers are not afraid to accept their humanity and to focus on what they are truly good at.

Toni Morrison, the Nobel Prize winning author, has spent a lifetime probing into weaknesses in society's moral fabric, exploring her own vulnerabilities, and turning her insights and lessons into a literature of hope, redemption, and pride.

Toni Morrison and the Power of Stories

Morrison crafts her ideas out of stark experience, searing pain, and naked vulnerability. As she puts it, "Generally, I respond to some disease or disquiet that's connected to some troubling image, an incident or a remark or an impression . . . that is serious enough to keep coming back." For an idea to become "bookworthy," it must stalk her. "I need to feel pursued by the question," she says. And when one chases and torments her, "I get out a legal pad, yellow, with a No. 2 pencil, and see what happens." She then sets out to explore the pain and vulnerability.

In 1993 Morrison became the first African American (and only the eighth woman) to win the Nobel Prize for literature. She has consistently said her work is not autobiographical. Yet all writers draw on their lives, their surroundings, and their observations when telling a story. Morrison is a master at turning adversity and vulnerability into strength, at describing the wounds of America's ugly history of slavery and the devastating impacts of racism. Her storytelling helps many to expose wounds and start the process of healing.

Vulnerability is, quite literally, the foundation of humanity. If we had not evolved the ability to give birth to and care for helpless infants, we could never have developed the large brain size which defines our species. We spend years overcoming this state of helplessness and are often hurt by others deeply while we are still weak as children. If we are honest with ourselves, this sense of vulnerability never completely goes away. There is always a memory inside, somewhere. The paradox of most human emotional development is that true power and influence come from acknowledging those wounds. If your power is built on denying them, you're powerless in truth, you just don't know it.

Some of us bury that voice of vulnerability from childhood. Others are obsessed with it, unable to escape its gravitational pull. Still others are periodically tortured by it but manage to muddle through life. Then there are those who embrace it, sharing in the common suffering that lies beneath the surface in all of us.

Toni Morrison had a goal in mind when she began to try her hand at writing. "When I began, there was just one thing that I wanted to write about," she said, "which was the true devastation of racism on the most vulnerable, the most helpless unit in the society—a black female and a child. I wanted to write about what it was like to be the subject of racism. It had a specificity that was damaging. And if there was no support system in the community and in the family, it could cause spiritual death, self-loathing, terrible things." This was the wound she chose to call out, name, and thereby cleanse.

Her Pulitzer-Prize-winning novel, *Beloved,* is a powerful and gut-wrenching tale of a runaway slave who'd rather cut her baby daughter's throat than let her lead a life enslaved. "I certainly thought I knew as much about slavery as anybody," Morrison explained once of her personal inward journey in writing the novel. "But it was the interior life I needed to find out about." There was terror in the writing of it. "I could imagine slavery in an intellectual way, but to feel it viscerally was terrifying. I had to go inside. Like an actor does. I had to feel what it might feel like for my own children to be enslaved."

When Oprah Winfrey read the novel, cover to cover, one night in her Lake Shore Drive apartment in Chicago, she paced around and around and picked up the book again. "Did I read that? Did I read what I thought I read?" She was so moved she tried to call Morrison, by then a Princeton University professor, at her New Jersey home but couldn't get the number on a weekend. So she called the fire department and told them to "call Toni and tell her Oprah called." Winfrey wanted to turn the book into a movie, and she did, playing the proud slave Sethe herself.

"It's my 'Schindler's List' and my 'Sophie's Choice,'" Winfrey said, explaining that the book had taken a situation that had a big, institutional label to it—slavery—and brought humanity to it. "Slavery meant your body did not belong to you. . . . The spiritual knowledge that you don't own you is far more devastating than anything you've been told about slavery." That profound insight, as it spread from reader to reader, revealed vulnerability as well as a potent sense of pride and strength shared with the book's heroine.

Wounds are often the other side of our greatest strengths. Just the way someone who is blind develops an acute sense of touch, our responses to wounds can become our strengths. And we should choose our heroes based both on the strengths we yearn for and the vulnerabilities we strive to overcome.

Every problem solver has some vulnerability. But successful Innovators take deliberate steps to confront their vulnerabilities. First, they stop trying to eliminate or deny them. They they identify them, explore their extent, share them, compensate for them, and move on with life. The best of them celebrate both vulnerability and the struggle to overcome it. (See Figure 1.3.) When you do celebrate both, you are in a position to light the fire of inspiration and innovation in others.

The ultimate act of courage is exposing and transcending weakness. Whether it is making fun of your own foibles, acknowledging shortcomings, or simply asking for help or advice, your action shows openness to improvement and helps create an environment that nurtures potential. When we see this courage in people who have overcome obstacles, we learn from them. These people become the heroes we always remember.

Toni Morrison was born Chloe Anthony Wofford during the Depression, in a rustbelt town not far from Cleveland. Her father was a shipwelder. Her

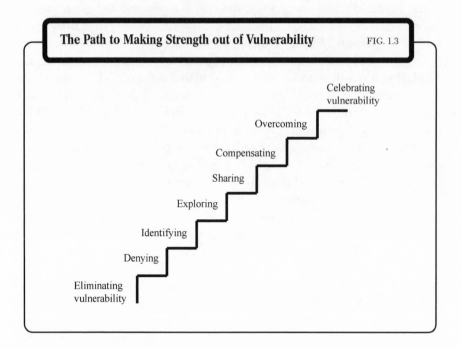

The Path to Making Strength out of Vulnerability   FIG. 1.3

Celebrating
vulnerability

Overcoming

Compensating

Sharing

Exploring

Identifying

Denying

Eliminating
vulnerability

grandparents on her mother's side were sharecroppers. She had a painful child-hood. While she was still a baby, her family fell behind on the four-dollars-a-month rent. The landlord set the house on fire—with the family in it. "It was this hysterical, out-of-the-ordinary, bizarre form of evil," she recalled once. "If you internalized it you'd be truly and thoroughly depressed because that's how much your life meant. For $4 a month somebody would just burn you to a crisp."

The family transcended the pain in the only way they could. "We laughed at the landlord, at the monumental cruelty of it," said Morrison. "That way you give back yourself to yourself. . . . That's what laughter does. You take it back. You take your life back. You take your integrity back."

That wisdom about the power of humor found its way into her fiction. In *Song of Solomon*, she explains that a street had come to be called Doctor Street after the city's only black doctor moved there. The city legislators didn't like it, and proclaimed with posted notices that the street had always been and would re-main "Mains Avenue and not Doctor Street." So the residents took to calling it Not Doctor Street.

Morrison has risen to prominence with storytelling that reveals, in a powerful and redeeming fashion, the flaws in America's social fabric. Applying her mind-set and lessons to the business and professional world is not as big a leap as it might seem. Once you've honestly examined and shared your vulnerabilities, your true strengths emerge; you become aware of your whole story, and through your newly understood strengths you learn how to contribute to a whole—a whole self, a whole organization, a whole community.

Morrison herself has come to a new understanding of the strengths of her people. She edited *The Black Book*, a look at three hundred years of black life in America, and she explained that she hoped that by doing so she would help blacks "recognize and rescue those qualities of resistance, excellence and integrity that were so much a part of our past and so useful to us and the generations of blacks now growing up." Sifting through photographs, newspaper clippings, and patents, Morrison found new heroes. The stories of black achievement, despite slavery and racism, that her parents had told her as she was growing up were true.

"I felt a renewal of pride I had not felt since 1941, when my parents told me stories of blacks who had invented airplanes, electricity and shoes," she said. "And there it was among Spike Harris's collection of patents: the overshoe. The airplane was also there as an airship registered in 1900 by John Pickering." "Morrison had," a biographer noted, "discovered a sustaining connection between her family history and habit of storytelling, black history and her own sense of identity."

It all comes back to stories. Stories like Morrison's are a viable and elegant way to reveal vulnerability that would otherwise be unbearable, and to celebrate strength that would otherwise stay hidden.

Innovation in Action: Creating and Telling Your Own Stories

Pick an area of your work where your instinct tells you a vulnerability exists that needs to be uncovered. It could be in yourself, your team, or even your entire organization. Step back and find the voice of disquiet. Explore the vulnerability and see if you can't develop a story around it. The story might involve how a customer was handled, how an employee was managed, how a stakeholder behaved. Now see if you can tell the story in such a way that it is redeeming, that the vulnerability or weakness or flaw is overcome. Let that story be your guide to how you may be able to turn the vulnerability you've identified into a strength for yourself or your colleagues.

HAVE IT BOTH WAYS
From Confidence to Determination

For me, walking the tightrope is living. Everything else is waiting.
—KARL WALLENDA (1905–1978)

Just as commitment can be undermined by inner vulnerabilities, it can also be weakened by the strength of external forces. When tough choices arise and trade–offs seem unavoidable, a sense of hopelessness can set in. Sometimes trade–offs are genuinely black and white—one thing must be sacrificed to obtain another. If this is truly so, the choice should be made quickly. But there is an inherent tension in such moments, a feeling of stress we try to relieve, sometimes by making a choice too quickly.

More often, trade-offs come in shades of gray and are subject to interpretation and analysis—it may be possible to have your cake and eat it too. When we resort to "either/or" decisionmaking in an attempt to relieve tension quickly, innovation suffers. Excellence often demands walking the tightrope of "both/and" thinking instead of "either/or." Customers want it both ways—low cost and high quality, customized and delivered overnight. Employees want workplaces with intense, competitive energy and great collaboration. By embracing both elements, even though they pull in opposite directions, Innovators learn there is always more than one way to do something.

Ron Barbaro, the former president, first of Prudential Insurance in Canada, then of Prudential Worldwide Operations, used "both/and" thinking to get around the hundred-year-old assumptions of the life insurance industry. By insisting on having it both ways, he was able to create "living death benefits" to help ease the suffering and perhaps even extend the lifetimes of AIDS patients in their final years.

Ron Barbaro and Living Death Benefits for AIDS Patients

Initially, Ron Barbaro felt the way a lot of people in the late 1980s did when it came to AIDS. A worthy cause, sure, but don't get too close. "Here's the corporate world, sending these few little bucks, but keeping twenty feet away," he recalled. As president of Prudential in Canada, Barbaro had long been active in the Toronto community. One day, a friend called up and urged him to get involved in Casey House, a new AIDS hospice. Barbaro agreed, and ended up raising more than $10,000 to add an elevator at the hospice.

When he brought the checks to Casey House, he was taken on a tour. Barbaro saw frail and shriveled men, meagerly living out their death sentences. "I was in a state of shock—these human souls, the suffering," said Barbaro. As he walked among those unfortunate people, he asked one of them, "Is there anything I can do?" He knew it sounded lame—just one of those polite things you say. "He belted me right back," Barbaro recalls. "He said, 'Yes. Help us die with dignity.' Wow! An instant feeling of helplessness and a sense of the impossible overcame me."

As the days passed, Barbaro asked after the patient and found he'd died. His remains were cremated, and the $25,000 his life insurance policy paid was sent to his parents in Germany. What irony. His parents hadn't been able to afford to come see their son before he died, and now, too late, there was $25,000. It set Barbaro to thinking. What if there had been a way to let that man have access to the money before his death?

What if there were a way? That is exactly how an Innovator's mindset begins. You open yourself to the possibility that something which seems inconceivable might actually be possible. You make the commitment to explore, to look for the answer. You cannot be rigid and absolute in your thinking. You cannot stop at either/or. You must ponder both/and.

The irony is that the either/or option seems easier at first—but gets harder as you experience the consequences of all you've given up. The both/and option feels harder at first—but as you push through and examine the real possibilities, it gets easier as perceived conflicts fade. With more information, you often find simple ways of accomplishing what you thought was impossible.

When Barbaro started mulling the possibility of death benefits for the living, he saw that the biggest obstacle was a traditional bureaucratic mindset. "It was a firmly entrenched attitude that payment follows death. An industry maxim, not a

government regulation," he says. "Death benefits for the living wasn't in the order of things."

"I got all my rocket scientists together," he explains, noting that he called in his
lawyers, actuaries, claims adjusters, and the company's medical director. He
shared his idea for accelerated benefits for terminally ill patients, so they might
have a better quality of life in what little time they had. "Everybody thought I'd
taken leave of my senses—Call 911," he recalls, laughing at the memory.

"All the lawyers, being lawyers, said, 'Well, why would you if contractually you
don't have to?' There were a hundred reasons not to do it, and we started eliminating them." There were questions of eligibility. How should they define terminally ill, and what diseases should be included? There were tax questions—would
beneficiaries have to pay taxes? Would it be discrimination not to offer a similar
policy to people who weren't dying? Would this create a nightmare for the company, and invite a stampede of the very sick to Prudential's door?

"Every time a black hat came up, we'd defeat it," Barbaro said, the tone of determination clear in his voice. He refused to believe that it couldn't be done, and
he was right. It could be done. A few companies had previously offered a "dread
disease" policy, which was purchased for a specific disease such as cancer. But
Prudential was the first company to consider offering life benefits for all diseases.

After Barbaro opened their eyes, Prudential executives set about hammering
out a proposal that would be good for its policyholders, but also sound for the
company. They settled on giving policyholders the option of adding an accelerated benefits rider, rather than making it standard. Existing policyholders carry-
ing $25,000 in coverage could add it retroactively for free. New policyholders
had to carry at least $50,000 in coverage. Prudential put together a formula for
the payoff that calculated lost investment income and administrative costs. Terminally ill policyholders would get about 95 to 97 percent of their benefits.

There were a few trial runs, but before long, regulators in several states had
approved Prudential's plan, with every state on board by 1992. The new approach brought mountains of publicity for Prudential, partially as a result of a
policyholder who called in the media. Life insurance sales shot up 25 percent in
the first half of 1990. And it has revolutionized the industry. Now, companies
holding 78 percent of the life insurance policies in America offer plans that provide accelerated death benefits to people still living.

During the initial global media blitz, Barbaro went to visit one of the policyholders, also named Ron. As he entered the sick man's house, Barbaro recalls his
own fear. "I hesitated touching the doorknob," he says. He remembers seeing a
brand new washer and dryer as he entered, and then he saw the gaunt man in a
rocker—"He looked like he weighed about 100 pounds." He had draped an
afghan over his knees.

Barbaro asked him how he'd spent his benefits, which came to almost $25,000.
The man had purchased a new drug to ease his suffering and possibly buy him

more time. "He had purchased the washer and dryer, because he was no longer welcome at the laundromat," Barbaro said. And the man had bought a train ticket, to take him home to make peace with the family that had once disowned him because of his lifestyle.

"I'm at peace," the man told Barbaro. He'd given his last $2,000 to the church where his sister was a nun. Barbaro—the man who had been afraid to touch the doorknob minutes earlier—hugged the man whose body had been ravaged by AIDS.

Innovation in Action: Applying Creative Determination

Pick a tension that is creating a lot of stress and strain in your life, a situation where you feel compelled to choose between alternatives but are tortured by giving something up. Maybe you don't have to. Allow yourself to imagine what it would be like if you could have everything you want. No matter how impossible that vision seems, hold onto it. Diligently evaluate every possible creative option that can help you achieve it. Work through all the apparent barriers one by one. By the time you've done all this, you may see how to make your image a reality.

TRANSCEND LIMITS
From Determination to Innovation

It is in working within limits that the master reveals himself.
—GOETHE (1749–1832)

With a mindset based on seeing opportunities, committing to their realization, making strengths of vulnerabilities, and applying that determination to finding "both/and" solutions, Innovators can begin to confront their true limits. The limits of their imaginations. The limits of their abilities. The limits of their resources. The limits of their professional training. The limits imposed by nature. Great problem solving demands transcending those limits, but adeptness at managing limitations is not always as simple as breaking through them. Sometimes, the creative solution of problems involves setting limits in some areas to generate extra energy and focus in others.

There are few institutions in the world that have the reputation for setting, protecting, and breaking through boundaries and limits like the U.S. Marine Corps. Taking the beachhead which no one else will dare is their defining maneuver. But even the Marines were tested when their most recent commandant, General Charles Krulak, designed "The Crucible"—the boot camp training regimen that has become famous for pushing even the toughest men past their limits to transform them into a new generation of Marines.

Charles Krulak and the Process of Forging U.S. Marines

It's 2 A.M. on Parris Island, and young Marine recruits—who've already endured ten weeks of punishing boot camp—are rousted from their bunks. This is the start of fifty-four hours in which they will be deprived of sleep and food and have all their psychological and physical limits tested. This is the Crucible. The tests take place at a series of "warrior stations," where the recruits will have to snake through live gunfire, cross rivers on a few planks of wood, and march forty miles with sixty pounds of gear on their backs.

It is a defining moment, a "gut check," as Krulak, former commandant of the U.S. Marine Corps, calls it. He brainstormed the Crucible in the mid-1990s, after studying what war might be like in the twenty-first century. He thought about what kind of soldier it would take to fight those wars, and he became convinced future marines would have to operate beyond the accepted limits of the past. The more you sweat in peace, the Marines like to say, the less you bleed in war. Krulak wanted even more sweat, less blood, and more thought.

To transcend limits in solving a problem, you have to know where the frontiers are. What are the existing limits you face? How are they changing? What frontiers have yet to be established? By moving into frontiers, Innovators not only explore new territory, they also discover new ways of thinking about their institutions. This kind of discovery is what Krulak wanted as he sought to understand the demands of future wars.

"It became pretty clear to me that the wars we would fight in the twenty-first century would be very chaotic," Krulak says. "There would be cultural, religious, and ethnic conflicts, highly complex and of widely varying scale. Conventional wars of nation-state against nation-state would be less likely." He looked at Somalia, the ethnic uprising in Chechnya, the civil war in Bosnia. He figured those were the models for future war—not Desert Storm, Vietnam, or the two World Wars. Krulak realized that soldiers of the future would not only make combat decisions on the battlefield, but moral decisions as well. "When you're fighting in villages and in towns and close terrain where the civilians are interspersed with your combatants," he says, "the decision to shoot or not to shoot is a tough one. It's a responsibility you're handing to a young man or woman and saying here, you make the call."

The Marines call it a "three-block" war—where a soldier may be faced with three different missions within three city blocks. "You've got a young marine who has a child in his arms at one moment. He's feeding it and caring for it, and it's called humanitarian assistance," Krulak explains. "And the next moment in time that same individual is forcing two warring tribes apart and it's called peacekeeping. And the next moment that same soldier is involved in a deadly firefight. It all happens within a twenty-four-hour period and within three city blocks." He adds, "How do you train someone to move seamlessly between those three types of problems and make a good decision every time?" Krulak saw these chaotic conflicts on the horizon that would require extraordinarily tough decisions by young people, but a society and a Marine Corps that were not producing the necessary young men and women of character. To transcend the limits of Marine culture, he realized, it would be necessary to push the limits of present-day marines.

There are two kinds of limitations. There are the limits we perceive are there. These limits are created by ignorance, lack of imagination, or just plain fear. Facts and tough-minded thinking can overcome those. Then there are the real limits, created by the environment, a lack of money, or people, or materials. Resourcefulness, innovation, and intelligent design are required to break through these.

Krulak was facing the perceived limitations of an old culture, old rules, and old conceptions of what a soldier should be. He also faced the very real limitations of the material that society was placing at his door in the form of new recruits. Krulak wanted to learn how to shape ability, decisionmaking, loyalty, character, and independence in a young soldier. He didn't know the answer. He just knew he had to transcend the current limits.

The key to thinking beyond existing limits—innovation—is to move to another point of view. Innovators understand rules and laws, but are not necessarily bound by them. It's like getting a good foothold before making a long jump. You need to know the ground well enough to decide where to plant your foot. But the plant isn't restrictive—it's what allows you to take off, to push off in another direction that offers a new vantage point.

To help him shape new Marines, Krulak began pushing himself and his commanders far outside their comfort zones. He brought in scientists, creative thinkers, and specialists in dozens of disciplines from around the world. Based on input from these free thinkers, his team analyzed what it would take to be a successful Marine and how such a person could be created from the material they had to work with.

The psychiatrists and psychologists they'd talked to about Generation X recruits reported that most young people "had never really had what is called a defining moment or a gut check, a period in their life where they really had to reach down to perform." Given Krulak's purposes, he decided that a "gut-check" was required for the new Crucible. This was the real breakthrough. He would give the young Gen X recruits exactly what they hadn't had—a moment in their lives when they really had to reach deeply. It would be a moment when they recognized their limits—and then transcended them.

Reaching one's limits and breaking down—whether it is an emotional or physical collapse—can lead to shame and embarrassment. It's an uncomfortable situation. But in healthy workplaces, people are encouraged to go beyond their limits and comfort zones. If they fail, they receive the support of the group to pick themselves up and try again. It's unhealthy workplaces, on the other hand, that discourage such creativity from the start or don't embrace the failures that are part of taking risks. Consequently, the organization never learns how great its collective capabilities could be.

In the same way steel is tempered by breaking down its molecular structure and rearranging it, the Crucible forces a breakdown that leads to a breakthrough. As the recruits arrive at each warrior station, the drill instructor appoints a leader, who has to put the squad together and come up with a solution to a daunting problem. "What happens, of course," explains Krulak, "is by now they're very tired and very hungry, they're cold and wet, and all the human factors that come into play when people are under stress are normally shown. Some are mad and some are despondent. It's up to the team to pull together and accomplish the mission. A leader must facilitate that." Things usually get worse before they get better, and breakdowns usually occur.

The challenges in the Crucible are based on team and individual efforts. None of the obstacles can be overcome unless the recruits pull together. And it's not always the appointed leader who shows the true leadership. "Slowly but surely in the first ten weeks of boot camp we develop self-discipline," Krulak says. In other words, learning to set limits. "Then, starting with the Crucible, we wanted to drive them toward what we call selflessness. You have self-discipline and then during the Crucible you become part of a team, part of the Marine family, and selflessness becomes the watchword." Self-discipline and selflessness blend in the Crucible to forge the morality and character required for a modern soldier.

At the end of the Crucible, the recruits—wet and smelly and tired and dirty—are Marines. In an emotional concluding ceremony, flags flutter and Lee Greenwood's "Proud to Be an American" plays in the background. "Now that may sound a little hokey," says Krulak, "but what we're trying to do is at this very emotional time—and believe me, there's not one dry eye in the house—we want them to understand: 'You are a Marine. But you are an American first.'"

The disciplined self, the unified corps, and the principled citizen, each level involves setting limits in order to transcend them. "That's what the Constitution is all about—setting limits to make freedom possible—and that is what's important," says Krulak. "People who say there's a disconnect between the military and society . . . well, one of the reasons we do what we do at the Crucible is to drive home that although you have this unbelievable allegiance to your fellow Marines and to the Marine Corps, behind it all you're an Individual, an American, and fully accountable for and capable of making the right choices in all those roles."

Innovation in Action: Transcending Your Own Limits

Create your own crucible by devising a test for teams in your organization that is related to your business (i.e., not just climbing a mountain or building a raft together). Make this a test that is very demanding, that is likely to create breakdowns and is calculated to confront just the kinds of challenges you expect to face in your business in the next five years. Then put together teams, especially of those first entering your organization, to face these challenges—with talented, skilled senior guides who will help them achieve their own breakthrough.

CHARACTERISTICS OF AN INNOVATOR

General characteristics and purpose: Innovators emphasize ideas. Their goal is creativity and innovation. They pursue creative formulations, play, ideas, concepts, and humor. Innovators like diversity and usually take a variety of approaches to something rather than just one. They value beauty, imagination, inspiration, and perspective. For them, time, structured knowledge, completed solutions, and practical resources are less important.

Strengths: Innovators can reconceptualize paradigms and develop creative alternative paths, solutions, and approaches. They refuse to be bound by existing ways of thinking. They are willing to experiment and play with totally absurd ideas. They can also achieve high levels of determination and persistence.

Skill Levels of Innovation   TABLE 1.1

Level 1   Has creative instincts and intuitions, but is unable to find any way to express them.

Level 2   Has creative impulses, and is able to express them in language, art, mechanics, music, dance or some other form.

Level 3   Can express creative impulses at a level of quality or ubiquity that make them outstanding amongst their peer group.

Level 4   Expresses creative impulses in a disciplined, not just an erratic fashion, continuously.

Level 5   Demonstrates innovative powers that achieve recognition beyond their field.

Level 6   Able to conceptualize, uncover and communicate a complete change in an existing paradigm or way of doing things that makes a genuinely rare contribution (e.g. Nobel prize winners).

Level 7   Able to conceptualize, uncover and communicate a complete change in an existing paradigm that alters the world as we know it (historic).

Weaknesses: However, Innovators can also have difficulty making choices and aiding in execution. They can be idiosyncratic and challenged in their ability to develop relationships with others. They can also be difficult to pry out of an area not bearing fruit.

Interactions with other types of problem solvers: An Innovator teamed with a Creator generates a potent combination of a conceptualizer and a more practical, concrete personality. Innovation encourages the generation of more creative options in the process of designing and constructing solutions. On the other hand, Innovators often clash with Performers, who sometimes have little patience for innovation. Performers thrive because of their focus and convergent thinking, which is in direct opposition to the playfulness and divergent thinking of many Innovators. Innovators, who see themselves as masters of ideas, may have little respect for Communicators, who operate in the "easy" realm of interpersonal relations. Innovators can also clash with Playmakers, who are authority figures and may seem too conservative and unwilling to take alternative points of view.

Typical ways Innovators are mismanaged: Not enough time or energy is invested in them because of the rush and resource-draw of execution. Other times, Innovators are asked to be creative, but only within certain bounds, which heavily constrains their abilities. Sometimes, a problem solver will attempt to keep a project team fenced off from a strong Innovator, for fear of too many inefficient conversations or divergent opinions.

Guidance for Innovation

Guiding Principles: Rules and Laws That Bear on Innovation
- The less you know about a problem, the more creative alternatives you can see.
- Problems and opportunities often come together, because they both involve change.
- Personal commitment creates change.
- Intrinsic motivation is the only thing that lasts.
- Untreated wounds don't heal well, if at all.
- Find what you're good at, stick to it and complement it.
- Innovation springs from inspiration, persistence, and relentless work.
- What is perceived is often real; what you believe is real may be only perceived.
- It often takes setting some limits to break through others.
- Absolute thinking will absolutely constrain your options.

Diagnostics: How Innovative Is Your Mindset?
- Are you capable of being both optimistic and skeptical? Do you look at problems from a variety of different points of view? Do you know your

own biases and those of the people you're working with? Do you consider both the absolute best and worst that could happen—and use that to assess situations?

- Are you really willing to do whatever it takes to achieve your vision? Why or why not? How much are you willing to sacrifice? Why? Have you considered the alternatives well enough to give them up?
- Do you know what your own wounds are? How deep are they? How severe are they? Have you ignored them or tried to cleanse them? Can you play as well as you can work? Can you laugh at absurdity as easily as you can search for meaning?
- Do you know what is causing you stress and strain? Is the level acceptable or not? Is it worth it? Have you chosen the right tensions? Are you confronting them and managing them? Do they embody real trade-offs or just perceived ones?
- Do you know the most important limits you or your organization face? Which are real and which are perceived? How do you know? Can some constraints be increased so that others can be relaxed? When people reach their limits in your organization, how are they treated? Are they encouraged to try in the first place? Are they supported when they fail, or just rewarded when they succeed?

Syndromes: Diseases Which May Plague Your Ability to Generate an Innovative Mindset

- "Playing the victim"—Inability to see possibility, take personal responsibility, or make commitments because you've labeled yourself a victim
- "A closed mind"—An inability to see opportunities because of bias, prejudice, cultural preconception, arrogance, insecurity, or haste
- "Submission to extremes"—Letting either extreme sensitivity or detachment inhibit your ability to commit
- "Counting on the muse"—Waiting for inspiration as opposed to working for it
- "Playing the cowboy"—Never asking for help and trying to do it all alone; refusing to acknowledge vulnerabilities out of pride or insecurity
- "Fear of fear"—Unwillingness to confront fears and get over old habits to fully commit to success
- "Permission syndrome"—Doing something because others think you should or failing to act because of a perceived need for permission
- "Been there, done that syndrome"—Believing that a problem fits a past experience when in reality it is something completely new

Going Further

Selected resources for further study. (See also sources and notes for Part 1 on page 265.)

Books

Adams, James. *The Care and Feeding of Ideas.* Reading, MA: Addison-Wesley, 1988. and *Conceptual Blockbusting: A Guide to Better Ideas.* Reading, MA: Addison-Wesley, 1986.
Arieti, Silvano. *Creativity.* New York: Basic Books, 1976.
Boden, Margaret. *The Creative Mind.* New York: Basic Books, 1991.
Camus, Albert. *The Rebel.* New York: Penguin, 1971.
Czsikszenmihalyi, Mihaly. *Creativity.* New York: Harper Collins, 1996.
De Bono, Edward. *Serious Creativity.* New York: Harper Business, 1992.
Doczi, Gyorgy. *The Power of Limits.* Boston: Shambhala, 1994.
Edwards, Betty. *Drawing on the Artist Within.* New York: Simon & Schuster, 1986.
Foster, Richard. *Innovation.* New York: Summit Books, 1986.
Ghiselin, Brewster. *The Creative Process.* New York: Mentor, 1952.
Goleman, Daniel, et al. *The Creative Spirit.* New York: Dutton Books, 1992.
Howard, V. A. *Varieties of Thinking.* New York: Routledge, 1990.
Koestler, Arthur. *The Act of Creation.* New York: Arkana, 1964.
Kuhn, Thomas. *The Structure of Scientific Revolutions.* Chicago: University of Chicago Press, 1970.
Miller, William. *The Creative Edge.* Boston: Addison-Wesley, 1987.
Van Oech, Roger. *A Whack on the Side of the Head.* New York: Warner Books, 1983.
Von Hippel, Eric. *The Sources of Innovation.* Oxford: Oxford University Press, 1988.
Wallace, Doris, and Howard Gruber. *Creative People at Work.* New York: Oxford University Press, 1989.
Wycoff, Joyce. *Mindmapping.* New York: Berkeley Books, 1991.

Websites

Creativity: www.gocreate.com
Creativity web: www.ozemail.com.au (search for Creativity Web)
Creativity: www.mindbloom.com
Creativity–Broken crayons: www.cre8ng.com
Creativity: www.enchantedmind.com
Brainstorming: www.brainstorming.co.uk
Innovation: www.likemindedpeople.com
The Innovation Network: www.thinksmart.com
Innovation: www.infinn.com
Innovation research: Mint.McMaster.ca
Innovation: www.fastcompany.com/online/resources (Choose Themes)

Part Two

⧳KNOW THE TERRITORY⧳

The Discoverer

Ask the Right Questions and Get Good Information

When you know, to know that you know, and when you do not know, to know that you do not know, that is knowledge.
—CONFUCIUS (551–479 B.C.)

Knowledge is the key asset of our age. Knowing a territory—the work of a Discoverer—means acquiring the right knowledge about the critical elements of the environment you solve problems in. It takes curiosity, awareness, insight, and a passion for learning. Discoverers ask the best possible questions and get timely information about their terrain. This skill builds on the Innovator's creativity and commitment and produces a better understanding of problems and opportunities and more insight into how to handle them. The right knowledge leads to new and often attractive destinations, while protecting you from dangerous routes and false paths. Knowing the territory helps problem solvers both to choose a worthwhile destination and to survive the journey.

The Lewis and Clark Expedition, July 5, 1803–Sept. 23, 1806

At the beginning of the nineteenth century, the great flood of European newcomers to America was beginning to push west. Learning about the territory ahead was vital for creating wealth, opportunity, and new settlements out of the wilderness.

The problem was, Thomas Jefferson had just bought a massive tract of land—the Louisiana Territory—with many real dangers, and people were surging into it without reliable knowledge. The nation needed Discoverers to map the new lands and send back information about what the settlers could expect as they trekked west. The opportunity was to expand scientific knowledge of the continent, to develop commercial relationships, and to uncover the means by which the national borders might stretch from one ocean to another. That was where Lewis and Clark came in.

Unlike Columbus, who was driven by a vision of riches and who innovated by uncovering an entirely new part of the world, Lewis and Clark were true Discoverers, who journeyed out for the sole purpose of mapping and understanding a defined territory in depth. Their expedition stands out for its focus on systematically gathering knowledge. That knowledge was to lay the foundation for a nation's journey across the continent.

Lewis and Clark exhibited the essentials of discovery in many ways. To prepare themselves, they gathered data from experts, enlisted guides, and pored over the journals of previous travelers. In this way, they determined what they knew already and what they still needed to know. They understood the full scope of the challenge, but focused on what was key to Jefferson, proving or disproving the existence of an easy Northwest Passage to support commerce. They spotted patterns in the new landscapes, the weather, the rivers and swamps, that would ease or impede their travels. They took account of all the key players in the territory, the Indian tribes and foreign powers that might compete for dominance or impede the progress of settlement. They learned as they went along, remaining open to the expanding boundaries of their own knowledge. They learned not to view new encounters solely through the lens of past experience.

There are many who work with the spirit of Lewis and Clark today. One of these modern Discoverers might be a market researcher, charting new Internet market space for a venture capital partnership. Or a laboratory scientist, studying the molecular and chemical foundations of the body in preparation for testing a new drug. One is a journalist, investigating a pattern of corrupt behavior among elected officials. Another might be an accident investigator, trying to uncover the causes of a disaster, to see not only who was responsible but also whether it can be prevented from ever happening again. They are motivated by the search for truth and disciplined by the understanding that what they discover will affect the work of countless explorers in the years ahead.

The Discoverer's Central Idea: The Best Insight
Comes from Balancing Perspective and Immersion

In the knowledge age, most explicit knowledge (i.e., knowledge outside our minds that can be given tangible form) will eventually be digitized. For the first time in history, our ability to store knowledge has outpaced its creation. As this knowledge is shaped and collected into databases, the best problem solvers will have extraordinary automated tools at their disposal to find patterns and thus identify problems and opportunities. Still, whether you are using a simple search engine or complex data-mining techniques, the quality of your insight and understanding will depend on whether or not you are asking the right questions.

Maximizing your chances of discovering useful knowledge requires simultaneously using top-down and bottom-up approaches to problem solving and questioning. (See Figure 2.1.) The top-down approach is problem-focused and uses deductive thinking: You ask creative and focused questions before looking at the data. The bottom-up approach uses inductive thinking. You make observations and use analytical tools to build patterns from the data, reorganizing it to find new trends and insights. Either approach without the other is far less effective than the combination. Together, they are a powerful means of developing the best possible understanding of an environment. Both approaches achieve their fullest potential if your questions are followed by working hypotheses about a likely answer, which are then tested and in turn lead to better questions. This type of "hypothesis-driven" discovery enables you to learn about a territory and eventually master it most effectively and efficiently.

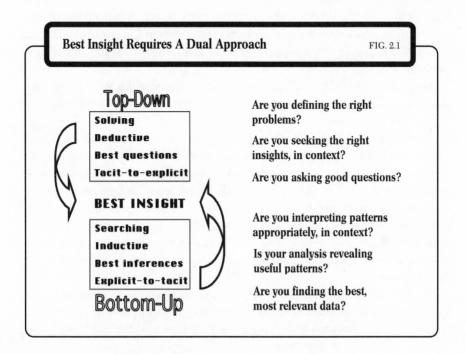

Best Insight Requires A Dual Approach   FIG. 2.1

Top-Down

| Solving |
| Deductive |
| Best questions |
| Tacit-to-explicit |

BEST INSIGHT

| Searching |
| Inductive |
| Best inferences |
| Explicit-to-tacit |

Bottom-Up

Are you defining the right problems?

Are you seeking the right insights, in context?

Are you asking good questions?

Are you interpreting patterns appropriately, in context?

Is your analysis revealing useful patterns?

Are you finding the best, most relevant data?

Discoverers in Action:
Monsanto and the Revolution in Genetic Engineering

If the Discoverer's central idea is that a flexible, focused approach is necessary to create the best insight, then how does it apply in practice? How does a Discoverer develop and apply the knowledge of a territory to create deep understanding? The following story of Robert Shapiro and Monsanto Corporation illustrates Discoverers in action. With their contribution, problem solvers can build on the ideas and inspiration of Innovators by adding strategic knowledge that moves a creative idea one step closer to the reality of exploiting an opportunity.

Monsanto is one of the many companies exploring how to influence life itself through genetic engineering. The entire biotech industry is charting new territory because of the new technologies that permit scientists and researchers to decipher and manipulate genetic codes.

Since earliest history, farmers have crossed one desirable plant with another, producing a crudely directed mix of both gene pools. The new plant may be hardier, but it may also carry on many undesirable genetic traits. With genetic engineering, on the other hand, only the genetic material for the desired trait is transferred. You know exactly the trait you want and the gene responsible for that trait. The new technology—assuming we know exactly what we are doing—allows agriculture to shift from reliance on external components, such as chemicals, to a system for producing better crops that's based on genetic information coded right into the genes of the plants. "Information," says Robert Shapiro, CEO of Monsanto, "is far more efficient than chemicals and much more sustainable."

Shapiro is a Discoverer who understands the nature of the quest before him. He started, as many Discoverers do, with a simple high-level insight buttressed by extensive observations.

The way he sees it, the Earth is a closed system with limits that are already within reach. There are roughly six billion people on the planet today, he says, and that's expected to increase substantially over the next few generations. Six million square miles of farmland cover the globe today, an area about the size of South America. But it would take millions of additional square miles to properly feed the swelling population in thirty years. That arable land isn't available. "The only practical answer," Shapiro says, "is to increase the production on existing farmland." And this goal leads to the key question: How can that be done?

Shapiro and Monsanto are betting the answer to one of the world's biggest problems lies in genetically engineered crops—boosting their nutrient value, yield, and pest resistance by unlocking the mysteries of DNA and transplanting bits of genes into plants. In short, they aim to turn knowledge into the commodity that feeds the world.

The historical pattern of human population growth juxtaposed with periodic hunger and famine reveals a potential threat to the species—and an enormous business opportunity. "We're getting, for the first time in our history as a species, to the point where our population is going to overwhelm the ability of the planet to continue to provide us with more and more stuff," Shapiro says. And that leaves two outcomes. Mankind either settles for "less stuff," as Shapiro puts it, which would affect the poorest the most, or "you find some way to create value for people without creating more stuff. And the only way that can possibly work is if you find some other commodity that's as valuable as physical, material things. And the only possibility that I know of is knowledge. Knowledge clearly has value, and it doesn't require an exponential growth in material things in order for a knowledge-based strategy to provide better lives for people." This is the heart of the problem and the most probable solution, as Shapiro sees it.

Armed with clear goals and questions, Monsanto has learned the new territory of biotechnology.

Already, it has such products as "Bollgard" cotton, which has been genetically modified to produce a protein that kills boll worms, cotton's biggest pest. There's also the "New Leaf" potato, which wards off the Colorado beetle. Biotech crops went from about 3 million acres around the globe in their first year, 1996, to over 65 million acres in 1998.

To build its knowledge, Monsanto's leadership assessed the key players and learned to recognize what was at stake for them. Starting in the early 1980s with Jack Hanley, then Dick Mahoney, and finally Shapiro, they assembled a team of stellar biologists and invested heavily in research and development. Although molecular biologists—with all the exciting work going on with the human genome—were in great demand, plant biologists weren't—until Monsanto targeted them as key players, and positioned itself as one of the few creative places for them to go. During his tenure, Shapiro continued to seek out the best and convince them to join. Many signed up because of Shapiro's personal vision and mastery of the subject. He had focused not only on what Monsanto needed to know immediately but also on how to continue discovering in the years ahead. For all these reasons, Monsanto was able to bridge the traditional management/scientist divide, and bring on board the key scientific players it needed to achieve its goals.

But Shapiro didn't just acquire talented people. He also bought companies and hiked research and development spending. In five years, he poured more than $10 billion into R&D and acquisitions. His goal was to build a superb knowledge base—an evolving foundation of learning on which Monsanto could draw for decades. His strategy was to learn everything possible about how genetic engineering could apply to food production. Many of these applications would be based on gene-splicing and insertion, a technology that had the potential to produce hundreds of new products in the years ahead. Shapiro understood how strategic knowledge gathering could lead to problem solving excellence.

The hardest part, Shapiro said, was convincing investors to come along. "There was very little understanding on the part of Monsanto's investor base as to why you'd want to spend a lot of money, for a long period of time, for things no one had ever done before and no one could really imagine exactly, and no one could figure out how you were going to get paid for whatever it was you were going to produce." Before there were any payoffs, Monsanto spent at the rate of about $1.5 billion a year on R&D, learning the new territory of biotechnology. "We had been investing in agricultural biotechnology for well over fifteen years before we made our first sale of anything," says Shapiro. "Which I love to point out when people talk about how shortsighted American corporations are, living only from quarter to quarter and so on."

And how do they keep their eye on the prize? "You have to keep learning, keep checking whether you still believe you're right," Shapiro said. "It's certainly possible to have a perfectly plausible theory as to why something's going to work, but as time goes on it may turn out you're wrong. You better know that quickly and stop at that point. The awareness and courage to stop is one skill you definitely need. But, conversely, you also need the conviction to stay with what you truly believe in. Dick Mahoney [Shapiro's predecessor] had that kind of courage in the face of a fair amount of criticism."

The first wave of Monsanto's genetically engineered products help farmers grow crops with fewer chemicals and at less expense. Bollgard cotton, for instance, achieves 85–90 percent reductions in insecticide applications for cotton budworms and bollworms. That is considerable, given that cotton crops use about a third of all the insecticides in the United States. Farmers using the Newleaf potato get about a 40 percent reduction in insecticides.

"The second wave will produce crops that are more nutritious, because they include more healthy oils, proteins, and other ingredients," says Shapiro. For instance, Monsanto is working on creating crops to produce beta-carotene naturally. This nutrient is particularly important in many Asian markets, where hundreds of millions of people suffer from Vitamin A deficiency. Supplements would work, but it's hard to get them to remote villages, and you can't force people to take them. The solution: Put beta-carotene, which the body metabolizes into Vitamin A, right into crops used in the country's ordinary diet.

Biotech crops have made important inroads in the marketplace but aren't universally accepted. In fact, many consumer and environmental groups are viciously antagonistic. Public acceptance in Europe is particularly low. The reactionary movement there has spread to the United States, and it's hard to know whether this is just a phase the nascent industry must weather or the death of Shapiro's vision.

The truth is, Monsanto drastically misestimated public support for genetically altered products and failed to take into account the role activists and politics could play in whipping up a media frenzy. That was one aspect of the territory that the company didn't take enough time to fully understand—a key set of players whose stakes weren't sufficiently understood.

Nevertheless, Shapiro's strategy is to keep producing smart innovations. "We're an institution that's fundamentally based on knowledge and science," he says. "The test of whether we've done our work well at the end of it is: Do we introduce products that people find helpful?"

In summary, knowledge has always been a source of power. But in the "knowledge age," achieving excellence is especially dependent on having the right strategic knowledge. In a recent survey of hundreds of American CEOs by the Department of Commerce's Baldridge Award, those polled said that after globalization, their greatest challenge—where the gap between their desired and existing capability was largest—was in knowledge management. In any industry or endeavor, there is core knowledge that is the key to the future. But you have to develop it before you can manage it.

For Lewis and Clark, the ultimate understanding and insight were based on determining whether or not a Northwest Passage existed, what the best routes of travel were and which tribes and lands would encourage or inhibit commerce. For Monsanto, the questions were which genes had which functions? How exactly did they execute those functions? What types of interventions would affect their activity, either by enhancing or dampening their effects? And which food products had the most to gain from applying those technologies? Both examples demonstrate that although knowledge is no guarantee of success, the better you know the territory, the smarter you get, the more options you have, the more potential rewards are identified, and the fewer risks you take.

The rest of this part covers in more depth and detail how the best Discoverers approach knowledge creation and problem solving so as to move from innovation to genuine insight. You can either skip to the next part, "Build the Relationships," on page 79, or proceed. Each of the following chapters explains one aspect of how Discoverers start with asking the right questions and progress to a posture of continual learning.

- "Know What and How to Know: From Ignorance to Information" shows how to ask the right questions and bring expertise to bear quickly in attacking a problem or opportunity. Examining the different approaches of Dr. William Haseltine and Dr. Craig Venter to the human genome shows varying strategies for knowledge acquisition and exploitation.

- "Spot the Patterns: From Information to Focus" pinpoints how to recognize patterns of change that define a specific problem or opportunity. The expertise of Dr. D. James Baker and Dr. Ants Leetmaa, key meteorologists from the National Oceanic and Atmospheric Administration, illustrates how techniques used to predict the weather can help you identify meaningful patterns.
- "Assess the Players and Stakes: From Focus to Interests," explains how to get a sense of who the key players are that may be affected, what is at stake for them, and what type of game you need to play. In this chapter Robin Allen, the director of the historic Barker Foundation, shares the approaches of the foundation's social workers to untangling the complex web of human interests in the process of adoption.
- "See the Whole, But Get to the Heart: From Interests to Understanding" illustrates how to specify the key leverage points or root causes that will give you the biggest bang for the buck in terms of impact per unit of resource. A lead investigator from the National Transportation Safety Board, Bernard Loeb, explains how the board gets to the root causes of airline accidents and ultimately develops constructive recommendations for potential solutions.
- "Learn to Learn: From Understanding to Learning" demonstrates the process of learning a territory and the awareness of learning styles and methods that makes it work. The executive in charge of corporate education at Xerox Business Services, Raymond Lammes, shows how successful learning takes place today in high growth, high intensity corporate environments.

KNOW WHAT AND HOW TO KNOW
From Ignorance to Information

Mankind may be divided into four classes:
those who know and know that they know–of them seek knowledge,
those who know but do not know that they know–awaken them,
those who do not know and know that they do not know–instruct them,
those who do not know but think that they know–they are fools, dismiss them.

–SALOMON IBN GABIROL (1020–1070)

Some Discoverers start their problem solving from ignorance, facing an uncharted territory, a literal unknown. Yet most problems needn't be solved from scratch. Usually, we can leverage existing knowledge to get us closer to the answer. Previous visitors may have information on the unknown territory. Natives of that territory—people who live or work in or around the area to be explored—may have expertise they are willing to share. Gathering such knowledge helps Discoverers distinguish what is known already and what questions must still be asked. It helps them define problems early and find solutions quickly. Without such knowledge, one is more likely to struggle over the diagnosis, treat symptoms rather than the cause, and deploy inadequate solutions that waste time and resources.

Yet in our present age of high tech information systems, we often put more effort into digitizing, manipulating, and searching within existing information than we do in pondering the right questions to ask. Individuals and organizations are often unwilling to make the long-term investment that high value knowledge requires. Instead, they rely on narrow viewpoints, superficial sources, legends, and stereotypes. They miss the benefit of deeper and broader general knowledge. Yes, specialized knowledge is indispensable. But because specialized knowledge can apply narrowly and go out of date quickly, general knowledge is also required to create a coherent approach to a question or problem.

One of the most strategic applications of knowledge in the world today involves the knowledge of life itself. Craig Venter and William Haseltine are among several scientists exploring the topography of the human genome. To help map this uncharted territory, they have brought together a dazzling group of scientists, ranging from mathematicians and computer specialists to biologists and financial executives.

Dr. William Haseltine and Dr. Craig Venter– The Human Genome Project

The mapping of the human genome is one of the most important knowledge-gathering events in history. By cataloguing the sequence of proteins in human DNA, then isolating the genes and learning how they operate to cause disease, scientists hope to usher in a new era of medicine. This knowledge promises to break the paradigm of diagnose and cure (a catch-up game once the disease has begun, using drugs that can have dangerous side effects) to predict and prevent (treating damaged or dysfunctional genes early, before they cause harm). The opportunities could be revolutionary. As William Haseltine, one of the key players, says optimistically, "Death is a series of preventable diseases."

The best maps are comprehensive enough to show all the landforms and their relationship to one another. But they also show the myriad details of a landscape. Their degree of accuracy and usefulness is judged by problem solvers who work with them in the field. The knowledge to make such maps is produced by asking questions. The most basic are: What are the real unknown areas? Who knows the most about them now? How much more knowledge is really needed? What is the most important knowledge to acquire? How will it be used in practice?

Haseltine wants to solve the problem of disease, but he doesn't want to do it by mapping the genome. That's more problem solving than is required, he argues. "If you have a crook in the jail, why do you need his address? You don't. Similarly, if you can find the gene that causes the disease, why do you need to know where it's located in the larger structure of DNA?" Haseltine says from the headquarters of his gene-hunting company, Human Genome Sciences (HGS), in Rockville, Maryland.

But in the race to fully decode and understand DNA, Haseltine is only one of the explorers who are trying to write "The Book of Life" as it has been called. Another is Craig Venter, a former colleague of his, who runs a high-profile corporation called Celera Genomics. Together, they exemplify two fundamentally different approaches to discovering knowledge. Haseltine's is problem-focused, independent of computers, and essentially top-down. Venter's is data-focused, highly dependent on computers, and bottom-up.

Haseltine defines his research projects in terms of his goals for solving the problem of disease. "The first thing you have to do in solving a problem is determine what it is you want to do," he says. "Then you must choose the appropriate questions, knowledge, tools, and methods to accomplish that goal." For Haseltine, the key question is, "How do certain genes cause disease—and what can be done to prevent this mechanism from activating?" To reach the answer, Haseltine is closely examining human tissue to see where certain genes have had a direct impact on the cellular machinery, possibly causing osteoporosis, cancer, or other diseases.

At Celera, Craig Venter also wants to have an impact on medicine and help resolve the problem of disease, but he has a different question to answer. Unlike Haseltine, he is less interested in identifying drugs. He asks instead, how is the entire genome constructed? How does it function to produce either normal physiology or pathological disease? The nature of Venter's question makes his effort much more dependent on computers and information technologies. He must rely on their calculating power to drive a "rapid analytical method" that will assemble a complete genetic map. This process breaks the genome into millions of overlapping fragments. The sequence of chemical units within each fragment is analyzed, and a super computer puts it back together, as though it were a jigsaw puzzle.

Venter contends that Haseltine will miss as much as 40 percent of the genes. And since genes interrelate, Hazeltine may miss key causal factors for disease. Venter says his own mission is the "big view . . . to look at the whole world of the genome." His is a grand scheme to see how life is built from the molecular level on up. But Haseltine believes he is already accounting for Venter's objection. He wants to solve specific problems, target specific diseases. He has already filed thousands of patents for genes, and hopes that this will lock in his company's rights on the commercial drugs that emerge from them. The potential drugs include one that shows promise in helping grow new blood vessels. It could allow the drug to replace coronary bypass surgery in some cases.

The HGS scientists look at the patterns of changes as tumors develop, as wounds heal, as tissues age. Haseltine argues that his way of accumulating information is better than that used by the government and biotech firms like Celera, which are taking a broad and comprehensive "genetic" approach, rather than a focused anatomical one. "They may answer a very fundamental question of deep scientific interest—why certain people get diseases, why people are different from one another. But they don't find cures and they don't treat diseases," he said.

Each of the competitors in the human genome race believes that his approach is best. And the truth is, both approaches are needed. Haseltine will learn more about individual genes and how they create disease, but he may miss information about how they work together. Venter will get a more complete picture of the genetic players and their interdependence, but he will miss detailed knowledge of how they cause disease. Ultimately, it will take the best results from both of them to fulfill the potential of the next generation of medicine. Both epitomize the essence of knowledge discovery, and the power of asking the right, or the wrong, questions.

There is no magic formula for asking good questions. The questioning strategies in the exhibit below are a means of accelerating an awareness of how you question to discover what you know and what you don't. (See Figure 2.2.)

Average Discoverers spend most of their time on the left side of this diagram. The best work on the right side as well. But most of them still spend a majority of their time in the research quadrant. The rarest of all are those who work the bottom right quadrant and have the combination of boldness, creativity, and innocence to explore, to ask the vague, powerful questions that truly open up whole new areas of knowledge.

Once you've formulated a question, then of whom do you ask it? Savvy Discoverers go straight to multiple experts to get in-depth knowledge, then put the pieces together to complete their whole answer. Although specialized knowledge may be the key to the future, one must remember that it can also become dated and its application, narrow. As Oliver Wendell Holmes once wrote, "To be mas-

---

Knowing What to Know–Questioning Strategies   FIG. 2.2

	Known	Unknown
Known	Known Knowns (Things we know or we know who knows) **VALUE and REFINE** Problem-oriented questions	Known Unknowns (Things we or others know are unanswered questions) **RESEARCH** Comprehensive, structured questions
Unknown	Unknown Knowns (Things that we know are known somewhere or by someone) **SEARCH** Selective, targeted questions	Unknown Unknowns (Things we aren't familiar enough with to formulate specific questions) **EXPLORE** Intuitive, bold questions

ter of any branch of knowledge, you must master those which lie next to it; and thus to know anything you must know all." Successful Discoverers have learned that the blending of specialized and general knowledge is a potent combination in problem solving.

In his discovery process, Craig Venter followed just this approach. He assembled a large team of specialists to help map the genome. He found people with business expertise to manage financing and operations, people who understood analytical methods to chart knowledge-producing strategies, scientists with gene-sequencing expertise, a computer specialist to tie together 1,200 Compaq computers, and a software engineer to write the programs. Venter even hired a Nobel-Prize-winning scientist to manipulate the DNA, as well as a physician to probe the link between the research and potential customer applications.

Knowledge, whether it's specialized or more general, comes in many textures and grades of quality. Most people believe the higher the stakes, the better, more precise, reliable, and scientific the knowledge must be. But sometimes it is speed, rather than quality, that is the determining factor. And in competitive arenas, trying too hard to get high quality information because of what's at stake can actually put you at risk. It inhibits early actions required to stake out a territory before it's completely understood. In the biotech arena, for instance, the "land grab" for genetic patents may have already given Haseltine the edge.

The secret is to realize that you can get rough, early knowledge now, and still establish the processes for creating more precise knowledge later on. There are no hard and fast rules for judging the trade-offs between the speed and quality of knowledge. The right knowledge too late is useless. The wrong knowledge, especially when it comes early, distorts your view of a problem just as you are forming it. Discoverers should search for the right balance, focusing on the questions that serve their goals, and making maximum use of existing expertise, for that combination of speed and quality that fits their needs.

As elite Discoverers, what both Venter and Haseltine are certain to succeed at is mapping and learning the territory of life in a new way, a way that will make new journeys possible, even though we don't now know what they may be. Venter once mused on the adventure as he flew in a Lear Jet, gazing out the window at a thick cloud bank surrounding the aircraft: "Visionary science is just like this. You can't see anything, but you can still get where you're going. That's something only the human mind is capable of, envisioning what it can't actually see."

Discovery in Action: Investigating a New Territory

Choose an area of unknowns that you would like to understand and start with the simple exercise of formulating and listing questions. Come up with all the questions you can, then organize them in a few logical categories. Try to make the questions mutually exclusive, but collectively exhaustive. Once you've done this, make sure every category contributes to the problem you're trying to solve, to your overall purpose. Then prioritize them and identify which questions you can answer, where you need help, and how much time and effort it is likely to require. Then either find experts and/or launch investigations. As the answers come in and you learn more, add new questions to your list and keep track of how your knowledge evolves.

SPOT THE PATTERNS

From Information to Focus

There is a tide in the affairs of men,
Which, taken at the flood, leads on to fortune.
Omitted, all the voyage of their life
Is bound in shallows, and in miseries.

—WILLIAM SHAKESPEARE (1564–1616)

Knowledge alone is only a resource—it doesn't define a problem for a Discoverer or generate focus on a specific opportunity. To make use of knowledge, a problem solver must spot a useful pattern in the noise of information and relate it to a human need or desire. Just as explorers adjust their travel plans according to the clouds and winds that presage calm skies or gathering storms, all problem solvers look for variations outside the boundaries of the expected and guide their explorations accordingly.

You can recognize a pattern only if you have reliable data and know what you are looking for. Some patterns are meaningful, whereas others are inconsequential. In business, the patterns may be in the form of fewer customer defections, more employee discontent, a rise in new competitors, or a decline in industry profitability. Patterns must be wisely read, however. If you're not well informed and can't recognize, verify, and understand the pattern, you won't know which problems are the right ones to solve. Distinguishing between the two requires some questions: Is there regularity in the change that makes it predictable? Is it a singular event? Is it getting better or worse? Accelerating or decelerating? What impact will it have? The questions are the same, whether the pattern has to do with a stock market plunge, an illness, a competitive threat, a social trend, or a gathering storm.

Today, some of the most sophisticated pattern spotting takes place among the meteorologists at the National Oceanic and Atmospheric Administration (NOAA). With an array of sophisticated observation equipment, tied to the latest supercomputing technology, they try their best to predict the unpredictable—the weather.

NOAA and the Challenge of Weather Prediction

After many years of data collection and increasing pattern recognition, U.S. government scientists can now forecast the severity of the phenomenon known as El Niño as much as nine months in advance of its appearance. For instance, in the spring of 1997, California—still recovering from the floods of 1995—had enough advance warning to fix its levee system before the next El Niño. Estimated savings: $1 billion. As much as one-seventh of the U.S. economy, or $1.4 trillion, is vulnerable to weather, the government estimates. Early warnings save lives and billions of dollars.

With good forecasting, farmers can decide what crops to plant, utilities can determine whether they should lock in on fuel prices, and other economic considerations can be more thoughtfully weighed. "What understanding climate variations gives you is fundamentally a new tool for managing potential problems," says Dr. Ants Leetmaa, Director of the National Oceanic and Atmospheric Administration's Climate Prediction Center. "You can start thinking about how to do things differently. There's a potential for mitigating disasters as well as for saving money and using your resources more wisely."

Dr. D. James Baker, the Department of Commerce undersecretary for NOAA, says having good, accurate data is the first step to accurate pattern recognition and forecasting. One's ability to forecast the weather is only as good as one's ability to recognize patterns, which is only as good as the data the patterns are based on. Good data starts with these key elements:

- what you're observing (unit of analysis—e.g., water or atmosphere),
- the attribute you're measuring (e.g., temperature or pressure),
- the unit of measure (e.g., degrees centigrade or millibars of mercury),
- the scale of measure (e.g., tenths of a degree changes per day), and finally,
- the benchmark you're comparing it to (e.g., previous month's temperature average).

To get that data, scientists have set thousands of remote temperature sensors in buoys on the ocean surface. "In the case of El Niño the big step was being able to say, 'OK. We think the ocean temperature variable is important,'" said Baker. That hypothesis, based on centuries of knowledge about global climate, made the investment in temperature-sensing equipment on a massive scale acceptable. Putting the temperature-sensing buoys in place took two decades of planning and development, and millions of dollars. The buoys, spaced hundreds to thousands of miles apart, have fiberglass and Styrofoam bases. Aluminum towers are perched on top. Wrapped with stainless steel bridles, the instrument packs include air and water thermometers, anemometers (which measure wind speed), and barometers to gauge atmospheric pressure.

But once you get quality data, how do you make sense of it? There needs to be a way to pull it together, analyze, and display it so that patterns can be identified and visualized. In the case of El Niño, this requires high-performance supercomputers that show changes in surface temperature over time (and in different colors) so that the emergence of an El Niño event can be spotted quickly and easily.

The El Niño pattern begins with a swelling of warm water off the Pacific coast of South America. But the water warms every season, so what makes it warm enough to be considered an El Niño? With an El Niño, the water warms more and over a broader area than usual. But how much warmer and over how much broader an area? Such judgments are the essence of discerning a pattern of change.

They form the basis of pattern recognition not just in meteorology, but in any other process of discovery. This process could be gauging the facial expressions of a partner during a business deal, predicting price movements in business, estimating adjudicatory trends in the law, or anticipating the directions of technical innovations in engineering.

What pattern you find is usually influenced by what you're looking for and what your point of reference is. There are many different identifiable patterns of change. These range from episodic events, like lightning strikes, which flash randomly, to repetitive events, like the tides and the pounding of waves on the seashore. A good Discoverer knows the different kinds of patterns well and is thus more likely both to see them in the first place and to choose accurately which one is occurring. There are four basic classes of patterns in the variation of anything, from a stock market to a heart rate. (See Figure 2.3.) The first two tend to be much easier to predict than the last two—an important practical distinction for any Discoverer.

Easiest to Identify

- Continuous change. This class includes linear, or evolutionary, change that increases or decreases over time: The life cycle of an individual, for

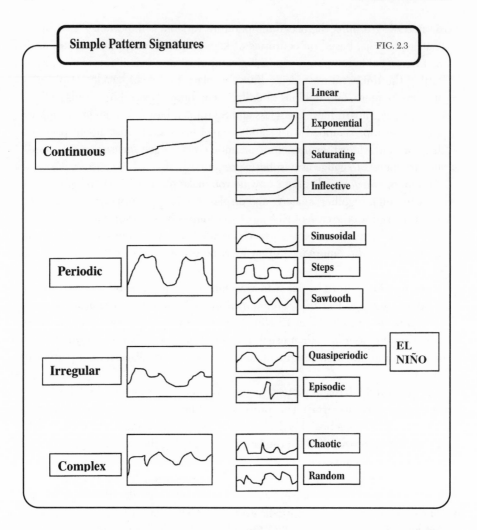

Simple Pattern Signatures   FIG. 2.3

example, in which immaturity leads to maturity, which leads to old age. It also includes exponential patterns, in which change starts out slowly and quickly ramps up, for instance in an outbreak of a disease. The exponential pattern is particularly deceptive , because it can initially look like linear change, until it leaps out of control.

- Periodic change. Patterns that repeat in a cyclical fashion with some regularity over time. Examples include fluctuations in the Earth's gravitational field over millions of years, long-term business cycles, and the seasonal spike in retail businesses over the Christmas holidays.

Hardest to Identify

- Irregular change. These patterns include events that are transitory or episodic—bolts of lightning or shooting stars. They also include harder-to-predict patterns, such as El Niño.
- Complex change. The systematic analysis of this class of patterns has been dubbed the science of "chaos" or "complexity theory." The study of chaos and complexity has revealed patterns in apparently random observations that were previously unrecognized. Alternatively, the behavior of a system may look regular in the short term but turn out to be chaotic in the long term.

Good problem solvers don't wait for an entire pattern to present itself, however. Judgments must be made about when to push hard on information gathering, and when to stop and combine the information you have, using experience and intuition to take some action.

But any action must be based on correct interpretation of a pattern's significance, any changes or alterations in it, and what or whom it can affect. This interpretation includes analyzing the difference between normal and abnormal patterns. How much of an impact could it have? How fast must you respond? What can you control and influence?

Interpreting the significance of changing temperatures in the ocean that signal a coming El Niño requires understanding the distinction between general and special causes of variation. General variation, which arises from the normal behavior of a system itself, is part of the expected pattern of change. Special variation is a deviation from that expected path, meaning a potential problem or opportunity. If you know the normal patterns, then the special ones are easier to distinguish. For example, in medicine, the study of physiology focuses on understanding the normal functioning of the human body. Pathology concentrates on the special variations, otherwise known as disease.

Computer models, which represent the normal or expected behavior of a system, are a great help in isolating the special variations, which can indicate a new and potentially useful or problematic pattern. They can help answer the question, is the water warm enough to signal an El Niño? Or, taking the logic to a whole new level, is the increasing frequency and magnitude of El Niños one more piece of evidence supporting the hypothesis of global warming?

With a good model, it's then possible to identify the basic patterns of a very complicated phenomenon. If the pattern is regular—periodic or continuous—then it can be relied on and used for future planning. If the pattern is irregular or complex it will most likely be difficult and expensive to predict. It may appear expedient to ignore such patterns—the cost of trying to predict them may outweigh the unreliable benefits. However, such patterns also represent an opportunity to the Discoverer who can be the first to decipher it, determine whether it bodes good or ill, and make use of the advantage that such extra knowledge of the territory can bring. This is certainly the case with the attempt to find evidence for "global warming"—a very difficult pattern to confirm, but one with tremendous consequences.

Leetmaa, his colleagues, and many others around the world are searching everywhere for clues to uncover whether warming trends are a real problem or just irregular change, even using such "proxy records" as tree rings and coral reef samples, both of which are sensitive to ocean temperatures—the same data that has been used to predict El Niño. "It's critical to have a long record," says Leetmaa, "We're just trying to piece together what we think the planet is really doing."

Discovery in Action: Interpreting Pattern Signatures

What are the most significant patterns of change taking place around you? Based on the data you have, which of the four categories do they fall into—the first two (continuous or periodic) that can be relatively easy to predict, or the last two (irregular and complex) that can be very difficult to predict? If you can't tell, what more would you need to know to be able to make a judgment? Once you know or have a hunch, take this into account as you consider the costs, risks, and opportunity of further data collection, modeling, or investigation into the patterns. If you're going to invest large amounts of resources in trying to capture an irregular or complex pattern, at least go into it with your eyes open. Make sure the result you're seeking is worth the effort.

ASSESS THE PLAYERS
AND STAKES

From Focus to Interests

Politics is not an exact science.
—OTTO VON BISMARCK (1815–1898)

Any survey of a territory is bound to turn up human players with their own stakes in the results of your exploration. Land masses are populated by indigenous peoples: hostile, friendly, and indifferent; diseases live in patients; markets for even the most technical products comprise customers, suppliers, and competitors. Even when you've determined what's happening in your territory and focused on a particular problem or opportunity, your understanding isn't complete until you know how it is affecting the players—those who have an interest in the system that's undergoing change.

Resolving any sizable problem involves decisions that affect people's interests. Since those interests are usually not the same, power plays a role in any resolution. In a competitive or a collaborative world, knowing where the power lies and what its dynamics are—knowing the key players, their interests and biases and their inclinations toward you and one another—increases your chance of success. Without this knowledge, the obstacles other players throw in your path can make progress painful, even impossible. Interests can be financial, physical, or even psychological.

In the professional world, few take time to consider complicated emotional dynamics. But those dynamics are there, and if you are unaware of them you will be at their mercy. Some of the best at discovering the complexities of human relationships are social workers—Discoverers such as those at the Barker Foundation, who deal with the challenges of adoption. It's worth learning from them. To take one example, a merger or acquisition, with its aftermath of integration, can reveal an emotional landscape surprisingly similar to that of an adoption.

The Barker Foundation and the Complexities of Adoption

Adoption is a complicated social phenomenon with four major players—the child, the birth parents, the adoptive parents and the relevant government and/or independent institutions. Here, the stakes are as high as they can get, the mix of emotional and empirical factors daunting, and the levels of power and influence subtle. The social worker must know the territory of the potential adoption and most importantly must assess all the players and their stakes in the game, in order to help all the parties involved make good decisions.

This thorough knowledge has become all the more important with "open" adoptions, in which there is some form of contact, often ongoing, among the three parties. "In these adoptions, a circle of people is brought together in a fantastic and beautiful way," says Robin Allen, director of the Barker Foundation. "Yet they have a relationship that society doesn't understand, and that they don't either. There is no model for it." So the quality of the decisions made must derive from how well each of the participants knows the territory as a whole, and how well they know their own unique internal landscape. It is the Barker social worker who must learn that territory and serve as guide. As Allen says, "Being alert to the interests at stake can not only prevent unforeseen conflict but also maximize the possibility of initiating mutually acceptable solutions."

Human behavior is shaped by what's at stake in a problem solving situation. The cornered individual becomes ferocious, the individual with guaranteed success becomes complacent. If you know the stakes and the odds—and what the other key players *think* the stakes and the odds are—you will likely know much of what you need to know to make judgments about their behavior.

At Barker, all the players have a unique stake. The individual players have to "make sense" of the adoption both before and after it takes place. Adoptees must come to grips with the "rejection" of being placed for adoption, must determine whether they are lovable and how to understand the life they missed with their birth parents. Then there are the birth parents, who, for whatever reason, placed the child. They often carry the "pain and sense of loss with them," as Allen said, even if they feel they've made the right decision. And there are the adoptive parents, who usually have been hardened by years of heartache—perhaps lost babies and lost pregnancies—and often wonder what their lives would have been like had they had biological children.

Then there are the institutional players—the government and the adoption agency. Government agencies have an interest in promoting professional practice, preventing fraud, and maintaining accurate legal records among other things. Adoption agencies have an interest in providing a demonstrably higher level of services than the many other independent parties competing to provide adoption services as well as in complying with regulatory and legal mandates.

"The stakes and the what-ifs are enormous," says Allen. "That's why it takes a particularly strong set of human beings to deal with them, especially the what-ifs. Because they come back at you at times when people are very vulnerable. They sort of look you in the face. You have to stare them down in order to remain balanced, in remaining a good adoptive parent and a good birth parent."

Identifying and accommodating the various interests is always challenging. Endless complications can and do arise. The interests of the birth mother and birth father may diverge. Or new court decisions may rest on ambiguous principles that make it hard for agencies to be certain they are meeting government objectives without undue burden to their clients.

At Barker, the most important task is to help the people involved stay flexible and maintain respect for each other. "It's like this," says Allen, entwining her fingers. "It's all hooked together: the best interest of the child; respect and flexibility; the lifetime nature of it. If you can establish at the very beginning a comfort level with the unknowns and a tolerance for the emotional climate—the fact that we don't know exactly how it's going to go, but we all care about the quality of the relationships we have with this child—that's what's important."

The state of play in a territory changes as the problem solving journey proceeds. Just as the weather in a particular country may be constant or highly variable, predictable or wild, so too the "human weather" of ongoing collaborations and conflicts in a particular territory will change over time. Warring factions make peace; isolated groups become trading partners. The same players with the same stakes may behave very differently at different times. It's difficult to honestly assess the state of play in a challenging problem solving effort. This is where science leaves off and intuitive human judgments begin. You will never know all the motives, all the calculations, all the interests, or all the potential scenarios. But without spending some time considering them, your decisions and actions will have a lower chance of success.

In the adoption process, Barker tries to help the parties increase their awareness of all the players' emotions and their interests. By understanding the behaviors of all the parties, Barker helps them make healthy decisions and build trust. For example, in an "open" adoption, there may be an agreement to exchange letters between the child and the birth parents. That may be fine for an eight-year-old. But at thirteen, the child may balk. In that case, Barker would urge the adoptive parent to write a letter saying, "You know, we have a budding thirteen-year-old who has now said he does not feel comfortable with the exchange at this point. And I hope you'll understand that I'm supportive of him in that." The birth mother might be devastated. "She may say, 'But I don't understand. I feel cut off. I feel blocked,' whatever she's feeling," says Allen. "Our job is to take her back to her role as a support to the family." Sometimes, adds Allen, it's the birth mother's needs that must be addressed. At another point, the birth mother might ask that she not be contacted for a while—that the letter be kept in a file. Perhaps she is getting married and she cannot handle it right then. "Life unfolds in unpredictable ways," says Allen.

The stakes get especially complicated when a teen wants to solve the problem of his or her biological origin and search for his biological parents. Barker will help in these searches. But they counsel against adolescents seeking their birth parents. "The adolescent doesn't have a long-term perspective; they're just living for today," says Allen. "They don't have enough life experience to imagine all the many things that could happen or the consequences they could have. But the parents do. It's just that the parents need support to take that position because they're going to take a lot of guff from that teenager. Very often that's our job—to help them."

When adult adoptees want to search for their biological parents, Barker sits down with them and discusses what they might find. Most birth parents want to be contacted, but not all of them. Some have never told their parents, spouses, or other children about their decision long ago to place a baby. "The mother's world could be just broken into a million pieces, from her perspective, by this knock on the door, this telephone call," says Allen. "That's why it's so important to use a neutral party. We can make that call, and provide a safe place for each party while they decide what they hope to have from this relationship."

Most importantly, as Discoverers, Barker social workers help adoptive parents make honest assessments of situations and talk honestly with their children. This honesty helps both parents and children sort out the real problems and issues from the perceived ones. And the more accurate knowledge of the emotional territory enhances everyone's chance of self-discovery.

One of the toughest facts to face is that for most parents, adoption was not their first choice. "Parents who acknowledge that fact, do well with it," says Allen. "The child can then say, 'Well, I wouldn't have set out to be adopted, either, but since my birth parents couldn't keep me, this is a pretty OK thing.' That moment of discovery is special. Then everyone can see the bittersweet quality of the decision and understand that it's part of the fabric of their lives. Yes, it might have been different, but that doesn't mean it isn't very, very good."

Discovery in Action: Assessing Players and Stakes

Focus on a challenging situation you face, know where there are multiple players and a confusing variety of interests. Make a simple list of all the key players and then rank them in priority by their significance, willpower, and capability. Then for each of the highest priority players, describe their interests, both in absolute terms and relative to other players like yourself. Using this information, try to identify the one or two major areas of common or conflicting interests that pose the greatest benefit or threat to your problem solving effort.

SEE THE WHOLE,
BUT GET TO THE HEART
From Interests to Understanding

*Whoever can't see the whole in every part plays at blind man's bluff.
A wise man tastes the entire Tigris in every sip.*

—GHALIB

Once knowledge has been acquired, focus identified, and interests assessed, a Discoverer must move to a deeper level of understanding to prepare for action. As it turns out, this understanding emerges quickest when one moves between different levels of analysis. When you see "the forest" you have a wide perspective on the territory, a general knowledge, but it's of little specific use. When you see individual "trees," in the form of particular patterns and events, you have a clear and specific area of impact, but you may miss other essential components of your overall problem. It's necessary to do both, to understand the whole but get to the heart of an issue.

Every system (or environment) has critical leverage points where small actions tend to have great impact. Engineers call them single points of failure (SPFs). A wise Discoverer should know exactly where these SPFs are and pay close attention to them. This is where the root causes of problems often lie, and where preventative maintenance can forestall them. Complex problems, however, don't have single causes, but multiple ones. Responding to them, then, is more difficult, and requires a knowledge of the whole as well as the various parts.

Because of complex technologies, shifting boundaries, and scarce resources, Discoverers who can define the right system from the very beginning, see the whole, and identify the leverage points quickly will be more successful. The National Transportation Safety Board (NTSB) is an organization that not only knows how to find the key points of failure, but also how to apply those findings to the whole industry which it monitors. Those skills are put to the test in every accident situation, for example in January of 1997, when Comair Flight 3272 nose-dived into a frozen field outside of Detroit killing all twenty-nine aboard.

The NTSB and Aviation Accident Investigation

There was no warning that a layer of ice, thin as sandpaper, had built up on the wings and was about to send the airplane lurching violently out of control. The airplane exploded into flames when it hit the earth, leaving its ghastly imprint over an area the length of a football field and twice as wide.

It was a routine, fifty-minute hop between Cincinnati and Detroit, operated by Comair, a Cincinnati-based commuter carrier affiliated with Delta Air Lines. Nearly every seat was taken. Of the 1.6 million Americans who fly every day, some 140,000 travel on similar twin-engine turboprops, sometimes called puddle-jumpers. The pilot, Dann Carlsen, forty-two, had an unblemished record in his nine years with Comair. He'd had the previous two days off, and spent them running errands and working on his computer. Those who'd flown with him described him as sunny and a fun man to work with.

As with all airplane accidents, the National Transportation Safety Board rapidly sent a "go-team" of investigators to the site to solve the problem of why the accident occurred and what to do about it. Since its creation in 1967, the NTSB has investigated more than 350 major commercial airline accidents and found a probable cause in all but a handful. The investigations can take as little as a few months and as long as a few years to complete, but the urgency is felt by everyone from the beginning. The families need answers. The airlines need answers. Could this disaster have been prevented? Are there mechanical problems out there that could endanger other fliers as well? The NTSB must get to understand this tree (the particular crash), other trees (other similar crashes) and the forest (the industry it supervises) to get to the heart of the problem: Can crashes of this particular kind be prevented in the future?

The crash site, next to a church campground, was tough and grisly going. Recovery workers had to work in fifteen to twenty-minute shifts because of the bone-chilling cold. The impact had buried the engine four feet into the frozen ground; several pick axes were broken trying to pry them out. A storm front was moving in, expected to dump an additional seven inches of snow. Tarps were brought to cover the wreckage from the lightly falling snow. The fiery impact had shredded the plane, a Brazilian-made Embraer 120, into shards of charred and twisted metal, barely recognizable from the air as parts of a plane.

From the start, airline accidents are studied on several levels of analysis. The lowest level of analysis is molecular—the reaction of standard chemicals in an unanticipated way that could have created a danger. Intermediate levels may have to do with errors in quality or manufacturing that can be traced to particular machines. Still higher levels may be traced to the faulty design of an airplane. And the highest level of analysis might be the political tensions between two countries that cause a terrorist to attempt to hijack or blow up an airplane.

Getting to the heart of a complex problem requires more than just an ability to see both forest and trees. As it turns out, the best strategy is to alternate between them rhythmically and regularly, moving from immersion in the details, to perspective from on high, and then down into the details again. This approach increases the probability that understanding will be accurate and thus solutions will work, not create new problems.

"A fundamental tenet is that you don't assume anything," says Bernard Loeb, the NTSB's Director of Aviation Safety. "You have to look at everything, at all levels, and eliminate them one by one—or rule them in as possibilities." Investigators look at the "four corners"—the nose, the two wing tips, and the tail—to see if anything could have fallen off in the air. They study valves and electrical components. The pilots' remains are tested for drugs and alcohol; their personal lives are explored. Did they have family or financial woes, or "stressers," as the NTSB calls such problems? Was either of the pilots someone who took risks or had trouble following rules? Had they been trained properly? "At some point you end up with maybe a handful of possibilities, and then the work really gets to be more difficult," Loeb says.

The trick is in knowing what types of failures tend to occur most frequently at which levels, and to compare this knowledge to previous patterns of failure, ruling out some causes and not others. Sometimes there is a fairly simple chain of cause and effect, as when stripped threads disabled the stabilizing mechanisms on an Alaska Airlines flight. Other times, it is more complicated. Experts recognize that the worst disasters are often a result of multiple levels of failure interacting, as when a failure in safety protocols and a missed cargo check, combined with poorly packed and designed oxygen canisters, caused the crash of the Valu-Jet plane in the Florida Everglades. This is why investigators must be able to move fluidly between the different levels until the facts tell them where something started and how the cause-and-effect chain came to occur.

Loeb explains that accident scenes simply offer information. Most of the discovery and problem solving is not done at the scene, but in the meticulous observation of the evidence. The on-site probe of Flight 3272 played a vital role in proving what didn't happen. "We learned a lot of negatives from it," one investigator said. And every negative lead ruled out a line of effort that would have absorbed scarce time, energy, attention, and resources. Every potential cause was held up to multiple levels of analysis.

Solving the mystery of Flight 3272 turned out to be extraordinarily difficult, because there was no "golden nugget," as Loeb calls it, no single piece of evidence that quickly told the investigators where to look. Instead, it was a matter of uncovering half a dozen pieces of evidence that by themselves were not sufficient to indicate a probable cause, but together told the story.

Constructing the cause-and-effect chain requires a series of "whys?" I call it the chain of whys. Why did the plane crash? Because it lost control in poor weather. Why did it lose control? Because the wing flaps were misadjusted. Why were the wing flaps misadjusted? Because the pilot believed the conditions required them to be in that position. Why did the pilot have such a mistaken belief? Because he was looking at faulty instruments. When you use the chain of "whys?" keep asking until you reach the leverage point that is driving the change. Each link in the chain requires evidence to support the relationship between one fact and the next one. Just like real chains, cause-and-effect chains are only as strong as their weakest links.

So what did cause the crash of Comair 3272? The weather was horrible that day. Visibility was at about 1.5 miles, according to the Federal Aviation Administration. Other pilots had reported icing conditions, which turned out to be one cause. The flight data recorder, or FDR, gave this clue to the second one: "Split torque." In other words, the plane's twin engines were producing different levels of power at the time of the "upset," making it difficult for the pilots to control the airplane. "That probably was the last straw and exacerbated the effects of the icing," said Loeb. "But the questions were: why was the split torque occurring? Why was the icing occurring? And why did these lead to a crash?"

To find out why the icing caused a problem, the team went down to the manufacturer's headquarters in Brazil to run computerized performance tests. The investigators also took a set of turboprop wings similar to that of the Comair aircraft to NASA's wind tunnel in Cleveland, Ohio, where water was sprayed on them in a fine mist and frozen so that they replicated the conditions investigators determined were present just prior to the crash.

The wind tunnel experiments told investigators that the Embraer 120 became susceptible to aerodynamic difficulties with fairly small amounts of fine, sandpaper-like icing—far less than the half-inch of icing that pilots of those planes are generally warned about. The pilots "may not have seen anything that was of any concern to them," said Loeb. Still, although the results of the Cleveland wind tunnel testing were important, "they weren't the golden nugget," said Loeb. "It was just a piece of the puzzle that fit with a whole bunch of other things."

The NTSB determined that the pilots were flying the plane too slowly—under 160 knots—and had not used their de-icing equipment properly. But those two facts, said Loeb, are "not fundamentally the root cause—the one that needs to be remediated to prevent that kind of accident." The question again is why? Why were they flying too slowly? Why did they not de-ice properly?

Complex problems almost always have multiple root causes, but finding the root causes of failure is not the last step. Once identified, the final, most important determination is yet to be made. Was this failure something unique to these particular circumstances? Or was it systemic? In the case of the Comair crash, was it representative of a fault in aircraft design or certification that could be corrected? To answer this NTSB used its database of accident investigations and consulted with the airlines. Were there other crashes with the same causes, crashes that that would give them a reason to believe a more widespread problem existed?

The NTSB's goal is to understand the cause well enough to be able to prevent future problems. Could those two pilots, somehow, in their final moments have been warned that they were in trouble? Did they have enough information to know they were flying too slowly, or that sandpaper-thin ice was so dangerous? "What we really try to do, and it is a painstaking process, is not just determine what happened . . . [but] look beyond that," said Loeb. "What really happened is the system failed them."

In this accident, the NTSB placed the cause in the higher level "system" because, the board stated, the certification standards for turboprops flying in icing conditions were inadequate. Among other things, the NTSB recommended minimum airspeeds for icing conditions. They also recommended that stall warnings—which alert a pilot to trouble—be set to go off earlier. The FAA, meanwhile, proposed that new ice-detector systems be adopted for the Embraer 120.

In making its recommendations, the NTSB considers unintended consequences. "That is always on our mind—that you fix this problem but that you create some other problem," said Loeb. Sometimes fixing a mechanical problem creates a human problem, said Loeb. "But you can create some problems most people don't think about—for example, mindset," said Loeb. "Anytime you make the pilots believe that you have now solved the problem, they may no longer be attentive to, attuned to, or aware of it," said Loeb. "A single fix is not always the answer. The system has to be tolerant of failures in both the man and the machine."

Discovery in Action: Getting to the Heart of a Matter

Do you truly understand the root causes in a major problem solving situation you're currently involved in? If you haven't yet done the analysis, start with your most painful symptoms and work through the why questions until you've found a few potential root causes. Just keep asking why. Consider all possible levels of analysis. If you have done this already, then work on identifying which of the root causes is the most sensitive—the one where the most impact comes from the smallest variation. Perform the analysis to determine these sensitivities, and then make sure most of your efforts are focused on the causes with the highest sensitivity to outcomes. Finally, while you're immersed in this investigation, consider unintended consequences of possible solutions. You'll be better prepared when the time comes to design one.

LEARN TO LEARN
From Understanding to Learning

I am still learning! (Ancaro imparo!)
–MICHELANGELO BUONARROTI (1475–1564)

It is no use asking good questions, spotting elusive patterns, understanding the heart of a problem and the human interests at stake if you can't learn from each journey you make in the territory you explore. Learning to learn is one of the most important skills you can acquire. Discoverers know that the better they are at learning to learn, the more momentum they'll gain and the faster they'll get the job done. They know that when one confronts similar problems regularly, one is able to reuse or adapt previously tested solutions and avoid reinventing the wheel. But excellence in learning is only possible if you understand how you learn best and if learning is in the context of doing.

Similarly, the difference between a company that is merely fast out of the blocks and one that can cover the distance and win over the long run is the ability to learn. It is this relationship between learning and action that is such an important focus in a fast-paced environment. The faster you learn about the territory you're in, the better you'll be able to manage your risks and find opportunities. Learning has as much to do with self-discovery as the transfer of book knowledge. Indeed, the best learning takes place when students face real problems—as is revealed at one of the leaders in corporate learning—Xerox Business Services.

Xerox Business Services and Corporate Learning

Xerox added thousands of employees in 1998–1999 and an equal number in 2000. As the manager of worldwide sales training at Xerox Business Services (XBS), Raymond Lammes must cope with a flood of new students who need to learn the business and the company fast and well. Lammes learned from his previous career as a calculus instructor that learning must be made fun. "You can kill 'em in class with boredom," Lammes said. "Education is part entertainment, part knowledge, and part motivation. If you don't have 'em motivated, all the skills and knowledge in the world are worthless."

To make learning fun, XBS has established "Camp Lur'ning" in Leesburg, Virginia, a place designed to teach new hires how to learn. Every new employee is sent to the 1,200-acre camp at the foot of the Shenandoah Mountains, where deer and other wildlife abound. The classrooms are surrounded by a 950-bed dorm—employees can roll out of the sack at 7:55 A.M. and still make the 8 A.M. class. Previously, before they had studied how their employees actually learn best, XBS would deliver dry lectures about the systematic, six-step method Xerox endorsed for problem solving. But no longer. The company began to recognize that most of the employees were not "information learners" who benefited from lectures. They were "people learners" and "active learners." Said Lammes, "We wondered how we could construct a doing environment, rather than dumping this knowledge on them and just hoping they take it back to the field."

Learning to learn is recognizing that learning itself is merely the hub of a knowledge cycle. (See Figure 2.4.) Without all the components, the cycle just doesn't work as well. A knowledge cycle starts at any point on the wheel, then advances as the knowledge is discovered, created (i.e., given form), applied, shared, organized, and even engineered. Learning is not accumulating piles of knowledge; it is a dynamic process, with all the elements in the diagram influencing one another. Learning is about a flow of knowledge, a continuously turning life cycle. The flow is everything.

For this reason, the Xerox classes stress dynamic collaboration in problem solving situations that force the use of various parts of the wheel. In one exercise, for example, forty-four employees are put in a class together, and given a very lifelike assignment: Xerox has been asked to produce a souvenir package for a convention center. The packages are to include postcards, sticker tattoos, brochures, and a cover letter. On the first run, the employees are given twenty minutes to put it all together. "Their first attempt was an abysmal failure," said Louis Olmos, an XBS "Learning Partner." Instead of forty-four packets, they hardly got one together.

The new employees spent the next day and a half repeating what had worked the first time and fixing the problems. By the second day, the processes were honed, and in the twenty-minute period, the class produced its forty-four

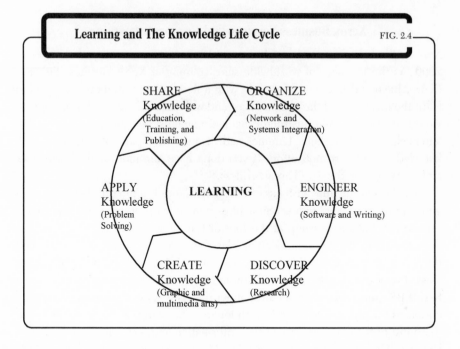

Learning and The Knowledge Life Cycle   FIG. 2.4

SHARE Knowledge (Education, Training, and Publishing)

ORGANIZE Knowledge (Network and Systems Integration)

APPLY Knowledge (Problem Solving)

LEARNING

ENGINEER Knowledge (Software and Writing)

CREATE Knowledge (Graphic and multimedia arts)

DISCOVER Knowledge (Research)

brochures. (XBS saves these for ninety days and mails them to new hires as a souvenir and a reminder of what they've learned.)

One of the most underestimated aspects of learning is unlearning. The well-prepared explorer sets out to learn the territory with all kinds of background information, accounts of previous journeys, and assumptions. Some of that learning will be of help in the field, but some will need to be unlearned, to make room for what the territory has to teach. Learning is about changing, about letting go of learned behavior as well as receiving it. But letting go is extremely difficult. It takes a deep personal willingness to change.

Pat Wallington, the former chief information officer (CIO) of Xerox Corporation (and a woman from whom I have learned much over the years) expresses it in this motto: "Learn to learn; learn to change." In other words, face up to the knowledge and habits that don't serve you any longer in a new environment and demonstrate the willingness to reevaluate them. Take the time to let them go, and then learn new ways of doing things. The older we get, the harder this is. It takes humility, looseness, humor, fun, and playfulness to let go of beliefs and knowledge.

To facilitate letting go, XBS creates a learning environment where students are encouraged to explore, share, and learn for the sake of learning. (See Figure 2.5.) The classrooms at "Camp Lur'ning" are modified computer labs, wide and open with plenty of space for students to move around. Employees are invited to bring their own CDs. Learning goes on with everything from classical to rock to rap

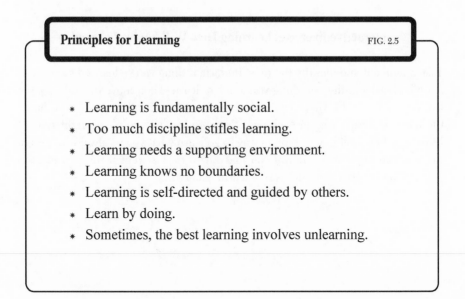

Principles for Learning   FIG. 2.5

* Learning is fundamentally social.
* Too much discipline stifles learning.
* Learning needs a supporting environment.
* Learning knows no boundaries.
* Learning is self-directed and guided by others.
* Learn by doing.
* Sometimes, the best learning involves unlearning.

playing in the background. "Some of them would prefer something else" to the hip-hop that the younger generation sometimes shows up with, said Olmos, "but somehow it all works out." The camp has a "Route XBS" theme, a takeoff on the legendary "Route 66" tune. The sessions are titled "On the Road to Customer First," and there's a "journey" motif running through it all. The facilitators, or teachers, are called "tour guides."

The environment allows for information learners, experimentational learners, cognitive learners, active learners, and others. These freedoms boost interest, curiosity, fascination, and a sense of wonder. XBS nurtures this spirit even when it doesn't relate to specific goals. Play and fun are as much a part of the equation as study and reflection, and the result is students who begin to enjoy the habit of learning and unlearning.

XBS knows it has hit on a golden strategy because its employees—and its customers—are happy. When XBS won the Malcolm Baldridge National Quality Award in 1997, it had an overall customer satisfaction rating of 95 percent, a customer loyalty rating of 94 percent, and an employee satisfaction level close to 80 percent. "These people come back to the workplace highly motivated," said Olmos of his students. "People begin to value learning, and then they seek it out for themselves." Once employees are in the habit of learning—a habit that is reinforced by the pleasure they take in it—they are primed to continue to learn as they encounter new problems to solve, with new territories to explore. The knowledge cycle becomes the wheel that carries employees across ever more ambitious stretches of territory, building momentum as they go.

Interactive Exercise: Learning How Well You've Learned

Take a moment and identify the most important thing you've learned recently as a professional and the one thing you'd like to learn. Then move on and pick the learning experiences where you've had the most fun and the ones you've hated the most. Describe why in each case. Now, to bring more of the right type of learning into your life, figure out a way to go learn what you've always wanted in the way you enjoy most. If you can make it work, just repeat the process and you'll be on the best possible type of learning curve.

CHARACTERISTICS OF A DISCOVERER

General characteristics and purpose: Discoverers emphasize learning. Their goal is acquiring and absorbing strategic knowledge in the right form at the right time on a regular basis. Discoverers love to understand. They are fascinated by the rich detailed tapestries of life and how things fit together, how they work together. They value curiosity, insight, truth, and science. They are less interested in how things could be than in how they currently are. They focus on completeness, depth and accuracy of knowledge, curiosity, and finding the connections between things. Play, concrete actions, and decisions are less important.

Strengths: Discoverers quickly master and enjoy working with detail and granularity. They are willing to take the time and effort necessary to understand intricate, dynamic cause-and-effect mechanisms in order to see how something

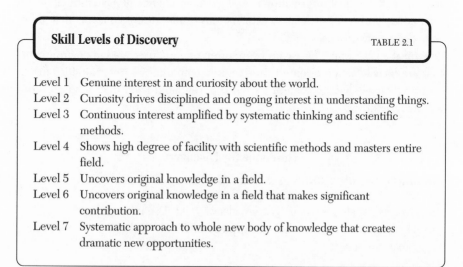

Skill Levels of Discovery   TABLE 2.1

Level 1   Genuine interest in and curiosity about the world.
Level 2   Curiosity drives disciplined and ongoing interest in understanding things.
Level 3   Continuous interest amplified by systematic thinking and scientific methods.
Level 4   Shows high degree of facility with scientific methods and masters entire field.
Level 5   Uncovers original knowledge in a field.
Level 6   Uncovers original knowledge in a field that makes significant contribution.
Level 7   Systematic approach to whole new body of knowledge that creates dramatic new opportunities.

works, what makes it tick and what affects it; to collect and organize data and information; to develop theories and to design experiments. They are able to marshal the mathematical and statistical tools necessary to formalize an understanding of a system or environment, including the ability to do sophisticated systems models or computer simulations.

Weaknesses: Discoverers can easily get trapped in low-level details when the point is not to understand perfectly but just to get enough knowledge to act. They can also focus on too high a level of precision and thus learn too slowly, when fast, rough knowledge is required. Specialization in a particular field, without general knowledge, can handicap Discoverers seriously in communicating with others on interdisciplinary efforts.

Interactions with other types of problem solvers: Discoverers make particularly good combinations with Creators, Playmakers, and Communicators, all of whom have important things to gain from the use of new knowledge. Creators use the inputs directly in solution design and are often able to target features or requirements more specifically because of better information about the environment. Playmakers get critical intelligence and insight that help them define opportunities, goals, and strategies more effectively, avoiding traps and false paths. Communicators derive knowledge about what's at stake for people that is useful in building or dissolving relationships. On the other hand, Discovers can conflict with Innovators, because of disputes over the point-of-view used to investigate or interpret knowledge. An Innovator may look at the same set of facts and information as a Discoverer and yet come to entirely different conclusions about their meaning, because Innovators take an alternative, creative point of view. Discoverers also differ from Performers, who are action-oriented, and often only in need of information, not knowledge and insight. The impatient Performer who likes small nuggets of information useful at the moment will have difficulty with a Discoverer who enjoys lengthy explanations of theories or concepts that are of little direct practical use.

Typical mishandling: Discoverers are often underappreciated in environments that are heavily action oriented. In scientific communities, their abilities in uncovering knowledge are sometimes not differentiated from their ability to lead and manage others.

Guidance for Discovery

Guiding Principles: Rules and Laws That Bear on Discovery

- Experts are always useful, but not always right. Use more than one.
- The search for knowledge can expand endlessly without problems and goals to focus it.

- You can usually act before you know all you need to know.
- The simpler explanation is usually the better one, as long as it's not too simple.
- Garbage in, garbage out.
- Prevent problems, rather than treat them; Treat causes, not symptoms.
- Most problems are overdetermined—there is almost always more than one cause.
- Know your sensitivities—some causes will have a much bigger proportional impact than others.
- Focus on the system, not just events.

Diagnostics: How Well Do You Know Your Territory?

- Do you know what you know? Do you know what you don't know? Do you have the right experts available when you need them? Are you asking the right questions? Do you trust the experts you are using? Are they manageable?
- Do you know what forces of change are behind the problem or opportunity? What's the pattern? Is the situation getting worse or better? How do you know? What is the system you are observing?
- Is your data accurate? Have you validated it from multiple, credible sources? By the appropriate methods? Have you observed things directly? Who is interpreting the data and defining the patterns? Are their biases evident? Do you have a model, with all assumptions accounted for?
- Do you know who is on your side and who isn't? Do you know what's at stake for the key players? What are their plans and how do you fit in? Do you know who has the real power? Who is doing what to whom? Do you know what you need from them and how to get it?
- If you've identified a problem or opportunity, do you understand the root causes or drivers, what's really necessary to produce change? How many causes have you identified and what are their relationships to one another? How many levels of "why?" have you been able to answer? Do you know which causes are most important? Which do you have influence over?
- What have you learned today? This week? This month? This year? How are you applying that lesson, today, this week, this month, this year? How is your learning different today than it was a year ago? What are you doing to improve it? What are you doing to make it more enjoyable and stimulate your own desire to learn?

Syndromes: Diseases Which Affect Your Ability to Learn the Territory

- "The know-it-all syndrome"—Wasting precious time and resources "reinventing the wheel," when you could ask for help or learn from others.
- "Tyranny of experts"—Overreliance on experts who cannot synthesize the knowledge and make sense out of it in the context of your problem.
- "Information overload"—paralysis from trying to collect too much information or shooting for unnecessarily high confidence levels.
- "Right answers, wrong questions"—Spending an inordinate amount of time and resources on data collection rather than thinking about the right questions to ask.
- "Focusing on the big spike"—Over- or underreacting to snapshots and recent events without looking at the overall pattern of change.
- "Playing ostrich"—Being unwilling to look hard enough at what's truly changing in the environment around you.
- "Fooled by Appearances"—Underestimating or overestimating players because of posturing or failure to recognize substantive elements of their capabilities.
- "The post hoc fallacy"—Inferring cause-and-effect relationship from mere association rather than on any statistical or organic basis.

Going Further

Selected resources for further study of knowledge and learning. (See also sources and notes for Part 2 on page 267.)

Books

Barton, Dorothy Leonard. *Wellsprings of Knowledge*. Boston: HBS Press, 1995.

Boorstin, Daniel. *The Discoverers*. New York: Vintage Books, 1985.

Davenport, Tom, and Lawrence Prusak. *Working Knowledge*. Boston: HBS Press, 1998.

Ericsson, K. Anders. *Towards a General Theory of Expertise*. Cambridge University Press, 1991.

Gardner, Howard. *The Disciplined Mind*. New York: Simon & Schuster, 1999.

Gelernter, David. *Mirror Worlds*. New York: Oxford University Press, 1991.

Gleick, James. *Chaos*. New York: Viking, 1987.

Goldstein, Martin, and Goldstein, Inge. *How We Know*. New York: Plenum, 1978.

Langer, Ellen. *The Power of Mindful Learning*. Boston: Addison Wesley, 1997.

Langley, Pat, et al. *Scientific Discovery*. Cambridge: MIT Press, 1980.

Machiavelli, Niccolo. *The Prince*. 1513. Reprint, Penguin Books: New York, 1983.

National Research Council. *Enhancing Human Performance*. Washington: National Academy Press, 1988

Nonaka, Ikukiro. *The Knowledge Creating Company*. New York: Oxford University Press, 1995.

Park, David. *The How and the Why*. Princeton University Press, 1988.

Porter, Michel. *Competitive Strategy*. New York: The Free Press, 1980.

Prigogine, Ilya, and Isabelle Stengers. *Order Out of Chaos*. New York: Bantam, 1988.

Senge, Peter. *The Fifth Discipline*. New York: Doubleday, 1990.

Stewart, Thomas. *Intellectual Capital*. New York: Doubleday, 1997.

Tufte, Edward. *The Visual Display of Quantitative Information*. Cheshire, CT: Graphics Press, 1993.

Wilson, E. O. *Consilience*. New York: Knopf, 1998.

Websites

Virtual library on knowledge management: www.km.brint.com

Knowledge management: www.knowledgeinc.com

Knowledge management: www.eknowledgecenter.org

Knowledge ecology: www.knowledgeecology.com

Online knowledge and exploration: www.exploratorium.com

Science and complexity: www.santafe.edu

Pattern recognition: www.ph.tn.tudelft

Root Cause Analysis: www.rootcauseanalyst.com

America's Learning Exchange: www.alx.org

Experiential learning: www.nsee.org

Professional training: www.skillsoft.com

Professional training: www.trainingregistry.com

Organizational learning: www.solonline.org

Part Three

❧BUILD THE RELATIONSHIPS❧

The Communicator

Cultivate Quality Communication and Interaction

Man is a knot, a web, a mesh into which relationships are tied. Only those relationships matter.

— ANTOINE ST. EXUPERY (1900–1944)

It takes people and relationships to solve problems and opportunities. But problem resolutions aren't meaningful unless they serve and advance the interests of people. Communicators build on the ideas of Innovators and the insight of Discoverers by creating a community that cares about one another and the problem.

The more challenging a problem is and the more people are involved in it, the more critical the right relationships become. Relationships are based on communication, and for this reason, problem solvers must be Communicators. Communicators know how to build, nurture, and draw sustenance from the essential fabric of human relationships, with or without the use of technology, whether it is instant messaging, video–conferencing, telephone, or radio. Some relationships are transitory—making quick exchanges with strangers or crossing paths infrequently with acquaintances. But long-term problem solving requires building deep, rich relationships. They underpin, fuel, and grow from the effort over time.

How do these deep, rich relationships form? Communication first leads to partnerships based on trust and free give-and-take. Strong leadership builds partnerships into a core team. The core team expands to propagate a network of allies who share a common sense of direction and loyalty. In time, the network evolves into a living community, with an identity and culture of its own. The length of that community's life will depend on its ability to enhance teamwork, intimacy, and a sense of common identity while retaining the vibrancy and variety of individual character.

The key to understanding the power of relationships in problem solving is recognizing that very small numbers of tight relationships can drive solutions to massive opportunities over long periods of time. It is these cores of relationships—whether founders of a business, igniters of a revolution, or creators of a family dynasty—that become powerful when they are associated with particular journeys. As the sense of identity, shared values, and purpose grows, others find out, interact, and are attracted into an expanding set of concentric circles that can propagate far and wide. One of the unique challenges of the Internet is that its rate of propagation has increased far faster than the rate at which authentic relationships develop.

The Long March of the Chinese Revolutionaries, Oct. 16, 1934, to Oct. 19, 1935

More than half a century ago, in the fall of 1934, the Chinese Communists were a loose band of 84,000 raw recruits and naive rebels. In operation and growing in strength for years, they were now on the defensive and in danger. The general leading Chiang Kai-Shek's Nationalist troops against them was pursuing a strategy of deliberate encirclement—cutting off all lines of retreat. The noose closed in tighter every day. Their problem was how to escape with their movement intact, fend off destruction, and find a new base of operations to continue their crusade. Their opportunity was to forge the country's next generation of leaders.

The solution was a long journey. At the end, one year and 30,000 miles later, they were 4,000 grizzled, toughened, wise, and savvy revolutionaries, more tightly bound together than a group of people could ever be except by ties of family. So tightly bound that for the next sixty years, until their entire leadership died out, it was the members of that march, the Long March of the Chinese Communists from October 1934 to October 1935, that ruled the largest country on earth.

The Long March has become legendary as one of the greatest retreats in history. Yet it was also an advance. That journey was as much about the relationships that were forged and destroyed, the factions that lost and won, the colleagues who were separated and then who found one another, those who made it and those who were left behind, than it was about the journey itself. It is a perfect example of how relationships play a vital role in problem solving. In such a history-altering enterprise, the formation of identity and mutual camaraderie was as important as the problem they faced.

The larger challenge of Mao Tse Dung, Zhou En Lai, Deng Tsiao-Ping, and their companions was one that has been taken up by rebels and revolutionaries for millions of years—a fight to the death for power and control over the direction of people and resources. Although today in business that struggle is much different, with the financial and legal mechanisms of corporations, takeovers, and mergers, many corporate titans have taught us that it is no less personal and that the same eternal games are still being played in another form. The drama of human relationships involves forming and dissolving ties, exploring and retreating, domination and submission. These aspects of personal and group relationships—the alliances and partnerships, competitions and rivalries—are what bring a problem solving landscape alive and fill it with both danger and promise.

It should be no surprise then that building and managing relationships is the third essential of great problem solving. More surprising may be the premise that the basis of all relationships is communication—not chemistry, not character, not complementarity. Becoming a Communicator, someone who is adept at the process of shaping and influencing human relationships, is one of the most intangible and yet valuable human skills.

Whatever one may think of their ends and means, the fact is Mao and his cadre of close allies exhibited the lessons of relationship-building throughout their adventure. Their relationships provided both the fuel for and the rewards of a great journey. The men and women on the Long March shared bitter cold, wet nights, tattered clothing, near starvation, and other deprivations that would conquer most of us in no time.

The slow weaving and tying together of the members underpinned the expedition's success. They opened new channels of communication between parties who had never truly listened or spoken to one another before. They built on those new channels to create a sense of give-and-take, the beginnings of mutual service that cement the bonds between people. They helped themselves by helping one another, filling in weak spots and building a force that was greater than the sum of the individual parts. They cultivated a network that strengthened the new channels of communication and relationships into a more permanent form of interaction for a purpose. And they evolved a social fabric that allowed for limited individual needs even as it shaped an enduring collective identity for themselves in the world.

Building effective partnerships, teams, and networks of working relationships has always been important, but it is especially vital today for two reasons. First, communications and collaboration technologies are creating opportunities to establish new connections and kinds of relationships. Second, those very technologies, along with the globalization and mobility that affect our lifestyles, are also separating and distancing us from one another. The flexibility and convenience of telecommuting, for instance, is balanced by the isolation and fragmentation it causes unless it is accompanied by pervasive efforts to feed and nourish human

contact. Many large business projects are conducted by groups of people distributed around the world who may have never met face-to-face, yet need to develop
trust, a common language, and a feeling of shared identity to get the work done.
Third, groups are forming and dissolving at a much faster rate in response to
rapidly changing problems and opportunities, putting a premium on understanding the process of forming relationships that makes an effective group.

The Communicator's Central Idea: The Best Relationships Come from Creating and Propagating Concentric Circles

The effect of a strong individual and/or a small core group on a larger environment is what I call the "Stone in the Pond" effect. (See Figure 3.1.) As the core
propagates, the webs and networks created by these interlocking waves of relationships form the field of possibilities and constraints that problem solvers deal
with as they choose or travel toward a destination. Ignoring some, selecting others and actively shaping, drawing from, and contributing to one's own web of relationships—independent of the particular problem you are working on—is
paradoxically one of the most vital abilities of a problem solver. Creating,
strengthening, and sustaining the web requires attention to individual journeys
in life simultaneously with the work you may be doing together.

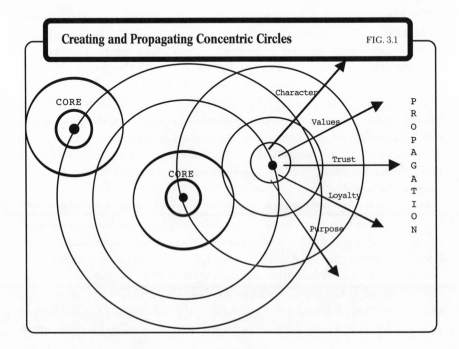

Creating and Propagating Concentric Circles   FIG. 3.1

Weak relationships sap the energy of a project or create new problems that overtake the ones defined at the start. They mislead you or inhibit your own process of personal growth. The consequences of weak relationships are more significant than ever, because the time, energy, and resources lost in lawsuits, project delays, or inadequate quality control are less affordable than ever. In contrast, a good relationship can help uncover an opportunity you wouldn't have considered or serve as the catalyst to help you get over the hump in tackling one you're afraid of. Strong relationships are necessary to get through tough times when motivation is flagging or disaster strikes. And they are what we all need to enjoy the peak moments of celebration or accomplishment when the wind is at our back and a resolution is finally reached.

Communicators in Action:
Orpheus Chamber Orchestra and the Ultimate in Music

If the Communicator's central idea is the importance of building a core that expands into concentric circles of relationships, then how does that apply in practice? How does building relationships lead to mutual devotion and collective identity? The following story of Orpheus Chamber Orchestra and some of the world's most beautiful music shows Communicators in action. With their contribution, a problem solver can build on the Innovator's ideas and the Discoverer's knowledge to create an inspired, intelligent, and living community.

It's concert night at Carnegie Hall. The moment comes, and the musicians file in and take their seats. The lights dim. A deepening hush follows, and thousands of eyes and ears turn toward the stage, where Orpheus emerges. The musicians position themselves as the audience waits for the moment when the conductor will confidently step out and take his place to lead. Then, with a barely visible gesture, the first violin takes up her bow, and the group bursts into the piece with perfect timing. No conductor. Members of the audience worry only a fraction of a moment about whether the lack of a conductor signals a problem with the performance, and then the beauty of the sound takes their breath away.

Julian Fifer and several fellow students founded the orchestra in 1972 out of their frustration with working as passive musicians under the domination of conductors. Their goal was to create a world-class chamber orchestra that would give each musician the possibility of reaching his or her fullest possible expression as a member of a community, a whole. Orpheus gave their first concert at a local church, after Julian's graduation, and total receipts were $111. Six years later, in 1978, they gave their first Carnegie Hall concert.

In Greek mythology, Orpheus was Apollo's son, who entered Hades, the land of the dead, and charmed the rulers of that land with his music to win back his beloved wife. As Milton puts it, he "drew iron tears down Pluto's cheek / And made Hell grant what love did seek.". Orpheus then, in the words of executive director Harvey Seifter, "represents singing, playing so beautifully that it melts hearts of stone."

Over the last twenty-eight years, Orpheus has become a legend in the musical community. They have built a worldwide following and stunned audiences with the quality of their sound, its feeling, and the timing and rhythm of their performances. Orpheus has charmed music critics and skeptics, who've come to believe the group's power lies in its very lack of a single authority. "The results," raved the *New York Times* in its review of Orpheus's opening of its 1999 Carnegie Hall season, "were uniformly excellent, as they should be in an orchestra in which everybody's a conductor."

How can it work? How is it possible that a couple of dozen of the world's most talented people, free thinking and creative by nature, fight out decisions—everything from speed and tempo of a piece to administrative details—and then perform together beautifully on the world's most storied stages? With no one in charge?

Communicating and listening to each other is the foundation of Orpheus's success. It has to be, notes Nardo Poy, who has played viola with the twenty-seven-member orchestra for two decades, since there's so much added personal responsibility. "When you're in a conducted orchestra, your role is a passive one. You're there to do what the conductor wants, to realize his vision. You're basically—I don't want to use the word slave—but you're there to do what he wants. With us, everybody's role is active. Everybody's ideas about music are incorporated and heard and considered. It's part of our role to be open about our ideas, to listen, interact, and communicate."

Communication is based on, as one member of the orchestra calls it, a "constant, rhythmic reciprocating motion back and forth." All questions are open for debate in Orpheus. Rehearsals become an open conversation, as they question one another constantly on points of interpretation. "Is it two-four or one-two?" "What should be the phrasing in this part of the score?" The most important quality of communication is shifting the bias toward listening rather than sending messages. Self-expression is important. But Orpheus musicians strive for being able to cue subtly, rather than lead with strong signals. This subtle communication requires attentiveness, awareness, knowledge of the context, and good listening on the part of every single player—without exception.

Orpheus, says Executive Director Harvey Seifter, can create one harmony from many voices, in part because everyone starts from a place of "mutual respect." And when the musicians listen to each other, they are fully engaged. Take the cueing, for instance. Most of it is done with breathing and eye movement. "This is a group," says Seifter, "whose beauty and power derives from its intimacy."

Orpheus prides itself on allowing musicians to confront each other—and the fact that friendships are not damaged by it. "There are times in rehearsal," says Poy, "because of the way we work, the intensity, the directness, often we do get pretty emotional, angry at each other. And yet, when our rehearsal is over, that's pretty much it, for the most part it's over. Either right after rehearsal or the next day, you're still friends. Whereas I see in so many groups that don't allow that kind of outlet of ideas . . . there are so many resentments that build up that it actually poisons the atmosphere, they won't speak to each other, there are enemies and factions. That's one of the healthy aspects of our group."

Trust and respect are created by the force of give-and-take. In turn, that trust and respect both nurture and protect relationships. It's about cultivating shared values and loyalty and identity. "Trust and respect are the cornerstones of the success of the organization," says Ronnie Bauch, a violinist who's been with the group nearly since the start, when musicians sorted out decisions at a Chinese restaurant. "Without that it doesn't exist. You can't go out on a stage without somebody [a conductor] standing in the middle, about to perform any number of complicated works, without knowing that you can rely not only on the person next to you but also on somebody sitting across the stage. And that underneath any agreement or disagreement is a basic understanding and vision about what you're trying to attain and achieve."

Of course, hashing it out takes time. Orpheus might spend thirty hours rehearsing for a two-hour concert—three times what a typical orchestra would take. "We don't make claims to efficiency, but that's not our point," Poy says. In the beginning, Orpheus' musicians would spend fifty or sixty hours rehearsing for a single concert. "They were leadership training seminars—that's what we were doing, training and developing each other," recalls Bauch.

"Quality control" is handled by the musicians themselves. Some are sent out to listen to the others rehearse. "You try to analyze out the important factors. Why does playing it fast sound better? Why does playing it slow sound better?" said Bauch. "And come up with maybe the underlying truth, OK, what's really important is the rhythmic integrity and the intensity of the phrasing and if you have that it can work at either speed. Once you've established what's really important about something, then nobody is really upset by how you got there." Interpretation by committee, a committee that doesn't shrink from confrontation, yields unexpected results. "What you get in the end isn't a watered-down, middle-of-the-road kind of interpretation which you could easily imagine—you know, General Motors decides to interpret music—but you get interpretations of extraordinary originality."

Orpheus musicians have to develop themselves through others, increasing their own contributions while improving the value of each other's, and thus build the stock of trust they share. "It's years of working with each other, understanding how that person works, what their capabilities are, and understanding their weaknesses," says Poy. "And knowing that everybody is in this for the right reasons, they want to do the best possible job."

The musicians constantly look to help one another. "When you're on stage," says violinist Eric Wyrick, "and you've been all over the world, sometimes it can be a very pressurized situation, whether it's Carnegie Hall or Musikverein in Vienna, with so much history. You go out there and you have to trust your people or things can go awfully wrong. Especially without a conductor, each line is so important, if someone drops the ball it can derail the whole piece." If the ball gets dropped, a fellow musician has to be right there to pick it up.

There are twenty-seven total in the orchestra. Originally, all the decisions about the repertoire and personnel were made collectively. The basic rehearsal principle was that anyone could say anything at any moment. This freedom attracted talented and individualistic musicians from all over New York. But things bogged down in practice. Many musicians were frustrated with the slow pace of interpretative evolution in the rehearsal process. So, they applied a classic solution and developed a system called the core. The core was an executive committee of musicians, with a concertmaster for each performance to serve as a sort of chairman. Each musical section elected a representative. It is this small core that works out the issues of interpretation and phrasing before the first big rehearsal, increasing efficiency and smoothing out interactions in the process. However, the only reason the core can function is because they take their responsibility for representing other musicians seriously and thereby earn their trust.

For Orpheus, choosing members is critical. There's not much turnover—about as much as the College of Cardinals, jokes Seifter. But in any given performance, a dozen or more of the regulars might be absent (the economics of the orchestra mandate that they all have other playing commitments or teaching positions), so "friends of Orpheus" fill in. The Orpheus network now reaches around the globe, to thousands of individuals who not only follow the group's performances assiduously, or contribute to its funding, and also to those who change their way of thinking about group work just by learning about them. These people are part of the web of those who have been introduced into the widening Orpheus circle.

On occasion Orpheus has invited soloists to perform who don't quite get the culture. Their mistakes and miscues typically start with clumsy communication. The soloists start cueing the other musicians with a bow or waving their hand. "It's an act of controlling—not trusting," explained Nardo Poy, who has played the viola with the twenty-seven-member orchestra for two decades. "The whole idea is to make it a group effort, not to have somebody up there showing you where the beats are. It's not necessary. We rely on our eyes and ears with each other." As soon as someone starts overtly guiding the other musicians, added Wyrick, "they're directing." "They're directing you how to play. They're telling you how they think you should play. We're not about that at all. This is completely against that. We're . . ." And Poy finishes the sentence: "for Orpheus."

It is just this level of intensity and mutual commitment that squeezes every last ounce of contribution to the group's enterprise—collective musical expression. All the ideas, the inspirations, the innovations, the cumulative series of delicate adjustments—all these ultimately are distilled out of the creative tension of this give-and-take. As one long-time observer of the group puts it, "Most of us who hang around with these musicians try to carry the group's values into the rest of our lives. You have to be willing to spend time talking; if necessary, to fight; if necessary, to disagree; if necessary, to draw blood. You have be willing to become Orphean."

This willingness is the root of the orchestra's greatness—the personal responsibility taken by each of the players for all the music, for the group's performance. The individual players think not just about how they sound, but how the entire composition is sounding. Their individual performance can only be judged in the context of the whole. They strive to play their best, but they always assess success as a group, constantly adjusting to one another in the midst of a piece, as rhythm and harmony ebbs and flows. All for one, one for all.

In summary, as Orpheus illustrates, relationships form the backbone of our ability to solve problems, to create and adapt, to change in pursuit of a vision, a destination. The people we know and love, work with and play with, constitute a field of potential and a web of support that mediates everything around us. The quality of the relationships we have and those we build either opens wide horizons or constrains one to narrow, cluttered pathways. A love relationship can change which problems we think are most important. A respected colleague can change our minds about what we know and how we know it. A trusted teammate can offer the assets and capability to get us places we could otherwise never go. The influence of a friend can keep us on track and comfort or inspire us in the midst of life's more challenging moments and situations.

Relationships are critical to problem solving because they motivate us to take initiative. They get us through the hard times and provide us with fellow travelers and companions to make the journeys more enjoyable. They offer us the expertise and experience of trusted colleagues who can help make certain we avoid mistakes and capture the highlights of a trip, or just provide someone to talk to and share stories of the road with. The relationships we build are both the ends and the means we seek. And they offer access to other relationships, and make us available to others, in the never ending web of human community.

Knowing when to emphasize and build a relationship and when to focus on the problem is the essential judgment. When should you make certain that the problem solving effort is serving people and when should you focus on the people contributing to the problem solving effort? These are the intangible challenges of building relationships as a problem solver.

The rest of Part 3 covers in more depth and detail how the best Communicators go about building relationships and solving problems. You can either skip to the next part, "Manage the Journeys," on page 119 or proceed. Each chapter in turn shows how the best Communicators start with the spark of a conversation and ultimately progress to the foundations of a living community.

- "Conversation Is King: From Isolation to Communication" shows how conversation is still the most fundamental mode of human interaction, no matter how complex technologies evolve. Franklin Delano Roosevelt and his fireside chats is the historical example that reminds us of this unchanging foundation.
- "Give and Take: From Communication to Relationships" illustrates how partnerships are built through interaction and risk-taking that eventually build trust. The software development teams at the United Space Alliance illustrate how this principle helps produce the world's best software.
- "Develop Yourself Through Others: From Relationships to a Core Team" pinpoints how mentorship, applied to both yourself and others, weaves the fabric from which a team emerges. Coach John Thompson and his well-known Georgetown basketball program illustrate how to build a team by improving yourself while coaching, mentoring and teaching others.
- "Cultivate a Network: From a Core Team to a Network" chronicles how a core team can grow into a large-scale network of people devoted to a shared cause. Billy Shore, founder of Share Our Strength, tells how he built from scratch a national organization dedicated to solving the problem of hunger.
- "All for One and One for All: From a Network to a Living Community" explains the values and culture required to turn a network into a living community. McKinsey & Company, the most elite consulting firm in the world, illustrates the cultural foundations of an enduring professional community.

CONVERSATION IS KING

From Isolation to Communication

The best of life is conversation, and the greatest success is confidence,
or perfect understanding between sincere people.

—RALPH WALDO EMERSON (1803–1882)

Good communication is the lubricant of a smoothly running problem solving team. The more challenging the problem and the more people involved, the more critical it becomes. Without effective communication, each problem solver is left isolated, alone, and far weaker than they could be. Friction, conflict, instability, and overall degradation inevitably occur in a problem solving effort when people under stress lose their ability to communicate. The significance of good communication has increased dramatically as more diverse workforces go through constant change and engage in collaborative work using new technologies over huge distances. In spite of that, many essential principles of communication remain the same.

Conversation sparks communication, which creates relationships. The many dynamic elements of human conversation, whether it is in a simple telephone call or in a multiuser video global videoconference, are still the same. As a result, one of the last century's great prizes for communication goes to the man who made a one-way speech he remembered as a two-way conversation—Franklin D. Roosevelt—the originator of the "fireside chat."

Messages flow best in conversations, and conversations drive work and problem solving—no matter what the medium. Communication is successful to the degree that it brings the participant into a conversation. No one understood this need better than Franklin D. Roosevelt. This is why his strategy for using the new technology of radio—even though that medium is very mature—is a perfect case study of what we need to remember in our use of any new technology we have at our disposal. He faced radio the way many face the Internet, struggling to understand how the medium could be used effectively to communicate with others.

Franklin D. Roosevelt and His "Fireside Chats"

It was early 1933 and a time that few of us can imagine who didn't live through it. Banks were closing all around the country. A full-fledged crisis confronted Roosevelt and the country within weeks of his inauguration. With decisive action from the Oval Office to keep banks closed until calm was restored, and with a debate on major legislation taking place in the Senate, FDR held the first of his famous "fireside chats." It began with the simple words, "I want to talk with the people of the United States for a few minutes about banking."

By the time the American public had gotten accustomed to these unique public addresses, they began to anticipate them. Around midday, perhaps even the day before, a family might start to look forward to the chat. Arrangements would be made to eat dinner a bit early, the house would be cleaned up, and there might even be a treat for everyone to eat with tea or coffee while they listened, listened to the voice that kept them together and gave hope the advantage over fear.

Roosevelt's success was combining a universal approach to communication—the conversation or chat—with sensitivity to a specific medium—radio. Everything he did, from choice of language, to the content of his message, to the style of his delivery, went into making his radio addresses like a conversation. The basic elements that FDR considered are still valid whether we are videoconferencing, teleconferencing, or in a chat room on the web: Simplify, take people seriously on their own terms, find a common language, teach and explain as well as listen, and be both honest and credible by linking words to actions.

In an information-rich, networked world, conversation is still king. Yet there are thousands upon thousands of highly advanced chat rooms on the Web where, if you observe closely, there is little real conversation going on at all. The fact is, a one-way communication conducted with feeling and understanding, so much so than it is accepted and felt by everyone to be a personal chat, is more successful than the most dynamic, "chatty" online exchange during which opinions and information are relayed but feeling and understanding take a back seat. FDR symbolizes what we most need to remember when faced with new technology: It's the communication between people that matters.

Every conversation opens a channel, and live channels are not just something you switch off or surf through with a remote. They are built or destroyed in subtle ways. The most basic goal is to keep a channel as broad and stable as possible and make sure that the information which gets through is accurate and undistorted. Opening a channel starts with good listening and ultimately rests on the more mysterious drama of human dialogue. What to talk about? How to talk about it? It's about subtle combinations of body language, verbal cues, and written symbols. How to establish the right rhythm? How to be efficient but do justice to the feelings of the person you're speaking with? How to make those thorny transitions from one subject to another, or from the beginning to the end? How to create a feeling of openness and candor so that the conversation not only communicates information but also builds trust and develops a relationship, which in turn improves the communication?

When most of us communicate, we blend two separate components—conversing and informing. The function of conversing is to keep bandwidth open and allow error-free communication when it is needed. If conversing works, then information can flow freely and is easily received—if the message is clear. Over time, if you converse well, you will have a channel open anytime you need it that you can use for mutual exchange of information. An example of such a high quality channel would be your best friend or your sibling, whom you can call in the middle of the night about anything.

FDR knew his audience and how to open a channel. His chats were aimed at specific groups of voters whose support he needed. He knew what he wanted to say and carefully crafted the message he wanted to get across in his conversation. Furthermore, he took the posture of a teacher, without being academic, lecturing, or preaching. He came across as someone who genuinely wanted everyone to understand, for their own good. Finally, he was completely involved in that communication personally, both in the delivery and in the visualization of the audience. As one observer described it, during a radio address, "His head would nod and his hands would move in simple, comfortable gestures." It was this genuineness which created the feeling of the fireside chat.

Genuineness keeps channels open, because we are all experts at identifying dissembling. Over and over again, research shows that much of a listener's reaction to a speaker is based on how genuine, relaxed, and forthright they appear, quite apart from the content of their message. So be yourself. Tell it like it is. Truth, value, and regular use build the credibility of a channel. Deception and unreliability destroy it.

One of the insidious causes of difficulties in communication is misinterpretation of meaning. Words are uttered and interpreted with different senses by different people, who walk away thinking they heard something accurately when the speaker meant something entirely, or subtly, different. Preventing this takes attention to developing a common language by actually talking about meaning. And this preventive strategy, followed consistently, is also the source of an elusive advantage that few organizations achieve—the power of a shared vocabulary. Shared vocabulary stimulates the creation of a pool of mutual knowledge, enhances joint learning, smoothes communication, and reinforces a common identity.

Even though he was describing complex issues, FDR simplified their essence without sacrificing truth and communicated it with vocabulary his average listener could understand. He chose the most common language to express even the most complex of ideas and made great efforts to simplify by reducing complicated issues to their essence. This approach is far from the norm today, when new acronyms and specialized technical jargon are taken by many as a sign of power and erudition.

Perhaps most importantly, he communicated in his tone and manner a feeling for how the public would hear it in the context of their lives, with their loved ones far away, fear in their hearts, tired from the exertions and deprivations of wartime. As David Brinkley said, "A great deal of Roosevelt's almost magical talent for persuading and manipulating the American people lay in his ability to state his thoughts in simple, homely phrases, in the language of the working neighborhood where visitors sat in the kitchen, with puppies frolicking under the stove, husbands wearing working clothes and wives in their one-dollar house dresses."

Beyond an open channel, a common vocabulary and clear messages, good conversation requires a sense of rhythm. There are times when spaces need to be created and times when they should be filled. Times when you need to take the lead and times when you need to step back. There are times when you need to be brief and to the point, and others when you need to slow down and relax. With a proper sense of rhythm, you will find the channels you establish with others growing and thriving over time. Forget the rhythm, conduct them at your own pace, and they will shrink and narrow over time.

There is no recipe for rhythm, but if you are aware of it and go into a conversation with only one idea—"take turns"—you can develop a sense of rhythm. It helps to have someone lead, and the leader is the one who chooses first to hear, then be heard. Communication is always a two-way street. Speak clearly and directly by formulating your own point of view and defining what it is you want or need. Listen and truly understand by taking the other's point of view and by questioning or paraphrasing. If you can be aware of, feel, and enjoy the rhythm, you can have a good conversation, a conversation that is the foundation of great communication.

Relationships in Action: Taking Conversations to a New Level

Identify the three people you care about most and have the easiest conversations with. In your next few talks, try to be aware of how you feel, what you do, and just what makes the conversation so enjoyable. Perhaps you go to the same place a lot to establish a comfort zone. Or you always start by asking how they are and really listening. Maybe it's just that you're more relaxed. Then take the simple step, once you're more aware of what's happening in those conversations, of trying to apply some of the things you're doing in conversations with others where you think your communication could be improved.

GIVE AND TAKE
From Communication to Relationships

"We receive but what we give."
–SAMUEL TAYLOR COLERIDGE (1772–1834)

Problem solving requires taking communication to another level, to the constant, mutually challenging push-and-pull interactions that are only possible within strong relationships. Over time, through the offering and taking of advice, the giving and receiving of gifts or praise, the sharing of intimacies, or the voicing and accepting of criticism, Communicators build knowledge, trust, and the bonds of loyalty. Through such intensive communication, in other words, we build the relationships that let us solve problems and that endure in spite of them.

Without fully participating in such give-and-take, we have only the shadow of a connection with another human being. Sometimes this participation comes easily. We call it "chemistry." But more often than not, it requires taking risks. Self-expression, conviction, and truth-telling put you at risk. Openness to others means letting down barriers and exposing vulnerabilities. This requires courage, faith, and trust that what you give will later come back in some form or another.

Yet in our increasingly diverse work environments, where different backgrounds and perspectives create barriers to openness and candor, true give-and-take is both hard to achieve and more essential than ever.

The key to this next level of relationship building is trust. Trust is the fertilizer and the soil, the nitrogen, oxygen, and water that feeds the growth of a friendship, a working relationship, or the love of a lifetime. Trust must be invested in carefully. A Communicator knows it is hard to build and easy to destroy, and depends on a heightened awareness on the part of all involved of the need to act and react so as to increase the stock of trust. In the workplace, the software engineers at the United Space Alliance have institutionalized a process of give-and-take that not only builds trust but also the highest quality software in the world, a world where software is embedded in nearly every device we use.

The United Space Alliance and Software Development for the Space Shuttle

None of us want a colleague looking over our shoulders, shadowing our every move, hunting for mistakes. That seems the essence of *distrust*. But for the men and women who write the software that flies the space shuttle, having a team to root out errors is key to shuttle success—and why the shuttle software is about as close to perfection as humanly possible. It has to be error free. Beyond the billions of dollars a space shuttle costs, astronauts are up there. "Human life is at stake and the environment is so unforgiving—it's not like you can make an emergency landing at the nearest airport," explains Keith Hudkins, the deputy chief engineer at NASA.

That's why the people who build the software, the United Space Alliance (USA), have set up a rigid series of checks and balances, along with inspection hurdles, to rid the software of errors. There is the development team, which writes the 430,000 source lines of code that fly the shuttle, and the verification team, which follows along behind and tries to find mistakes. The last fourteen versions of shuttle software had just thirty-two mistakes—and three of the last four systems delivered had no errors at all. Commercial software of similar complexity could be expected to have twenty times as many errors. The shuttle software group is one of the rare organizations to achieve the Software Engineering Institute's Level 5 rating—its highest—for sophistication and reliability. It has operated at that level consistently, and for longer, than any other group in the world. One reason: the deep level of trusting give-and-take in professional relationships that is built into its culture.

Each and every interaction, even in relationships that have endured over a long time, has a greater potential to destroy trust than to build it. All it takes is one lie, one deception, one betrayal, and so much can be lost.

The software engineers at USA respect this same principle as it applies to software production: There is no such thing as an insignificant error. "We have come to believe two things—any line of code can have an error, and any error can be very severe," says Tom Peterson, project leader for the shuttle software. "Other people try to parse or categorize their code as to critical or noncritical, benign or active. We have taken the attitude that every line is important, every error can be severe. Most errors are not severe. But if you believe that all errors can be severe, you don't lull yourself into thinking this isn't important or that isn't so important. For us, every error is bad, every error has to be treated the same."

And then there's the way errors and defects are viewed, as learning opportunities. "The discovery of an error, rather than something to cringe about, is actually a positive event in the sense that you can use that to further improve the process and or take some action that may enable you to go find similar errors that exist out there," says Orr.

In the same way that engineers view every defect as an opportunity, so should anyone trying to build a meaningful relationship view a mistake. Trying to hide them, lie about them, or avoid them only increases the probability of failure in the end. Confronting them, bringing them out in the open, and dealing with them, if it is done sincerely, creates the potential to learn and get the relationship to a new level. In the building of a long-term relationship, an error handled well can be transformed into an opportunity.

That's where the give-and take is critical. What results at USA is a healthy rivalry, a friendly adversarial relationship. "When we spread out into a team there is team ownership. If an error is found, we use a team approach; it becomes the team's failure or the team's success," says Peterson. "And that's why the rivalry between the development and verification teams works so well." "The secret and success of the product," adds Jim Orr, manager of project coordination, "is not the single individual as superstar. Our success is really based on two components—good people and a very good process with a lot of give-and-take."

The men and women on the verification team (the Red team), have to have the right personality, says Hudkins. "We pick them with good people skills because they're likely to ruffle feathers with their work. Just showing up and asking a development team [the Blue team] member how their day's going might set them off. The reaction might be, 'Well, I'd be doing a lot better if you weren't here bothering me,'" said Hudkins. The team doing the assessing "has to go into a controversial environment, keep exchanges constructive, and not let it turn into mudslinging."

Giving and taking are like two pistons in the engine of a relationship. Each stroke brings another counteracting one and once the cycles have begun, they can generate their own momentum. But in the rhythm of give-and-take that takes place in any relationship as it builds over time, there come moments of truth. These are times when what one does or doesn't do can block progress, degrade the relationship, or, alternatively, catapult things forward and take them to a new level. Moments of truth multiply the effects of normal actions. They occur when a combination of events and emotions brings some major issue to a head, where a decisive judgment or behavior change on the part of one or more of those involved is required to move things forward.

It could be a moment of chaos and strife, or an imbalance of power, when someone needs to take a firm hand and exercise control in everyone's interest. It might be a time when a difficult subject has been in the background and is getting worse but is so volatile that no one will talk about it. Someone may need to confront it head on. Or, it might be a time when—after many confrontations or at a particularly delicate moment—the relationship cannot bear the weight of the controversial issue any longer. Deflecting, diffusing, or delaying it with humor, or calling a time out by some other means, might then be the most effective thing to do.

To move through most moments of truth requires surrender, domination, confrontation, or deflection. The art is in choosing the right ones for a particular situation. To handle them, USA offers a "negotiating" class for its employees. "We're trying to put them in confrontational situations with different goals and then teach them to give and take while negotiating to a win-win situation," says Peterson. In these classes, employees learn to anticipate the "moments of truth" in their relationships, so that they can make the most of them when they arise.

During actual quality inspection, there's a "moderator" on hand to iron out differences between teams. "Our process is written toward roles," says Orr, noting there are developers, verifiers, and in almost all meetings, moderators. "They [the moderators] are accountable to keep the process on track. They are the ones, probably more than anybody else, who would handle any kind of conflict that comes up."

Moderators receive training not only on how to conduct an inspection, but "how not to let personality, if you will, interject," says Orr. It's a balancing act, Orr says, to keep the verifiers involved in the process of building software, involved in relationships with their counterparts, but still totally independent for the purpose of quality control. "You get the most intense emotion in the process if the verifier perceives that their independence is being eroded beyond some invisible line. They tend to react very strongly to that."

Effective Communicators often use a simple but powerful model of group dynamics to guide their thinking on moments of truth, called the Storm Model. According to this model, any relationship goes through four phases: Forming, where people orient themselves to one another; Storming, where conflict arises and arguments occur; Norming, where people move beyond the conflict to establish common operating principles; and Performing, where those shared values underpin improved performance.

Most relationships get stuck in phase two, and it takes both poise and flexibility—the ability to surrender or dominate, confront or deflect as necessary—to get through it. Sometimes you need to give in. Other times, when there is no progress and things are stuck, it can be necessary to step in and control things to move them forward. Still other times, breaking the tension with humor is what's needed. A colleague of mine used to always pick these moments to declare, "I think we're all in violent agreement here."

In the best groups and relationships, when "storming" doesn't take place, look for ways to get it started in a constructive manner. Once healthy conflict has taken place and people have lived through it, they are not only more cohesive, they are more confident and more knowledgeable about what their friends or colleagues actually think and feel. They know the group and its limits and possibilities better. As a result, they tend to be more willing to invest the effort and make the sacrifices and compromises necessary to maximize the group's accomplishments. The absence of conflict is not harmony, it's apathy.

Relationships in Action: Improving your Give-and-Take

In your most important professional relationship—a work group, your department, or your company—choose which of the four phases of relationship building your organization is in. Forming—orienting to one another, with low levels of conflict and superficial interaction. Storming—high levels of conflict, much substantive interaction, strong points of view expressed. Norming—Initial formation of shared values and principles that help the group make collective choices and resolve conflict more easily. Performing—Strong shared purpose and principles, along with sense of personal freedom of expression, which combine in high-intensity, efficient work and effective outcomes. When you've identified which stage you're in, take action to get it to the next level by choosing a mix of confrontation, submission, domination, or deflection.

DEVELOP YOURSELF
THROUGH OTHERS

From Relationships to a Core Team

Some players you need to kiss their butts.
Some players you need to kick their butts.
Some players you need to pat their butts.
And other players, you just need to leave their butts alone.

—PETE ROSE

When all the members of a group are simultaneously helping themselves and help-ing others, something magical happens. A core team comes alive with a spirit of participation that knits multiple relationships together in a dynamic fashion. They move together toward a future in which the challenge is not only their joint accom-plishment but also their greater capability and fulfillment as human beings.

For this reason, Communicators invest significant time and energy in nurturing their own and other's abilities. These are not contradictory notions—the process of developing individual ability is the foundation of a team's ability and the catalyst for developing your own as well. Concentrating your attention and intuition on help-ing others in their life journey contributes to an open environment where mutual assistance and support occur. In such an environment, good communication and free give-and-take are encouraged. At the same time, openly pursuing your own goals of self-fulfillment sets an example for others to do the same.

This is the art of mentoring. You make the commitment to help others grow, and in so doing you coach your team and yourself through a process of personal and professional development. Mutual learning and growth can inspire the best in everyone. For John Thompson of Georgetown, one of the best known college coaches in the country, mentoring his players not only built his storied basketball dynasty, it also spurred his own journey of development.

John Thompson, Georgetown Basketball and the Art of Mentoring

In Thompson's career at Georgetown, where he had one national championship, three Final Four appearances, two dozen postseason appearances, and has since been voted into the Naismith Memorial Basketball Hall of Fame, he is known not just as a coach but as a mentor. For the sake of appearances, he doesn't like to be called a father figure—that's an insult to the boys' true parents, he says. But for a generation of young men he has been a nurturing, guiding light. And he uses the language of parenting, in all its most positive senses, to discuss both how he feels and how he works. He has, as *Washington Post* columnist Michael Wilbon wrote upon Thompson's resignation in 1999, "used the moral authority of his position to inspire a segment of urban America thought by many to be unreachable."

When Thompson was coaching the Georgetown University Hoyas, he heard that a reputed drug lord in the nation's capital was going out on the town with a couple of his players. Thompson ordered his players to stop the fraternizing and put the word on the street that he wanted to sit down with the drug lord, Rayful Edmond III. Now serving a life sentence without parole, Edmond sauntered in to Thompson's office one day at McDonough Gymnasium "Do me a favor," Thompson said he told Edmond. "If you see anything going on out there, use whatever resources you have to stop it from happening."

For Thompson, it was what any caring parent would do. "Those players are under my supervision, and I was trying to do what my mother or father would have done." Thompson said afterwards. "If there had been a problem that concerned me, I could see my mother taking that apron off and going down the street and saying, 'Well, let me sit down and talk with this young man and find out just what this is about.'" The act of mentoring begins with such courageous acts of caring and protecting.

Making the commitment to mentor involves not just helping someone along their road in life, but actually showing them the way because of how you live. Just passing on the savvy moves, the key skills and critical knowledge isn't enough if you can't ignite passion and motivation. And the spark of motivation never just comes from commitment, it has to be seen, observed, and watched in action. Only then can the flame of your own conviction and purpose be passed to another. Such spirit is not something that can be taught, but it can be modeled, it can be expressed and celebrated, it can be inspired, and environments can be created that bring it out in people, that create a sense of freedom and adventure.

Thompson always kept a deflated basketball in his office. Why? It's a symbol, he said, of his commitment and passion about developing whole men. It was a visible message to young men of what their life would be once basketball was over, if they hadn't properly prepared themselves for the real world. When Thompson arrived at Georgetown's brick-and-ivy campus, known as a destination for young people interested in law or medicine, but not sports, his challenge was daunting. The Big East school was not exactly a powerhouse in NCAA basketball. But Thompson's first move wasn't to hire a hotshot recruiter, or a skilled floor assistant. It was to hire Mary Fenlon, a former nun and English and Latin teacher who oversaw the players' academics.

At 6 foot 10 and with a signature white towel draped over his soldier, Thompson could be tough. At times, he had a my-way-or-the-highway style. He ran his program like the Kremlin, one sports columnist wrote. His players had to maintain certain standards or they were gone. One of the kids who had been hanging out with the drug kingpin, John Turner, didn't heed Thompson's warning to stay away from Turner. Thompson sent him packing. Recruits were told they had two years to show they could put a Georgetown education to use, or they were gone. During Thompson's reign, 97 percent of his four-year players graduated.

But Coach Thompson was also compassionate, his love for his players shining through at painful times, just like a parent's might. There's a scene involving Thompson that is seared into the minds of Final Four fans everywhere. It was the 1982 NCAA championship game, and Georgetown trailed by one point as the clock ticked. With just seconds to go, Georgetown junior point guard Fred Brown took the ball up court and threw a pass to his right side, thinking the ball was going to a teammate. But instead Brown put the ball into the hands of North Carolina's all-American forward, James Worthy. That errant pass killed any Georgetown hopes for the title.

As the buzzer sounded, Thompson threw his arms around Brown, consoling his player in a portrait captured by cameras and beamed across the country. Bill Bradley, the former New York Knick player and New Jersey Senator, cited it in one of his books as the most character-building demonstration he'd ever seen in sports. Tennis great Arthur Ashe said tears poured down his face that night.

What John Thompson demonstrated was a deep level of caring about young men who were not his own sons and a firm commitment to help them develop as human beings, not just to win basketball games. He distinguished himself by his posture as a mentor, by his determination to develop others in a multidimensional fashion, outside the bounds of any one particular problem or opportunity.

At the heart of the mentoring role is the ability to develop a personal authority with someone else so that you can send real messages, which are heard at a deep level, and learn lessons together. Mentoring, in other words, creates the environment that sustains communication and effective give-and-take and then builds teams out of individuals. Such personal authority comes only with a combination of competence and caring. And it comes especially if you're the kind of person who has taken the trouble to develop yourself and come a long way in life. For this self-development, there is no substitute.

It's hard to help others find their dream if you haven't found yours yet. The starting point for great mentors and achievers is the same place, learning how to develop yourself. Last year, I went to the wedding of a friend who counted former secretary of defense William Perry as one of his mentors. Perry, in his tour at the Pentagon, had a reputation as a leader of substance who cared about his people and developed them naturally and with ease.

When he spoke at the ceremony, he gave the couple, and the audience, two pieces of advice. The first was to find ways to tap into your true nature and let it shine forth in all its brilliance. "Be dazzling," he said, you don't serve anyone well by hiding yourself or suppressing your talents. The second was to remember that life is about joy and companionship. "Never forget how to dance," he said, even in the midst of the most trying times, never forget that the most treasured asset you have is the short time you spend on this earth and the people whom you spend it with, enjoy it. Enjoy just being alive.

There's something important here that bears on the process of developing oneself and others. When you dance, truly dance, no matter what step you may be performing, you bring an important piece of your heart and soul to the fore. And when you help others dance, you are more credible and effective if you do some dancing yourself every once in a while. We should all strive to seek a calling, a profession that both puts bread on the table and lift in our steps.

Thompson took the first steps towards his dream of helping kids at Providence College, where he played ball and studied economics. He was a student teacher at a local junior high during his senior year. His assignment: kids with low IQs. "I like to see the smiles come across their faces when they finally understand the point being made," he said at the time. "They appreciate the help so much, it gives you a feeling of great satisfaction. I don't know if I have the right temperament or the necessary patience to teach these children, but I want to try."

He played for the Boston Celtics for a couple of years, but with a wife and new baby, decided the pay wasn't good enough to compensate for being a nomad. And he said he wanted to add meaning to his life. So he headed home to Washington, D.C., and took a job with a program tied to President Johnson's war on poverty. He volunteered as a Police Boys Club basketball coach and put on basketball clinics for inner-city kids. A local high school hired him as coach, but he kept his other jobs, too. Even after he went to Georgetown, Thompson reserved seats in an area behind the home bench called the Coach's Corner for inner-city kids.

Thompson was mentored himself by Dean Smith in North Carolina. When he took the Georgetown job, he went to Chapel Hill for a few days, picking the brain of the more seasoned coach for tips on everything from alumni to academics to time-outs. "The most meaningful gift a man can give another man is his knowledge," Thompson said once of his gratitude to Smith. "So much insecurity exists among people in this business that they don't reveal, as honestly and as openly as he did, the things one needs to know . . . I was able to learn from his experiences and his failures."

Mentoring, then, is not just an altruistic gift, nor is it merely enlightened selfishness, by which the mentor in turn gets mentored. Mentoring involves a deeper, mutual interdependence, which fuels the self-improvement of everyone and helps transform mere partnerships into a team of mutual companions that can tackle multiple opportunities over time.

For Thompson, part of nurturing another soul is giving something back. The relationship between two individuals who help one another develop is a deep bond that is hard to break. Years after Patrick Ewing played for Thompson and turned Georgetown into a national force, his old coach was still traveling to every one of Ewing's play-off games with the Knicks. Meanwhile, Ewing had stayed involved in Georgetown, calling up players in trouble he'd never met, taking part in alumni affairs.

Thompson and Ewing exemplify how two problem solvers can come to help one another develop throughout the journey of life in many different ways. But what binds them together is more than their personal relationship, it is also their common caring about the program at Georgetown, the environment, the place they helped create. It was a place that encouraged young people to be great players, but also to grow as individuals. This is a characteristic of growth-oriented environments. There can be no limits on developing potential. You try to create the freedom to fail and take risks. You allow people to grow the way they truly want to. You don't try to change them or shape them except in a supportive way. You help them to make good decisions, but once the decisions are made, you support them in success or failure. In doing so, you can reach one of the most satisfying and enduring forms of relationship that two people can achieve—fellow travelers in life.

Relationships in Action: Developing Protégés and Mentors

If you don't have a protégé, spend some quality time thinking about who you might like to mentor, if you're really up for the commitment, and then, if it appeals to you, develop a short list of potential protégés, rank order them, and develop one. At exactly the same time, think about who you would like to have as a mentor. Write down the criteria that would make such a relationship worthwhile for you. Then make your own short list of potential mentors, rank order them, and then approach one with the idea. Doing both of these simultaneously can prove tremendously fulfilling.

CULTIVATE A NETWORK

From a Core Team to a Network

"Never doubt that a small group of committed people can change the world. Indeed, it's the only thing that ever has."

—MARGARET MEAD (1901–1978)

The greatest asset in any problem solving effort is usually not on the balance sheet. It's not the capital or technology, but rather the thriving network of people that is generated by the core team and committed to its success. The foundation of such a network is always a small, tightly knit core group of individuals that gets a project started. Their own individual networks of relationships can then begin to combine and recombine to form a larger whole. Nodes are added, and the network grows steadily and gradually. That small group of founders can expand its influence to create a web of global dimensions. In this way, even a very small group can solve problems on a vast scale.

Bigger, tougher problems and opportunities mean these core groups and their networks are even more vital. Most organizations are woven tightly into a web of interrelationships with suppliers, complements, distributors, customers, stakeholders, strategic partners, and competitors. In the same vein, every individual is part of a larger professional web. The degree to which Communicators cultivate a network successfully may determine not only whether they are aware of problems or opportunities, but also whether they can marshal the capability to solve them. Few examples of network building are as creative and noble as that of Billy Shore, a former political advisor who has revolutionized the philanthropic industry through his unique approach to the problem of hunger—an organization called Share Our Strength.

Bill Shore, Share Our Strength and the Power of Networking

When Billy Shore started Share Our Strength, he operated his fledgling anti-hunger organization out of a one-room basement office in an old converted house on Capitol Hill. His core group included his sister, Debbie, and a pair of kindred spirits from the Gary Hart presidential campaign. Steve Wozniak, who invented the Apple Computer, sent a couple of computers and his assistant to train the Shore team on the machines. Shore's wife, Bonnie, gave them her Visa card, from which they took a $2,000 cash advance to buy a typewriter, purchase stencils from a five-and-dime to make stationery, and pay the rent on the basement office. The office window was high on the wall, near the ceiling, so that the ankles of anyone walking by were at eye level. That included the mailman.

And every day Shore waited for the mailman, expecting a stack of letters in response to the thousands of appeals he'd sent to chefs, restaurateurs, and hotel owners. He got to know the mail carrier's ankles well. Sometimes they never even slowed down. In one bleak stretch, twenty-five straight days passed with no mail at all. Shore chased down the postal worker and asked gently if there'd been a mistake. The next day, he demanded a trace be put on the mail he was convinced had gotten lost. "We just couldn't believe there couldn't be mail—there had to be a mistake," recalled Shore, one of his frequent grins lighting up his face.

Finally, a letter came that turned it all around. A respected chef in California, Alice Waters, sent $1,000 and asked how she could help. Shore—tapping into a lesson about building networks that he'd learned in politics—asked her to contact a small handful of opinion makers in the restaurant business who would be impressed by her call to arms. "The light bulb went off that we'd be a lot more effective if we made it peer-to-peer," Shore said. Her letter to fellow chefs brought in nearly $20,000. Every time another well-known chef joined the cause, Shore would ask them to appeal to their friends in the restaurant business, too.

There can be as few as two or three and as many as eight people in a core group of founders. In business startups, the core often includes an investor or two, a few key board members and the two to four initial members of the management team. If it works well, the group develops strong bonds, trust, and an interdependence that transcends both friendship and professionalism. Among other things, this common identity and mutual obligation plays a critical role in building consensus on controversial issues and sustaining morale in difficult circumstances. This networking is not the superficial kind that involves collecting names and making shallow acquaintances. It is the development of deeper inter-locking relationships, all brought to bear on the project at hand.

It was the theory of "concentric circles" that Shore's old boss, former Colorado senator Gary Hart, had used in his 1984 presidential campaign in New Hampshire. Before walking away from politics to devote his full energies to Share Our Strength, Shore spent years as the "Body Man," first constantly at the side of Hart and then serving that role for Sen. Bob Kerrey of Nebraska. "He [Hart] always used to say, 'Our campaign in New Hampshire is a campaign for twenty-five people, and if we get the right twenty-five people, we'll win the primary,'" Shore said. Because those twenty-five people could each bring in a circle of supporters, who in turn could bring in a new circle, and on an on. Hart won the state's primary.

Share Our Strength has come a long way since those dark days when the mail-man walked by and kept going. It has distributed more than $60 million in anti-hunger and antipoverty grants and is now perhaps the best-known such group in America. Shore remains as down-to-earth as always—instead of using a desk, he still sits at the same folding table he used when they started.

Once a founder's group is established to tackle a challenging problem, it faces the task of expanding and replicating itself while maintaining its cohesion. Essentially, the goal is to start a chain reaction, including others who become part of the family and get involved in trying to achieve the founder's goals. Each founder brings in several other key individuals, who each bring in several others, and the reaction starts. For the chain reaction to generate a large amount of energy, choices about the people to extend the founder's network are vital. If they have the right level of competence, chemistry, and common interest, the reaction gets very hot very fast. If they don't, it will die out quickly or simply smolder and be impervious to attempts to energize it.

Shore found that chefs and restaurant owners were more willing to donate $1,000 in food and talent than to write a check for $100. So "Taste of the Nation" events were born, where chefs got a high-profile chance to strut their stuff in the community. "We had a couple of dozen [chefs and restaurant owners] at the core who reached out to another couple hundred and then eventually it turned into six or eight thousand volunteering every spring," Shore said. The other key to drawing in the restaurant community, Shore said, was giving them ownership. "We created it not as an antihunger organization but as an organization of chefs and restaurateurs fighting hunger, so that they really felt that the ownership was theirs," Shore said. By the time Hart's second presidential bid collapsed in 1988, Shore had moved his family—and Share Our Strength—to Denver.

Shore's subsequent reach into corporate America has been described as a Japanese-style *keiretsu*, or a web of affiliated companies. This web started when American Express became a key partner in 1991 as the lead sponsor of the "Taste of the Nation" events. It was a chance for the credit card company to mend fences with restaurateurs who had been boycotting American Express, complaining of high fees and below-par service. Starbucks Coffee and others have joined in, too, because these events created marketing opportunities for them with restaurants. American Express then wanted to do something larger, and created "Charge Against Hunger," donating three cents of every dollar charged the last two months of each year. The visibility Share Our Strength received with AmEx put Shore in touch with a host of other companies, like Gallo Winery and Calphalon Cookware. He reached licensing agreements that put the Share Our Strength logo on bottles of wine and sauté pans, and gave the organization a slice of the profits to add to their resource base.

Creating a web is about networking, and networking is about creating, adding, linking, and managing nodes. The vibrancy of a network always depends on the foundation of communication, and communication feeds on trust. Trust is a subtle underpinning of the relationship between number of nodes, quality of channels, and network growth, a relationship expressed in Metcalfe's law: The value of the network grows exponentially in proportion to the number of participating nodes. Just as trust sparks the give-and-take between people, it is also fans the flame and spreads it. Trust is a network propagator.

As the World Wide Web expands, it is creating mountains of data, of highly variable quality, and billions of new interactions between individuals and organizations that have never known each other for longer than a mouse click or a flirtatious chat. As a result, the age-old issue of trust is in the foreground again. Companies and leaders that are aiming for more hits, transactions, and page impressions, or stickiness, rather than building loyalty and trust through value and service, are more vulnerable than ever to competitors only a hot link away.

This problem leads to the final challenge of growing a network—scale and sustainability. Networks that operate effectively at a small scale easily break down at a large scale. This vulnerability happens surprisingly early on as a network grows, and it requires deft and consistent management and attention to keep a network working effectively as it spreads. Starting a network, like founding a company and then getting it going, is one thing, but bringing it sustainably to scale is quite another. Keeping channels open and information flowing, managing the web and increasing the stock of trust, these tasks mean a constant demand in terms of energy and skill. The more heterogeneous and varied the network, the greater the required reliability, and the more effort will be required by a Communicator.

Share Our Strength also confronted scaling issues as it grew. Charities around the country were contacting them and, instead of asking for grants, were asking to be trained so they could create wealth, too. "Finally a light went off that we ought to create a formal capacity to do it, and practice what we preach, which is use one of our assets . . . for profit," Shore said. "We wanted the free market to shape our products and services to make sure that what we were putting out there were things people really wanted and would pay for, which is a pretty good way of judging."

So Share Our Strength recently branched out into the consulting business to grow its global network even further. It hired a top consultant and go-getters from Stanford Business School. The goal—teach other nonprofits how to market their assets. This attention to management is actually part of their strategy to make their chain reaction sustainable. By focusing on how to help enhance each of their network nodes, Share Our Strength makes the network itself more robust. It is the institutional equivalent of mentoring—improving oneself by coaching newcomers to fulfill their potential. But now the "team" is a nationwide network of charities. The underlying principles of building relationships to foster problem solving have been taken to a national level of impact.

Shore has never issued a press release about the consulting arm, Community Wealth Ventures, Inc. That's because he still believes in concentric circles. "Our whole strategy has been to get four or five of the right clients," Shore said. "Try and hit a double to triple on their behalf and let that build the business."

"You always want to have a story to tell before you go out and tell it. It requires patience. In a town where everybody is basically, in one way or the other, pitching their story, I'd much rather have our story be discovered when it's really there and real for people to see. It's just like a discovered truth is better than one that's been sold to you."

Relationships in Action: Throw a Stone in the Pond

Pick a problem or opportunity where you'd really like to make a difference in the long term. It could be a volunteer effort in your community, something at work, or an idea for a new venture. Then do some brainstorming on three or four other people, at the most, who would make the perfect core group to get it off the ground. If you don't have someone specific in mind, write about the qualities and skills that you need until your vision of the core team is clear. Then try to enlist just one or two of those people. Take your time. Cultivate them. Inspire them. Ask them. And then once you've got partners, work with them to get the other two. You'll be surprised how fast your new venture can take off.

ALL FOR ONE AND
ONE FOR ALL

From a Network to a Living Community

If individuality has no play, society does not advance;
if individuality breaks out of all bounds, society perishes.

—THOMAS HENRY HUXLEY (1825–1895)

The growth, richness, and enduring character of relationships, from the simplest two-person partnership to the largest organizations in the world, depends on having the simultaneous capability to exalt the individual and to recognize that individuals can only find their fullest expression within the group.

Maturing relationships revolve around questions and tensions of identity. Who am I? Who are you? Who are we together? What are we now? What will we become? The core of the relationship rests with how you view yourself, how well you know yourself, and how deeply you believe in your own worth. Everyone in an organization should be dedicated to the individual fulfillment of each member. And yet, to develop any effective team or organization means that individuals need to generate a collective identity. The hard-fought achievement of individual self-esteem and confidence is not the final destination. It only allows us the strength and inner resources to make the final leg of the journey to interdependence, putting ourselves in the service of something greater than ourselves. Institutions are built on the foundation of individuals. But individuals only achieve their full potential within the context of organizations.

The characteristics of any strong network, as it matures into a living community, allow for individual identities to flourish within a clear common set of values and vision: all for one and one for all. Realizing the full potential of a group requires balancing these two vital tensions—a sense of individuality and a sense of collective identity.

McKinsey & Company and the Nature of Corporate Culture

Communities and cultures that encourage the principle of all for one and one for all are especially long-lasting and dynamic. Whether they tend to err on the side of the individual or the group, it is the balance that matters. Few business organizations in the world have a more resilient culture and a more widely recognized success than McKinsey & Co. Its organizational values and philosophy are to a large degree driven by this fundamental principle. And its success depends on it, since the firm relies on a continuous stream of high quality people working well together to feed its "up or out" philosophy and to underpin its premium prices.

Nothing defines a community more clearly than how members enter and the way in which they leave. Looking at exactly how one enters and leaves McKinsey brings this into high relief. First, picture the entrance—joining the community. In the interview process, applicants meet between 7 and 14 different associates, managers, partners and senior partners in a well-tested selection process that has already screened out 95 out of 100 applicants just to get you in that room. By the time you're finished, you will be 1 out of a 1000 and have met a complete cross section of the firm. This thoroughness is no accident. They want every perspective on you and want you to have every possible perspective on them, to ensure a good fit.

During the interview process, the applicant is told that the firm will never hire anyone whom they cannot envision as a future partner in the firm. In that first encounter, there will be a respect shown that at once embraces your potential as an individual and links it to the destiny of the firm as a whole. Once you join, the tables are turned.

After hiring, the emphasis shifts from your potential for the future to what you can do today and how to move towards that future. You are expected to know yourself and work hard to fulfill your individual potential—irrespective of whether that keeps you in the firm or not. Many of the most senior partners, who have been there for decades, will tell you over and over again that they reevaluate and question—every two or three years—whether McKinsey is really still right for them and then make the choice to join all over again.

At the same time, McKinsey is always reevaluating you as well—no matter how good you are—and deciding whether it wants to hire you again. This orientation immediately breeds an intense sense of freedom and purposefulness that subtly binds you to the group. Your job, once you've joined, is to learn the ways of the firm, the values, the processes for doing business, the style and image, the history and culture—to take that on as part of your persona. You will be put through training courses and evaluated after every assignment for what you've learned and what you still have to develop. Your progress will be tracked against a "development path" so that everyone can assess whether you are on track or not in developing the next level of skills and knowledge.

But you will be expected to think independently, to assert your own point of view on defining and solving problems, to take personal responsibility for the quality of your work, to openly dissent when you disagree with a direction the work is taking. You will also be assigned a senior partner who is dedicated to your personal and professional development. In sum, from the beginning of your entry into the firm, there is a dual emphasis on making you part of the whole and encouraging you to enlarge the whole through the expression of your own individuality and professionalism.

Between the time you enter and the time you exit, which I'll cover in a moment, there is the great "in-between"—your career at McKinsey: tackling some of the toughest problems and opportunities in the world; traveling through many time zones to do it; working with dozens of different nationalities and often guiding hundreds of clients.

At each step of the career journey will be three primary fixtures, or images around which life and work pivot. One is the father of the modern firm—Marvin Bower. The other is the guiding principles. The third is fear. All of these encourage the dynamic sense of community that underpins the firm.

First, there is Marvin. Even the newest associates call him by his first name as if they've known him all his life. For decades, he was there when new associates were trained. He interviewed many of them when they exited. He took the pulse of the firm far into his old age, serving as the conscience of the partnership. Everyone in the firm of McKinsey & Co., at some level, feels they have a relationship with Marvin, even though most can't possibly know the first thing about who he really is. No matter where you are in the organization, people talk about him. Comments on his presence vary from expressing deference to a legendary figure to the compassion one feels for a mascot, or even the antipathy felt for a member of an Old Guard. In a global firm, in which people are traveling constantly and relationships are hard to develop, the relationship with Marvin is perhaps the most effective subtle binding force of the institution.

Second, there are the principles. McKinsey has—in every one of its offices around the world—a set of twelve guiding principles that drive behavior and symbolize the values of the institution. Two in particular epitomize the idea of "all for one and one for all." The first principle is "Accept the rights and discharge the responsibilities of self-governance." The second is "Uphold the obligation to dissent." Everyone is expected to take responsibility for the whole firm, and thus all its members. At the same time, consultants count on one another to speak up and bring the full weight of their personality to bear in solving a problem.

Third, there is the fear. A former leader in the firm once sat down with a group of new associates to answer questions about their career development and how performance was measured. He heard many comments about the competitive intensity, the difficulty of finding true mentors even though the system was supposed to provide them. He also heard about fear—fear of not making the grade, fear of not living up to the ideal the firm's leaders represented, even fear of speaking one's mind. In the end, after all the discussion and much wise counsel, he said something surprising and blunt. "Look everyone, this firm has a rich, complex culture. But even though our principles and values are real, it's not only the high-minded things that make this place work. One of its foundations is the fear and competitiveness that throwing a bunch of insecure overachievers together can produce. Understand that, but don't mess with it. Transcend it."

Out of many different "ones" there is the potential for an "all." The question is just how that happens. Creating identity can be done in a positive fashion or in a negative fashion. In the positive form, there is an opportunity, or a common interest and tradition, that binds people together and encourages the formation of identity. In the negative form, there is a threat or a problem that forces a group together that was hitherto not unitary, and creates a new level of identity. The best communities are built on a combination of both inspiration and fear, just the way the United States was built out of thirteen colonies based on fear and the need to construct a unified defense as well as the higher ideals of the "more perfect union." The more your teams, families, and professional communities are imbued with the ethic of all for one and one for all, the stronger and more robust they will be.

In the end, when your career there is over, leaving McKinsey is roughly the same whether you've been there for three years or for thirty. Most importantly, no one ever tells you to leave. It is always, always the individual who makes the decision to go. This is even the case when there is a clear performance problem, with no doubt about the firm's point of view. It is always left up to the individual to assess the situation and realize that things are not working. There is respect for the individual at every point in his or her career.

Then, once you've made the decision to leave, you're given plenty of time—proportional to your years of service—to decide what you want to do, to take advantage of firm career counseling and to use placement advice on actual positions that the McKinsey network makes available. Even then, it is not over. In fact, if you've absorbed the culture, it is never over. Once you've joined McKinsey, even after you've left the intimacy of the active firm and are pursuing a separate career, you become part of the Alumni Network—the extended community.

Being part of the McKinsey Alumni network is special. Its directory is published regularly and religiously kept up-to-date. There is always a measure of deference given to someone who has worked, survived, and thrived at this organization. Naturally, McKinsey Alumni tend to be successful in their separate careers and, as a result, often hire their former employer to help them succeed further. And at this point, the relationship has come full circle. The former firm hire has now hired the firm. And the relationship bears witness to the fact that the one supports the all, just as the community has supported the one all along.

As younger, technically savvy, and highly individualistic new generations enter the workforce and are fought over by corporate America, it becomes more vital than ever to have cultures that exalt the individual while knitting them together to create wholes greater than the sum of the parts. These are the only types of organizations that can attract and retain the best human resources and thereby develop sustainable advantages in the marketplace.

Whether it is a family, team, enterprise, or nation, the ultimate challenge of communities is to weave together a group in which both the individual and the group can find their greatest expression. In such a group, problem solving potential can be fully realized. The sustainable culture of the group becomes a recognizable part of the landscape, a place where individuals will continue to be drawn to maximize their self-expression. The secret is to see that the drive of both individual and group springs from the same source—the desire to create and realize human potential.

Relationships in Action: Assessing Your Own Community

In your own work group or workplace, consider the things that are done to encourage individual rights, self-expression, and fulfillment, completely apart from the company's stated goals and mission. Then look at the things that are done to reinforce mutual obligations, collective identity, shared values, and common purpose. First ask yourself, is there enough being done in both areas? And then ask yourself, have we got the balance right? Is the culture skewed too far in one direction or the other? If you think there's an opportunity to improve, get a group together and give them the job to take your culture to another level.

CHARACTERISTICS OF
A COMMUNICATOR

General characteristics and purpose: Communicators emphasize human relationships. Their goal is building trust and loyalty. Communicators love to be involved and engaged with people, especially people who are willing to share and
participate in the full range of human emotion, passion, and spirituality. They
value sharing, fellowship, teamwork, compassion, and synergy. They focus on
people, organizations, feelings, communication, language, and group identity.
Problems, strategy, and complete solutions are usually less important to them.

Strengths: Communicators are the glue that helps create common identity in
groups. They often infuse their chosen communities with energy and cohesiveness
that could not otherwise be achieved. They improve the quality of human bonds,
and they reduce stress and tension by organizing events and lightening the work

Skill Levels of Communication   TABLE 3.1

Level 1   Able to express ideas and listen to others in a two-way, engaging fashion.

Level 2   Able to internalize knowledge gained and use it to influence formation of
          groups.

Level 3   Able to influence formation of groups and enhance their functioning as
          well.

Level 4   Able to enhance a group's functioning, over an extended period of time,
          and its cohesion.

Level 5   Able to have this affect on many different types of groups, irrespective of
          domain.

Level 6   Able to exercise catalyzing affects across cultures, and groups at a deep
          level, incorporating work and life.

Level 7   Able to articulate ideas of millions, facilitate and catalyze identity on a
          massive scale.

environment. They contribute to clarity and mutual understanding by interpreting and harmonizing messages that flow through an organization. They tend to be fluid at all forms of communication and are often helpful in conflict resolution.

Weaknesses: Communicators have a hard time saying no or disappointing others, because of the deep empathy they feel. As a result, they often have difficulty with intensive decisionmaking. They are also not likely to be strong at breaking new ground in terms of innovation. Communicators tend to work better in groups than on their own and normally do not enjoy creating high profiles for themselves.

Interactions with other types of problem solvers: Communicators work especially well with Playmakers, because their abilities complement one another so well. While the Playmaker develops and communicates a plan and vision, the Communicator builds participation around it, giving it life and sustenance. Communicators also typically are a good match with Performers and Creators, who both recognize the need for lubricant in a smooth-running machine. Both are deadline, quality, and cost driven and depend heavily on not only good working relationships but quality individuals to get the job done. A Communicator who can make connections to good players and help keep conflict to a minimum is a prized asset. Communicators also work well with Discoverers, who often need significant help translating their ideas, theories, and insights into a form where they can be understood and accepted. Communicators can encounter more conflict with Innovators, who frequently change perspectives or points-of-view, which are the basis for communication.

Typical mishandling: Communicators are typically valued more between organizations than within organizations, who often downplay the value of this ability. They are often labeled as superficial, when their ability is one of the fundamental elements needed to achieve scale in any type of problem solving.

Guidance for Building Relationships

Guiding Principles: Rules and Laws That Bear on Relationships

- In communication, both sides are always accountable.
- Trust is much easier to destroy than to build.
- Separate the people from the problem, or the problem will be the people.
- Focus on influence, not control.
- Be constructive, and give away credit.
- To thine own self be true—your own sparks of passion and motivation ignite relationships.
- Institutions are the way individuals reach their full potential.
- Individuals are always the foundation of an institution.
- The founder's rule: The quality of the founders in a core determines the total potential size and quality of a network.
- The protocol rule: The quality of the network's communication protocol determines sustainability.

Diagnostics: How Well Are You Building Working Relationships?

- Do you have the relationships you need to build the capability and solve the problem or opportunity? Why or why not? Who are your fellow travelers in life? How will solving your chosen problems add value to your relationships?
- Do you have the right communications channels open when you need them? Do you regularly use your most important communications channels? How well are you listening to the people who are important to you? How well understood do you feel by them? How well do they feel understood by you?
- What degree of give-and-take have you achieved with your closest relationships? Are you really reaching out to help as well as opening up to be helped? Is it just as easy for you to surrender as to dominate? What about your partner or colleague? How do you deal with conflict, as an opportunity to push the relationship to a new level, or as a threat?
- Are there people in your life who you are committed to coaching and developing? How are they doing, where are they going, and how are you helping? How well are you coaching and developing yourself?
- How high is the quality of your founders' group? Does it need any additional elements? Are you working closely and well together? Are you building trust? How strong is your network? Is it propagating well or stagnating? Is the scale sustainable? What network management practices are you putting in place to ensure it? Do you encourage culture, behavior, and incentives that both reinforce individualism and reward collective effort?

Syndromes: Diseases That Affect Your Ability to Build Relationships

- "Insecurity"—Lack of self-confidence and boundaries that inhibits formation of lasting relationships
- "Narcissism"—Overwhelming focus on what you get out of relationships as opposed to mutuality; superficial interaction without taking any risks
- "Benign neglect"—Focus on problem solving to such an extreme that relationships are left to wither
- "You messages"—Blaming someone else habitually for problems in the relationship
- "Booby traps"—Hidden resentment that comes out in passive/aggressive behavior
- "Use or be used"—Manipulation, submission, or lack of trust that results in heavy use of code words, spin, and indirect communication
- "Falling short of scale"—Collapse and burnout due to low energy, poor management, inadequate values, proprietary focus, or fragmented power
- "Holding back"—Not giving people enough autonomy to contribute in their own way

Going Further

Selected resources for further study of building relationships. (See also sources and notes for Part 3 on page 269.)

Books

Ashkenas, Ron. *The Boundaryless Organization.* San Francisco: Jossey-Bass, 1995.

Auerbach, Red. *On and off the Court.* New York: MacMillan, 1985.

Axline, Virginia. *Dibs: In Search of Self.* New York: Ballantine Books, 1964.

Blais, Madeleine. *In These Girls, Hope Is a Muscle.* New York: Atlantic Monthly Press, 1995.

Blanchard, Ken. *The One-Minute Manager.* New York: Berkley Books, 1981.

Carnegie, Dale. *How to Win Friends and Influence People.* New York: Pocket Books, 1994.

Case, James P. *Finite and Infinite Games.* New York: Ballantine Books, 1986.

Chomsky, Noam. *Reflections on Language.* New York: Pantheon Books, 1975.

Coles, Robert. *The Call of Service.* Boston: Houghton-Mifflin, 1993.

Elgin, Suzette. *Success with the Gentle Verbal Art of Self-Defense.* New York: Prentice Hall, 1989.

Fisher, Roger, and Scott Brown of the Harvard Negotiation Project. *Getting Together: Building Relationships As We Negotiate.* New York: Penguin Books, 1988.

Goleman, Daniel. *Emotional Intelligence.* New York: Bantam Books, 1995.

Gray, John. *Men are from Mars, Women are from Venus.* New York, HarperCollins, 1992.

Hagel, John, and Arthur Armstrong. *Net Gain.* Boston: HBS Press, 1997.

Handy, Charles. *The Age of Unreason.* Boston: HBS Press, 1989.

Hasling, John. *The Message, The Speaker, The Audience.* New York: McGraw-Hill, 1988.

Hayakawa, S. I. *Language, Thought and Action.* New York: Harcourt Brace Jovanovich, 1990.

Minsky, Marvin. *The Society of Mind.* New York: Simon & Schuster, 1986.

Peck, M. Scott. *The Road Less Travelled.* New York: Simon & Schuster, 1978.

Rheingold, Howard. *The Virtual Community.* Boston: Addison Wesley, 1993.

Rousseau, Jean Jacques. *The Social Contract.* New York: Penguin Classics, 1968.

Shore, William. *Revolution of the Heart* and *The Cathedral Within.* New York, Riverhead Books, 1995.

Weisbord, Marvin. *Productive Workplaces.* San Francisco: Jossey-Bass, 1987.

Yalom, Irwin. *Love's Executioner.* New York: Basic Books, 1989.

Websites

Emotional and social intelligence: trochim.human.cornell.edu

Communication skills: www.coopcomm.org

Organizational communication: www.openbookmanagement.com

Team communication: www.workteams.unt.edu

Personal development and team building: www.outwardboundpro.org

Team building: www.oxfordchallenge.com

Interpersonal skills: www.interpersonal-skills.com

Negotiation: www.pon.harvard.edu

360 Degree feedback: www.360-degreefeedback.com

Part Four

⧫MANAGE THE JOURNEYS⧫

The Playmaker

Choose Destinations and Set Directions

The superior leader gets things done with very little motion. He imparts instruction not through many words but through a few deeds. He keeps informed about everything but interferes hardly at all. He is a catalyst, and though things would not get done as well if he weren't there, when they succeed he takes no credit. And because he takes no credit, credit never leaves him.

–LAO-TZU (C. 604–531 B.C.)

Every problem or opportunity is a potential journey. There are usually many destinations to pursue, with multiple paths to choose. A problem solver needs to get oriented to the choices, prioritize and select what to work on, plan and initiate action on the most urgent opportunities, and guide a team through the stages of resolution. This is the realm of the Playmaker. Playmakers take the Innovator's ideas, the Discoverer's insights, and the Communicator's community and concentrate them on a specific journey for a compelling reason, then show them both where to go and how to get there. Playmakers excel at the essentials of initiating and guiding change in constantly shifting terrain. They juggle multiple projects, identify destinations, set directions, and chart courses to the endgame. Their skills range from defining missions, crafting strategy, and setting priorities to portfolio management, measuring success, and leading effectively.

When journeys are managed poorly, priorities will be confused, success or failure will be uncertain, solutions will be rashly chosen, and routes recklessly plotted. When they are managed well, you take on problems you're capable of solving and those that stretch your abilities without pushing past the breaking point. Your priorities are clear. Scope is managed. Course corrections are regular and accurate. And you'll know when you've been successful and can move on to the next problem.

The United States of America's Journey to the Moon, July 16–20, 1969

It was 3:17 P.M. Houston time, on that day in 1969, and most of us remember exactly where we were when the first manned landing on the Moon occurred. We all knew our silvery friend well, even took it for granted. We'd gazed at it and fallen in love by it and traveled by it. But few thought we could ever *go* there. And then Kennedy said it, he said we *would* go there, within a decade. We would go to the Moon. Born of the kind of unusual convergence of fear, inspiration, technological possibility, and the opportunity for tangible gain that often gives rise to great adventures, the journey to the Moon in 1969 changed our view of ourselves, our world, and our place in the cosmos forever.

It qualifies as the supreme adventure of mankind to date—the first time we left our home, went to another place in the universe, and returned. At the time of JFK's announcement, there was no Saturn V rocket, no lunar module, no Apollo program. Only Sputnik and a fast-growing Russian space program with limitless confidence and boastfulness to match. It's hard to imagine what it must have been like back then to conceive of the goal, much less announce it to the world. But that is what great Playmakers in history have done. At the right time and in the right way, they have chosen destinations that were just entering the realm of possibility and made us believe that we could get there.

When he challenged America to go to the Moon, Kennedy led in a way that made people feel as though they could lead as well as follow. He chose the right problem to solve at the right time. An aggressive move into space would not only marshal national energy and manage fear in the age of ICBMs, it would develop technology needed for military defense and for industry as well. He focused on an inspiring place to go and articulated how we might get there in a believable way. Choosing the Moon meant choosing an extraordinary challenge that was far enough out of reach to be a major accomplishment, but not totally impossible given the technological evolution at the time. In fact, he made sure it was feasible before he would even consider the idea. This was no leap of faith. He defined success clearly and unambiguously, to put a man on the Moon and bring him home safely, before the decade was out. And he had the right people put a plan together that anticipated the scale and degree of difficulty of the problems that needed to be solved.

Conceiving and managing journeys is the fourth essential skill of problem solving. Every adventure needs someone to lead it and make it happen. Leadership is at the heart of managing journeys. Playmakers see the opportunity to make a dramatic and inspiring journey possible in a way that no one has before. In doing so, they motivate us to go in that direction, perhaps for many years, striving to achieve it.

Playmakers today are shooting for Mars, rather than the Moon. They range from social activists and business leaders who are working to eliminate hunger to scientists who are working to eliminate disease. They include financiers who help create entirely new industries to defenders of our environment who envision new ways to achieve economic well-being while protecting the planet.

The Playmaker's Central Idea: The Best Leadership Comes from Managing Problems As Journeys

Moving to a higher level of performance as a Playmaker means learning to think about problems in new ways. You can't think of them as static, waiting to be analyzed and dissected. Every problem is a journey. And every journey has phases, from the moment the idea is conceived and the destination is chosen, to the initiation of the voyage and actually making the passage itself. (See Figure 4.1.)

Phases of a Problem Solving Journey FIG. 4.1

	Orientation	Selection	Initiation	Momentum	Breakthrough	Evaluation
Question	*What are the problems and where are they occurring?*	*Which problems will you solve or prevent?*	*What are your goals, plans and how to engage?*	*How to make it happen?*	*How to "break the back" and make it stick?*	*How to learn and improve?*
Activities	Recognition Identification Location Confirmation Generation	Definition Preparation Prioritization Prevention	Planning Design Sourcing Budgeting	Prototyping Piloting Adaptation	Concentration Consolidation Closure	Assessment Reflection Implications
Objective	Clarity Visibility	Specificity Proactivity	Maximize rewards, minimize cost and risk	Movement Transform	Persistence Control	Learning

Any problem or opportunity in any profession, from the smallest to the largest, the simplest to the most complex, the shortest to the longest, goes through the same phases over time. These phases start with orientation in a new environment, when problems and opportunities first present themselves, and finish off with closure and evaluation of what has been accomplished, what has been learned, and what it means. Once you understand these essential phases, you can position yourself in any problem, no matter how big it is, and gain an ability to navigate through it—knowing where you are at each step of the journey.

Playmakers in Action: Kleiner, Perkins Venture Capital, and the Technology Industry

If the Playmaker's central idea is the notion of problem solving journeys, then how does that apply in practice? How do they manage the right journeys and continuously choose the right destinations and set the best directions? The following story of Kleiner, Perkins Venture Capital and its success in the technology industry shows Playmakers in action. With their contribution, a problem solver can build on an Innovator's ideas, a Discoverer's knowledge, and a Communicator's relationships to create an inspired, intelligent, living community with a sense of vision, direction, and priorities.

Although lives are not usually at risk, there are few more challenging problems than starting and growing a new business. Many start the journey, with hopes high, but most eventually succumb to failure, whether it is because of an unwanted product, lack of capital, inability to recruit talent, poor focus, or any number of other flaws.

"Across the nation," John Doerr, a partner at Kleiner, Perkins, Caulfield & Byers (KPCB) says, "four of five new businesses fail. But when backed by professional venture capitalists within 20 miles of this office, four of five new ventures succeed. Think of Silicon Valley as an effective system for getting people, projects, and capital together." The people who drive that system, whether they are venture capitalists like Doerr or CEOs, are Playmakers.

KPCB is one of the best Playmakers in town. They helped found such cornerstones of the technology industry as Genentech, Sun, Compaq, and Lotus and in the process built 10 of the Fortune 500. Their returns are regularly ranked in the top 5 percent earned by venture capital (VC) firms across the country.

Fortune Magazine estimated not long ago that the twelve partners at Kleiner, Perkins, Caulfield & Byers, the venture capital firm in Silicon Valley, had divided $210 million in pure profit from one year of high-risk investing. Two questions immediately present themselves: How do you get a job like that, and why do the people who have them keep working year after year?

The answers to both questions are basically the same. At the hottest money shop with the biggest hype in the hottest industry in the world, what matters is not just making money. KPCB is also about forming teams, building companies, creating new leaders, and undertaking great adventures.

KPCB partners don't just read business plans, give money away, and then relax. They aren't just financial wizards. They have all built, or helped to build, successful businesses. They've learned how to define, measure, and deal with success and failure before joining a company that thrives by helping others succeed.

Although estimates vary, the partners at KPCB read and receive about 2000 plans per year, choose 300 for closer study, meet with 100 teams, and invest in about 25, for a shakeout rate of 99 percent. Every business plan they read is a proposal for a new problem solving journey. Their challenge is to decide which opportunities will be most profitable, who should make the trip, and how much help they will need. KPCB must act to rescue endangered but still promising voyagers when they get lost, and say goodbye when it comes time to part ways.

To choose the right opportunities at the right time, KPCB looks at more than companies. For them, the unit of analysis is a new industry or a technology that could influence an entire industry. The key is to target an emerging industry sooner than anyone else. Once they have defined the right overall problem, then choosing companies is not only easier, it is done from a perspective that sets them apart from their competitors. As Doerr puts it, "There are 400 venture firms. How can any one firm develop significant market share? Only by focusing on initiatives, which means several KPCB partners working together to help build companies and opportunities in specific areas, such as wireless communications, interactive media and Internet/online services." He continues, "What we do is look for markets that are going to change at least by an order of magnitude, technologies that can make it possible, and great teams—because strategies are easy, it's execution that's everything."

The partners who decide which problems are the right ones to solve base their decisions on a long personal history of previous success and failure. Vinod Khosla, for example, cofounded Sun Microsystems before joining KPCB. The rest of the KPCB team boasts similar backgrounds. Most famous of all is Doerr. In twenty years as a financier he has backed such start-ups as Sun and Compaq, Lotus and Intuit, Netscape and Amazon.com.

How do these Playmakers manage the journeys of their companies so well? It starts with clear and rigorous definitions of what problems they are trying to solve and for what customers, what value a business is intending to deliver, and whether the timing is right or not. They've developed elaborate formulas for evaluating a proposal's worthiness. Up front, there is a strong focus on the business problem, the markets, and the technology, and especially the team that will make it happen. According to Doerr, "We think hardest about the team. . . . In the world today, there's plenty of technology, plenty of entrepreneurs, plenty of money. What's in short supply is great teams."

As far as KPCB is concerned, choosing direction and strategy is straightforward, it's refining the strategy through execution, to lower risk, that is the toughest part, which is why they religiously adhere to Kleiner's first law, get risk out of the way early. As Doerr explains, "There's technical risk: Can we split the atom? There's market risk: will the dogs eat the dog food? There's people risk: Will the people who founded the company stick around? And there's financing risk: Can we get the money?" As their companies' management teams confront these issues, a KPCB partner is usually right there with them as a strong board member, not only figuring out course corrections but how to make them happen. They challenge, push, facilitate contacts, and catalyze mergers or other relationships. By managing risk so aggressively, they work to increase the probability of success.

KPCB works with a company to get it up and running and to help it become self-sustaining. But that goal is understood in the context of a longer-term strategy of building a portfolio of mutually beneficial companies. It guides the new company to maturity and an initial public offering (IPO), and then it seeks to integrate it into mutually beneficial relationships with other KPCB-funded ventures. Generations of KPCB successes are then woven into still larger teams on shared journeys.

Take Excite, for example. When KPCB decided to back the new company, they placed proven KPCB stars like America Online's Steve Case and Intuit's Bill Campbell on the new company's board of directors. In another example, Epiphany's top man, Roger Siboni, has been such a hit inside KPCB he has been added to the boards of Active Software, Pivotal Software, and Macromedia. KPCB works with whole companies, as well as people. Doerr and his partners weave KPCB-backed firms into networks and teams. Excite was partnered with Amazon.com and Sportsline USA, for example, before being blended with @home to create Excite@home.

But no matter how hard the people at KPCB work, on the surface they appear to fail more often than they succeed. KPCB always has a short-term goal of seeing return on investment in three to four years. But most of the companies in the portfolio fail to make it big.

"I often say that training a venture capitalist is like crashing a few F-16s," Doerr says. "It costs about thirty million, straight down the drain." GO computing was one of Doerr's most spectacular failures. But there was another recently. Investors put in $15 million in four rounds. Then it was just written off. The losses, however, have been more than offset, year after year. Conservative estimates suggest that KPCB sinks hundreds of millions per year into start-ups. Some fail. Many succeed modestly. A few succeed stupendously. The huge university endowments and other institutions that make up the core of KPCB's investors get an annual return of at least 40 percent after the partners have taken nearly one-third of the profits off the top.

KPCB's approach works for two reasons. One, they have defined success in terms of the portfolio as a whole, not in terms of the individual ventures. Success is reached by multiple routes, through multiple vessels. Just as in the old days of round-the-globe exploration and trading, a single big score covers a half-dozen or a dozen ships lost at sea. Second, even if a company doesn't make it big, if KPCB at least gets it to IPO, their preferential position means they can usually make a 300–400 percent return, just because their cheap stock gets a bump from the public offering. So the recipe for success is actually a group of such "moderate" return companies and just a few that bring in twenty to one hundred times KPCB's investment or more. At one point last year, of the 79 companies KPCB took public between 1990 and 1998, 25 percent were trading above the NASDAQ index, 5 percent just below it, and 70 percent were trading below the first-day closing price of their IPO.

Keeping its eye on success, KPCB watches its portfolio closely. The partners meet one day per week to review current investments. Every quarter, a longer session looks at their most active 100 investments. Companies are rated on seven parameters, including financial status and officer performance. Then the partners agree on how to update their three goals on how to help the company going forward.

But in spite of all the focus on numbers and money, there's another angle on success. The partners consistently claim it's about more than money, it's about creating opportunities, solving problems, and building companies and industries—the act of creation and making change is as important as the money. Doerr explains, "The best entrepreneurs don't focus on success. They focus on building a company that can be a leader in the global economy. They know success will follow. If you focus on success, you won't get there. If you focus on contribution and customer value, then you can win."

To achieve their high levels of success, KPCB must do more than minimize risk early with careful analysis of each venture, or spread risk widely with their long-term, portfolio-based definition of success. They also plan aggressively and make the best out of failures when they occur.

The combination of their extensive board memberships, personal networking, planning sessions every six months, and multiple conferences has the effect of a private intelligence agency with ideas about what is going to happen in the future. Extensive effort is put into planning and figuring out what industry might be the next winner. But they are also prepared to be surprised, as when Bill Joy told Doerr that someday a twenty-year-old software programmer would change his business. They thought it would be computer games, but it turned out to be Marc Andreesen and the browser. As one of Doerr's colleagues, Vinod Khosla, puts it "We are on the board of everything from Sun to AOL to Excite. As a group we have developed a sense of how to forecast the future before the market researchers can."

The company must make opportunities out of unexpected losses, planning for the chance events they know will occur in spite of all their efforts. When they wrote off one $15 million company, they still had forty employees to take care of. Rather than treating the people as losses, though, KPCB viewed them as valuable assets to be used elsewhere in the portfolio. "Other companies in our portfolio have already offered jobs to over half the team. The investors are circulating resumes to help all of the employees get great jobs. As long as you work hard with the team and don't lie, the venture industry doesn't penalize failure."

Perhaps the most interesting perceived difference between KPCB and many other more passive investment firms is the leadership they sometimes offer. The firm doesn't like to make money the old-fashioned way—by investing and collecting the dividend checks. The partners often roll up their sleeves—targeting new industries, teaching, cajoling, pushing, dumping, and recruiting the managers who can make a success of a high-tech company.

As Khosla puts it, "60–70 percent of our time is spent with our existing companies, another 20 percent is spent getting educated." The rest goes to looking at new businesses. So of their total time, three-quarters is spent in helping to make the company a success and one-quarter is spent in determining what problems to solve. "Once we make a judgment on how a new technology is going to develop, we work the space to influence it." And although collaboration is the focus, they're willing to take the tough leadership positions if necessary. Khosla says, "My job as a board member is to ask the tough questions, force management to anticipate tough issues and . . . be a real pain in the butt." In contrast, they also have developed a reputation for leading from behind, for being constantly available, with pagers and cell phones, all hours of the day or night, to struggling entrepreneurs trying to solve a problem or grasp an opportunity.

Above all, KPCB has made a name for themselves with their focus on choosing leaders. That recruitment may be the most important leadership KPCB provides. "We're always looking for great leaders." As he puts it, "Great leaders are great communicators. They have incredible integrity. They're usually the first to recognize problems. They're ruthlessly, absolutely intellectually honest. They are great recruiters: They're always building their network of talented people. And they're great sales executives: They're always selling the value proposition of the enterprise." In the same way, Doerr and his colleagues are always selling the value proposition of KPCB: twenty-four years, roughly a billion dollars to more than 300 companies, $500 billion in market cap, more than 250,000 jobs created. Based on their general reputation and the numbers, they are indeed doing well.

In summary, Kleiner Perkins exemplifies the idea of a Playmaker. Playmakers manage journeys by picking the problems that are most worth the time, that have the most synergy with one another, then define success for each one and map a route to get there that has a high likelihood of succeeding. They specify destinations. They make choices about direction—which route to take and how to break the trip into manageable legs. They exercise leadership, at every stage, to direct a team and align them with an overall purpose. They have to adjust goals when it becomes apparent that original plans have failed to anticipate critical circumstances. A combination of clarity, flexibility, and precision in leadership ensures a minimum of confusion about where one is going and exactly why or how to get there.

The rest of this part covers in more depth and detail how the best Playmakers go about managing journeys and solving problems. You can either skip to the next part, "Create the Solutions" on page 159, or proceed. Each chapter in turn describes how Playmakers start by choosing the right problems and eventually progress to direction-setting and leadership.

- "Solve the Right Problems at the Right Time: From Disorientation to Selection" examines how Playmakers select the right problems to work on. An emergency room physician at one of the nation's leading hospitals, Dr. David Nicolaou of Johns Hopkins in Baltimore, shows how their techniques for patient triage help keep priorities straight.
- "Choose Where to Go and How to Get There: From Selection to Direction" explains how to determine your ultimate destination and develop a strategy for making it there, a strategy that, in turn, will help define the kinds of solutions you'll need. The story of one of the world's leading design firms, IDEO, illustrates this stage, focusing on how it helped Amtrak choose a vision and a strategy for the next generation of high-speed rail transportation in the United States.
- "Define Success: From Direction to Defining Success" pinpoints how a Playmaker defines and deals with success or failure. In this case, the story of Nelson Mandela and the freedom movement in South Africa illustrates the power of a clear and high-minded definition of success.
- "Plan for Chance: From Defining Success to Planning" develops the idea of how to forecast and create a real plan for how to achieve your goals. Using one of the world's leading planning systems at Sabre, Inc. and American Airlines as an example, this chapter shows how the combination of human judgment and computing technology keeps American one step ahead.
- "Lead the Way: From Planning to Leadership" shows how Playmakers get out in front at the beginning of a problem solving effort and then move to leading from behind. Colin Powell and his new movement of volunteers across America illustrates a tested leader in action attempting to solve the problem of how to improve the future of a nation's children.

SOLVE THE RIGHT PROBLEMS
AT THE RIGHT TIME
From Disorientation to Selection

*The older I get, the more wisdom I find in the ancient rule of
taking first things first–a process which often reduces the
most complex human problems to manageable proportions"*

–DWIGHT EISENHOWER (1890–1969)

Life and work usually present us with multiple problems and opportunities constrained by limited time, resources, and attention. Many roads beckon, and a Playmaker must set priorities about which journeys to take, which problems to solve.

Consequently, managing journeys well has to progress from orienting oneself in a territory to selecting which journeys are the most important and why. This way, you can solve the right problems at the right time. Rapidly changing terrain and evolving competition make choosing the right opportunities and setting priorities more challenging than ever. At the same time, the opportunity cost of focusing on the wrong areas—in lost time and resources—is more painful.

The quality of the sorting and prioritization process, called triage, has a strong influence on problem solving effectiveness. Triage strategies that have their origin in the methods used by battlefield medics to prioritize treatment of soldiers can be applied anywhere today in successful businesses, from managing stock portfolios to routing incoming phone traffic from customer service lines. If there's one place where, every single day, professionals make some of the toughest decisions about which problems to solve first, it's the emergency room at Johns Hopkins in Baltimore.

Dr. David Nicolaou and Triage in Johns Hopkins Emergency Room

It's evening rush hour, both on the streets of Baltimore and in the emergency room (ER) at Johns Hopkins Hospital. Hopkins is the top hospital in the nation, according to *U.S. News and World Report*, coveted ranking of excellence within the industry. Wealthy heart patients have been known to charter 737s to be treated by Hopkins' cardiologists.

It's been busy at the ER all afternoon. Mondays are like that. Folks tend to let ailments slide over the weekend. Dozens of sick people cram the waiting room, looking miserable. They are stuck until some of Hopkins' forty emergency room beds open up. The ER itself is a noisy place. A handful of psychiatric patients lie on gurneys along the walls; one of them howls every few minutes. You might hear a woman softly chanting a mournful prayer for a family member; a man retching loudly into a trash can. Medical monitors chirp their warnings.

Suddenly, a frantic paramedic's voice sounds over the dispatch box at the desk. "Double trauma on the way. Female in her thirties . . . full arrest . . . blunt trauma . . . ETA three to five minutes!" The second victim is not as serious. A semitrailer truck has plowed into the passenger side of a taxicab.

Dr. David Nicolaou, the attending emergency physician on this shift, moves into high gear.

The two trauma patients are expected in less than five minutes. Taking the handset, Nicolaou asks the paramedics, "Do you have an airway?" his voice calm but urgent. The doctors working under him are in motion. They stride quickly down the hall to the trauma room, gathering plastic yellow gowns and masks as they go. Nicolaou goes to a closet for an ultrasound machine, which can help determine if a patient has internal injuries.

Then the paramedics rush in with the gurney. Doctors and nurses surround the motionless victim. "How long?" a doctor asks, meaning how long has she been without a pulse. Fifteen minutes, a paramedic answers grimly, or since the moment paramedics arrived at the carnage. When there's instantaneous cardiac arrest from blunt trauma, there is little hope. It's usually from an irreparable injury, like aortic disruption or brain stem laceration.

Her jeans are cut away. The soles of her feet are dirty, as though she's been playing barefoot outside. The young doctors begin CPR, lines are hooked up, and nurses call out numbers. There is no response from the body on the table. Nicolaou watches for a few moments and gives direction. Then, abruptly, he makes the ultimate triage decision. He exits into the adjoining trauma room to be ready for the second victim.

When you first become aware of a problem or opportunity, there's a premium attached to making a quick, thorough assessment. "The trick," says Dr. Nicolaou, "is not so much getting the questions answered quickly and the rush that comes from that, as defining the questions correctly. You can spend a lot of time chasing after the answers to questions that turn out to be unhelpful in deciding what to do with the patient. Determining exactly what information you need and what order you need it to make decisions about priorities is probably the epitome of what this specialty is." Recognizing problem types becomes the basis for triage decisions.

A native of Kalamazoo, Michigan, Nicolaou found his way to medicine by accident. He was a political science major in college with his sights on law school. His mother, a nurse and hospital administrator, got him a summer job transporting patients at a local hospital. "I walked into the emergency department and said, 'Wow, this is great.' You've got very little time to figure things out," recalls Nicolaou. "Even the data that you're going to base your decisions on has always got to be suspect. Most of the decisions that you make matter a lot to somebody. That's what fascinated me—the problem solving aspect of it."

The set of problems any Playmaker chooses to focus on can be thought of as a portfolio. (See Figure 4.2. The circles represent individual problems, with the size varying according to the amount of resources required for resolution.) When Nicolaou starts his shift, he surveys his portfolio of patients in front of a wipable

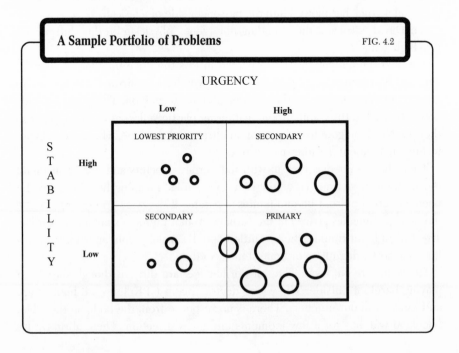

A Sample Portfolio of Problems   FIG. 4.2

URGENCY

Low   High

STABILITY

High

LOWEST PRIORITY   SECONDARY

SECONDARY   PRIMARY

Low

black board. Patient names, the bed they occupy, what's wrong, and whether they're waiting for admission to the hospital are marked in hospital code. Doctors who've been working the previous shift flesh out each patient's story for Nicolaou.

There's a woman with an ectopic pregnancy awaiting transfer to the operating room. An elderly gentleman who gets dizzy when he stands up. His rectal exam has revealed blood, and the doctor attending him fears it's colon cancer. A man with pleural effusion—fluid in his chest, but outside the lung. An asthmatic woman short of breath. A woman with five days of abdominal pain and a high fever.

Prioritizing problems (in this case, patients) is very different from sorting out tasks. You can be doing the right priority tasks on the wrong problem. Or you can be doing the right problem but pursuing the wrong tasks. Problems always come first. Unfortunately, many professionals take the opposite approach, letting their daily calendar and micro time management get in the way of much higher level decisions about what's really important.

By concentrating on tasks rather than issues or opportunities, people waste large amounts of time and resources. A hospital is a perfect place to illustrate this issue, because if a doctor or nurse is doing the right task on the wrong patient, the consequences are stark and immediate.

The triage nurses on the front lines make the initial priority decisions. They give the walk-ins a preliminary examination, draw blood, check temperature and blood pressure, and take an oral report. They assess vital signs—heart rate, blood oxygen level, pupil dilation, blood pressure, temperature, breathing, and circulation, among others—and determine which are the right problems to solve at the right time. Which cases are most urgent? Which are most serious? Which will probably get better on their own? Which need more detailed diagnostic treatment to gather the information necessary to make a confident assessment—to define the problem clearly and accurately?

The nurses have a triage guidebook and make immediate choices. The first dimensions are urgency, importance, and stability. Patients are put into categories. Level One means the patient needs to be seen within five minutes; Level Two means within an hour; on a busy day, the patients placed in Levels Three and Four are in for a long wait. An urban ER can only do so much. At the end of a busy day, there is sometimes a two-inch stack of the sick who've grown tired of waiting and have just walked out.

The prioritization by both nurses and physicians is informed by guidelines but is largely driven by "experienced gut instinct." Much of it depends on highly skilled guesswork, based on a deep understanding of statistical risks and past experience, rather than being governed simply by rigid rules. As Nicolaou puts it, "The guidelines for determining a patient's priority are fairly loose but based on protocol and specified, algorithmic, highly deterministic branch points." But there's only so much information that can be contained in guidelines. It is the

---

Universal Triage Criteria   FIG. 4.3

Principle	Implications
Urgency and timing	The amount of time available before a critical change in condition could occur.
Importance, significance	The overall threat or benefit of the problem situation.
Cost, risk, return	The economics of the situation—cost to fix, potential benefit if repaired, opportunity cost.
Stability	How predictable and stable is the problem? Does it need constant observation?
Ownership	Who's responsible? Can you pass it off to another responsible professional?

---

combination of guidelines, a willingness to take in the full pattern of a patient's condition, and experienced pattern recognition that makes for the best triage decisions.

If you can define problems well and prioritize your portfolio, you've already won most of the game of solving the right problems at the right time. (See Figure 4.3.) But if the portfolio is volatile, it needs to be rechecked again and again, to allow you to reprioritize if necessary.

Nicolaou always surfs the chart rack occasionally, to make sure patients with urgent problems have been triaged correctly. He finds a Level Two—a pregnant woman who's bleeding, with a blood pressure of 90 and a pulse of 106—that he bumps to the top of the pile. There's a man back in acute care, at the highest level of priority, who needs to be intubated. Nicolaou goes to the waiting room and gathers the family, bringing them back to the ER to gently deliver the bad news. The man is very sick. He has a rare bacterial infection from eating under-cooked seafood. A relative begins chanting a prayer. The patient makes it through the night, but dies three days later. Good prioritization increases a patient's chances and uses scarce resources most effectively, but unfortunately, it still falls far short of guaranteeing a positive outcome.

Playmaking in Action: Prioritizing Your Portfolio

Make a list of the top ten problems or opportunities you are facing at the office at this point in your career. Step back a little and take a longer-term perspective. List the ten things you're working on this year. Once you've got a list of the items in your portfolio, decide how you'd like to rank them. Which of the triage criteria are most important to you? Once you've done that, either rank the list or create a matrix that helps you view your portfolio according to the criteria you've selected. Highlight the problems and opportunities that really stand out as the ones you should be spending time with and then look at your calendar for a week. Are you really spending time with the priorities in your portfolio?

CHOOSE WHERE TO GO AND HOW TO GET THERE

From Selection to Direction

To get to any destination worth reaching, you better have a road map. You better know where you're going and how you're going to get there.

—BILL PARCELLS

Once a Playmaker selects a problem to invest time and energy in, the problem solving journey depends on a clear conception of where to go and how to get there—destination and direction. Business professionals have the pressure of competition and customer expectations, which stimulate the setting of "stretch" goals. On the other hand, nothing can deflate a business or project faster than setting high expectations and failing to deliver, or setting out aggressively in one direction and then having to change course too frequently and too erratically as you try to build momentum. One of the prime reasons that projects tend to go off course is that the sometimes baffling complexity of technology solutions interferes with a clear view of the goals and the strategy for getting there. All too often, the most sophisticated technologists are hindered in their playmaking ability by the very technology they've created.

Developing creative alternative goals and strategies is one of the least understood aspects of direction-setting. When Amtrak decided to build a next-generation high-speed rail system in the United States to parallel the successful ones developed in Japan and France, they hired IDEO—the world's leading design firm. Their goal was to formulate a direction and strategy for moving into a new era for train travel in America.

IDEO and Designing Business Strategy for AMTRAK

Two businessmen were standing on the platform at the Philadelphia train station discussing how they traveled the busy Northeast corridor. "Oh, I never take Amtrak," said one of the men. "I just ride the Metroliner." When Aura Oslapas overheard the remark—erroneous, since the Metroliner is part of Amtrak—it summed up a big chunk of her mission: Help Amtrak set a direction as it looked ahead to making its new high-speed rail service a competitive force against the airlines. "That tells you a lot about people's perception of Amtrak," Oslapas said of the businessmen's misguided statement. "That's because Metroliner is somewhat successful, it must not be Amtrak, right?"

Oslapas is a designer with IDEO, the highly successful design company based in Palo Alto, California, founded by David Kelley, a Stanford University professor. In 1991, Kelley merged his engineering background with that of friends who were industrial designers to start IDEO, the Greek word for idea.

Amtrak went to IDEO looking for a strategy to convince travelers that riding the new high-speed trains, especially from Boston to New York, is preferable to taking an airline shuttle. The problem was, how to position a company and product with such a poor reputation to be a leading competitor in the cutthroat metropolitan shuttle business.

Playmakers spend a good deal of time choosing, defining, and communicating their endgames—where they want to go, but also why and for whom. Change takes energy and effort. People who are going to come along for the ride have to know why they should sign up. Setting meaningful objectives requires having real evidence of a problem, as well as of the potential benefits of a solution. It usually requires having a reason to leave as well as a reason to arrive.

Many different terms are used to refer to a destination: vision, objective, goal, endgame, target, future state. They vary primarily by their degree of specificity. Vision is a general description, usually unmeasurable, of what one wants to achieve in the long term. Future state, endgame, objective, goal, and target are each progressively more specific and narrow and more likely to be in the short term rather than the long term. One might picture them as a ladder, a hierarchy with vision at the top. (See Figure 4.4.) Milestone at the bottom is the narrowest, most specific rung and nearest to you in time.

IDEO began at the very top of the ladder, by searching for the right vision for Amtrak. Oslapas and about twenty others from IDEO spent four months on a service strategy, to frame the problem and set a direction before they got to redesigning the product. As they gathered evidence, they found Amtrak had a set-

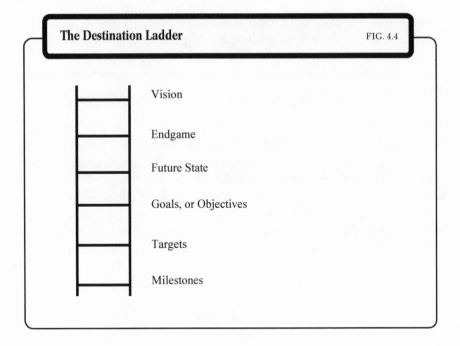

The Destination Ladder   FIG. 4.4

Vision

Endgame

Future State

Goals, or Objectives

Targets

Milestones

tled, technology-centric, way of viewing the direction of their business. The train and its routing was the centerpiece. From Amtrak's perspective the issue was how to become ever better at getting the passengers on and off the train. The product was the focus, not the service, not the problem. The IDEO team felt that overcoming this outdated vision was the challenge.

IDEO came up with a new direction—a vision of the journey based on the passenger's experience, rather than on managing the technology. "Since we're going out to gather evidence on passenger journeys, why don't we use that as a tool to break down the problem for the client?" she explained. "That's how we came up with the idea of the customer journey. It got the message to Amtrak executives that service, or service strategy, really means from the moment you learn about the service all the way through to the moment at which somebody leaves a station and arrives at their destination." In other words, from the time a customer starts to solve a problem, until it is resolved successfully.

IDEO broke down the customer journey into ten steps. "It was a really big 'Aha!' for Amtrak to recognize that all this energy had been spent on the train, and what happens on the train. They were able to finally see that you're not riding the train until step number eight of ten." Of course, IDEO didn't want passengers thinking about ten steps. So the "seamless customer journey" became the vision at the top of the destination ladder. At the next rung was displacing competition in the metropolitan markets—the endgame. The smoothly integrated ten-step operation was the future state that would realize the endgame and make progress toward the vision. As a result of all this, Amtrak's corporate destination would change from managing the logistics of entering and leaving a train to providing an attractive and seamless journey that would have travelers coming back again and again.

Of course, even though the IDEO team focused on a completely new vision, there were still many things about Amtrak's current operations that were working and would stay the same. Train logistics were still vital and didn't need to be fixed. Often, so much time and effort goes into defining what's supposed to change, especially during major transformations, that playmakers don't take the time to define what will stay the same. This causes anxiety, because people aren't sure if all the cards are being thrown up in the air or not. The chart below can eliminate confusion and decrease tension by forcing you to confront the issue of the difference between the end (i.e., resolution of the problem) and the means (i.e., the immediate solution), as well as to decide what will change and what won't. (See Figure 4.5.)

With their new destination and general direction, the IDEO design team now set out to get more specific and consider a strategic path for wooing passengers away from alternative modes of travel. The first thing they did was what you might call a reconnaissance mission out into the new marketspace they were moving toward. They took a journey themselves to brainstorm strategic possibili-

---

Clarify What's Going to Change   FIG. 4.5

	END	MEANS
CHANGES	The new outcomes that will take energy and effort to produce (e.g., a seamless passenger journey)	The new means that will have to be adopted to get where you want to go (e.g., better customer interface, train design, and information systems)
REMAINS CONSTANT	The elements of the current situation that you want to keep and not change (e.g., well-running trains)	The things you're doing now that will still work in getting to the new endgame (e.g., train handling and logistics)

ties. They started with "I want to go to New York City, what are my options? How do I find out about high-speed rail, where do I find out about it?" They finished with step number ten, helping folks get to their next destination.

After they returned from their reconnaissance mission, the strategy began to take shape. In strategy, the challenge is to figure out, given your available solutions and resources, how to actually make it to your endgame most successfully. Strategy is thus more than merely choosing routes, it is an integrated set of actions that will govern how you move through the terrain to get to your goal.

The best strategies are unified and integrated around a concept, an idea or a theme that expresses something about how the different sets of actions will interrelate. It is this idea of an integrating theme, the most intangible element of strategy, that is most often misunderstood and most challenging to come up with. A unifying idea—a campaign theme—keeps your execution cohesive and ordered even under pressure. Without one, strategies can unravel very rapidly in the heat of implementation.

IDEO's strategic idea for winning over new customers and capturing market share was *time*. They wanted to push the idea that the train lets people be in charge of their time. Oslapas noted that if you're in Boston and are taking an air shuttle to New York, it's a jagged multistep process with little sense of control— especially when the weather is poor.

"In sum the trip is probably three to three and a half hours long. With the train, you're in downtown Boston, you wait at the gate, or maybe you've already got your ticket so you get on the train and you've got three hours. For three hours you're in control of your time. You're not buckled into a seat. So we used this overriding theme of sit back, relax, and breathe. You're here for a while, you're in control of your time. Think about all the things you can get done."

The new strategy guided serious changes in how Amtrak did business and, subsequently, how they designed their product. IDEO had a team in Canada for about a year, working on the design of new trains to build on the theme of making better use of your time. They redesigned the seats for more legroom and the café cars so that each was truly a café, with seating, and not just a counter in the last car of the train. They put power outlets at each seat, so that travelers could plug in their laptops.

For the ultimate in efficient use of time, "My dream was that you get Kinkos in all these stations," says Oslapas. A passenger working on a report could beam it to the next station, and when they arrived, there would be a nice printout of their report. Amtrak chose not to make the investment, but perhaps some day.

Playmakers in Action: Choosing Your Destinations

Choose an important problem or opportunity you're working on and create your own goal ladder. Start with the highest level vision you can imagine, at least several years in the future, and then work down systematically through endgame, future state, goals, targets, and milestones. Each time you move down a rung, you *must* get more specific and closer in time to the present. When you finish, your milestone should be no more than a month away, and it should be quantifiable or measurable. Now, keeping in mind that most people overestimate what they can do in the short term and underestimate their long-term potential, are you reaching high enough? Are you grounded enough? Confirm your point of view with your colleagues and readjust the ladder if necessary.

DEFINE SUCCESS

From Direction to Defining Success

Failure is the foundation of success; success is the lurking-place of failure.

—LAO-TZU (C. 600–550 B.C.)

Once a problem is chosen, a goal identified and a direction set, a Playmaker must define success, what it means to everyone involved, and how you'll know when it's been achieved. Success comes into focus when you start talking about how fast, at what cost and risk, and to what level of quality you intend to get to your destination. To define success, it's important to make clear both what you will and won't accomplish. It's also necessary to define the other side of success—failure.

You'll need a means to measure results and a plan about how to explain those results to your community of interest, because success can be as much about perception as about substance. Success appears in different lights depending on one's point of view. It will look different from outside and inside your organization, to founders, investors, and employees. And it will look different from the shop floor than from the executive suite.

Given how far and how often the bar of success is being raised these days—for individuals and for companies—few things are more vital to good problem solving than defining success. So it's surprising how often problem solvers spend time choosing a destination but neglect to define success or failure. Too often, after agreeing on a general problem and goal, average Playmakers launch an effort and then define success on a piecemeal basis as they go along. Disorganization and futility can build quickly, sapping momentum when it should be building. Sometimes this omission is all it takes to kill a new initiative at birth. Nelson Mandela, on the other hand, in leading the rebellion in South Africa, thought through the definition of success at every stage of the long journey, and used those definitions effectively to keep on track to an historic accomplishment.

Nelson Mandela and the Free Nation of South Africa

On the surface there was little doubt for Mandela and the African National Congress (ANC), throughout the many years leading up to their ultimate success, about their destination. They wanted what many rebel movements want: freedom—pure and simple. And yet so many of the other rebel movements in Africa had failed to achieve real freedom, even when they had achieved that basic goal of independence from outdated colonial governments. Their problem was assuming that they would know it when they saw it. Mandela's movement wisely engaged in all the elements of defining success and failure:

- How precisely can I define success? (accuracy, speed, net benefits, cost, risk, quality)
- How will I measure my success in an objective fashion? (goals, metrics, systems)
- Success compared to what? (absolute and relative)
- Success as judged by whom? (founders, investors, stakeholders, employees)
- How will I handle success or failure? My own, or that of others? (incentives, relationships)

Early on, Mandela and his fellow revolutionaries were frustrated by their lack of progress in making social change and the high human price of delay—the lives stunted, spirits crushed, people killed. Their sense of urgency, and their assessment of their adversary's strength and tactics, led them to debate the need for armed struggle and more speed.

In the summer of 1961, Mandela and other ANC leaders reluctantly decided that peaceful protest was not enough. As he says, "[We] came to the conclusion that as violence in this country was inevitable, it would be wrong and unrealistic for African leaders to continue preaching peace and non-violence at a time when the government met our peaceful demands with force."

As most of the world now knows, Mandela unlawfully left the country and began organizing training for guerrillas. He was arrested upon his return and imprisoned, then charged with sabotage in the historic Rivonia Trial. From the dock, he vowed that he was prepared to die for the ideal of a democratic and free society, in which all men lived in harmony and with equality.

Mandela's and the African National Congress's definitions of success were high risk, high cost, and high-minded from the start. They showed themselves willing to pay the ultimate price in human life because they were outraged at the cost of their people's virtual slavery and because, in their own mind, their goal justified the means.

But the hardest question may have been the question of precision. How much freedom did they really want? Did they want to control the whites the way they were controlled? Did they simply want participation in government? Or something in between? These questions sparked the debates that raged throughout the fight for freedom in South Africa. They pointed to the tough decisions that had to be made to define success or failure.

By the 1980s, Mandela had developed a single-minded focus and determination in spite of serious internal dissension. At that point "He said, 'Everything is negotiable—except one person, one vote in the unitary state,'" explained Princeton University professor of political science Jeffrey Herbst. "That is how he defined his baseline demand." Accuracy and quality were what counted, to lay the right foundations for democracy. In the chaos, confusion, and conflict of a massive problem solving effort, his clear-eyed definition of success helped him win.

Playmakers must not only define success and failure, they must be able to measure their results in terms of that definition. Success is sometimes absolute, but more often it is relative—success compared to what or whom? Even though the ANC had socialist roots, Mandela ultimately looked to multiparty democracies around the world as his point of reference. Ultimately, it was his decision to be more like these models that helped confirm a definition of success that would, in turn, become an example throughout the entire African continent of how to transcend the tribal past.

One of the most critical measures of success for the movement, and for the country as a whole, came down to the issue of free elections. If a free, monitored, multiparty election could be held, then one of the major elements of success would have been achieved. Ultimately, this happened in late April, 1994. But it was the product of years of intense negotiations on systems of representation, the numbers and types of deliberative bodies that would make up the legislature, veto power, and several other major issues. In everyone's minds, however, there was the developing common knowledge that until the world witnessed a free election in South Africa, little else mattered.

The South African election was attended and verified by multinational observers from the UN and other countries. Similarly, whether it is in business or in politics or in science, the best measures are independently observable and verifiable. Different stakeholders and perspectives need to be able to interpret them in similar ways, and there must be sources for the information and a process open to verification by independent outside parties. The measures need to be at the right level of detail and precision. Sometimes, adequate measurement can be done based on intuitive observation. Other times, it requires statistically valid and experimentally proven observations. What level of precision is required depends on the circumstances, what's at stake and what decisions are being made.

Mandela—and the world—showed the greatest wisdom in the way they described the ultimate success of the ANC. Mandela did not claim that he or his movement had achieved success, nor did others claim that for them; rather there was an attempt by all of the more enlightened leadership to portray the outcome as a success for all of South Africa and for the world. Everyone knew, that if there were perceived losers (even though something was in fact lost) victory could not be achieved. The Nobel Prize was given to both negotiators, both Mandela and de Klerk, not just one. The government may have been elected by a majority of blacks but it was the government of all South Africans.

In pushing for reconciliation and redemption rather than revenge, Mandela and the ANC saw to it that the past became everyone's, that the two sides were not defined as victims and criminals. The entire issue of success or failure was transformed into a mutual success, and failure was clearly identified as the inability to complete this transition into a new era of peace for the country. Ultimately, it was this ability to define success and failure so masterfully, by making both collective and by immediately setting a new goal of building a country together, that set Mandela apart as a historic figure.

As soon as Mandela acquired power, he faced the problem of how to govern. Playmakers know that both success and failure are ephemeral, and that once you reach a certain level, work needs to begin soon on how to get to the next one. Standing still is all too often falling behind. In the ebb and flow of a problem solving effort, the states of success and failure tend to fade into the background, making the journey, the struggle, the effort to achieve what is most important.

But, without the marking points of success and failure, problem solvers aren't able to gather the information they need to make course corrections and assess progress. Success can easily lead to complacency. Alternatively, failure should be viewed as not only something to learn from, but something to persist through. The real danger of failure as a concept is giving up too early when all that is necessary is more work, more learning, more change, and improved problem solving.

Mandela showed just this attitude at the pivotal point of his success—negotiating with de Klerk over the future of the country—after many previous disappointments and setbacks. A lesser man would have been impatient, but Mandela and de Klerk both emphasized relatively slow, steady progress. "I understood that nothing was going to be resolved that day," Mandela wrote. "But it was extremely useful, for I had taken the measure of Mr. de Klerk just as I did with new prison commanders when I was on Robben Island. I was able to write to our people that Mr. de Klerk seemed to represent a true departure from the National Party politicians of the past."

Mandela said he felt about de Klerk as Margaret Thatcher had felt about Mikhail Gorbachev. "Mr. de Klerk . . . was a man we could do business with," Mandela said. And what amazing business was done.

Playmaking in Action: Defining Success

Pick the most important problem or opportunity you're working on today. Define what success and failure will mean at the end of the project and how you'll know. Then, think about what failures you will have to have in order to achieve success. Similarly, write down the new possibilities of failure that will loom once you achieve success. Now, make a short list of the most important players (e.g., stakeholders, colleagues, customers) who need to understand all these things, and have conversations with each one until they do.

PLAN FOR CHANCE
From Defining Success to Planning

Le hasard ne favorise que les esprits préparés.
(Chance favors only the prepared mind.)

—LOUIS PASTEUR (1822–1895)

Once you've chosen a problem, set direction, and defined success, you need a plan. Planning forces you to think through issues and anticipate possible scenarios and their consequences along the way. Common sense and experience tell us that, at least to some extent, we make our own luck. With the right type of planning, you can anticipate possibilities and thus be better prepared. Planning forces you to think through issues and anticipate possible scenarios and their consequences, to prepare for them along the way.

Up to a point, better planning means better preparation. But ultimately, your plans must allow for chance—both bad fortune and good—especially in fast-moving environments. No plan can account for every possible development along a journey. For this reason, Playmakers plan for surprises, for chance, having a healthy respect for uncertainty and unpredictability. They conduct a "directed" exploration that not only allows for exploration's inevitable surprises but consciously tries to stimulate them.

In this mold, there are few more advanced planning approaches than that applied by American Airlines and its offspring, Sabre, Inc. Their Integrated Forecasting System (IFS) is the epitome of what the leading edge of business planning looks like today.

American Airlines and Sabre's Integrated Forecasting System

The center of Sabre is its main data center. This vast concrete bunker hidden somewhere in the Midwest seems more appropriate for nuclear missiles than airline travel. It is the world's largest private database and real-time information system—second only to the Pentagon. With nearly 300,000 devices, it processes upwards of 150 million transactions per day, or about 5,000 messages per second.

It is the heart and soul of one of the most consistently successful applications of technology in the last thirty years, the American Airlines (AA) computer reservation and information system. Although it was written about extensively for its first decade, many do not understand just how powerful and vast this organization has grown. Simply by virtue of its staying power and consistent growth through decades of changing technology, it illustrates the best of what it takes to succeed in the information age.

Good planning is based on the ability to forecast and anticipate. Forecasting minimizes the harmful effects of chance by giving planners the most reliable view possible of the future. How far out you look and how much meaning you can attach to that outlook varies tremendously depending on how predictable your environment is. If planning a week or two ahead has one confidence level, planning a year or two ahead has a tiny fraction of that confidence level. The farther you go out in the future, the lower your probable accuracy. And this relationship is an exponential, not a strictly linear one. One solution to these fundamental problems of probability and capturing complex relationships comes with technology, and it is because of its use of technology that American Airlines has such a strategic advantage over its competitors—it has the best planning technology in the industry.

At American Airlines, the Integrated Forecasting System (IFS), created by Sabre, is the closest thing you could have to a crystal ball. Given a set of input assumptions, IFS can forecast the entire worldwide network of AA flights in thousands of markets in a total of three minutes. Every airplane, every flight, every passenger, even fuel usage. And that's not all. It not only builds the entire flight network, it calculates market share, determines implications for passenger traffic, and distills the implications for costs and revenue of the airline as a whole.

But it is more than just technology. It is the synthesis of human judgment and computer calculation that is the real power behind AA's approach to planning. AA's senior management team drives the process. It takes many smart people to exercise judgment based on the forecasts that are made by the IFS and develop actual plans. Airline transportation is a very complex business, where the computer can never capture everything. It is competitive, price sensitive, with low margins and a highly perishable product (an airline seat) played out across the globe on a real-time basis.

AA uses the blended planning approach to forecast schedules, loads, yields, revenue, and profitability for AA and any of 200 competitors. AA's people have an unparalleled ability to peek into the future and evaluate alternative futures. For example, they can focus on a competitor airline and test different scenarios. IFS can help assess the profitability of different types of aircraft fleets. It allows management to evaluate the impact of macro events and decisions (e.g., mergers or hub openings). It also improves the quality of micro decisions on aircraft choices, fleet retirements, and timing of certain flights.

The real reason the blended approach adds value, however, is by pushing past the conventional wisdom in decision making and encouraging managers to think of new, more profitable options. It offers a more complete analysis of a problem or opportunity in less time. It does this based on facts and equations that have proven themselves increasingly reliable over the years. The teams behind IFS use the lessons they've learned to constantly refine the models, the algorithms, and the data they use.

When American is making especially large decisions—such as a potential merger with another airline or a major capital investment—they may use the IFS to troll through thirty, forty, or even fifty scenarios in one day. There is extensive board discussion and argument. They formulate alternatives and questions. At that point, the analysts go back and run another model, returning in minutes with the results.

No matter how much we plan, chance occurrences can always surprise us. Not only do events take unexpected turns, but the terms in which we conceive of our problems and opportunities can shift radically. The core of planning wisdom is to balance precision forecasting techniques—with their built-in assumptions of control and sufficient knowledge—against looser, more open experimentation, exploration, and analysis.

I think of this approach as "directed evolution." It's designed to ferret out unknowns and maximize the possibilities for innovation, earlier than the competition. Getting the right balance between detailed planning and serendipity requires anticipating the possibility of chance events that could completely overturn expectations and send you in a different direction. But it is more than just being ready to respond with contingency plans or hedges when an unexpected event happens. It means identifying potential paths of evolution that are relatively more likely to have good surprises and investing in them to create future options.

There is no better example of this approach than Sabre itself. In the beginning, the airline used color-coded index cards and a lazy Susan to keep track of seats, flights, and reservations. The next generation system, the Semi-Automated

Business Research Environment (SABRE), added simple data processing technology to the basic system. By the 1960s, Sabre had already moved beyond travel agent reservations to include an online catalog of theater tickets, gifts and other travel services. It was spun off from AA in the fall of 1996, almost forty years after its humble genesis.

Now, it offers decision support systems and consulting to the travel, transportation, and food service industries and government agencies. It handles 25 percent of the world's airline reservations and a similar percentage of rental car bookings in the United States. What no IFS forecast could have shown was Sabre's potential to become a full-fledged independent company, in fact the vanguard of an entirely new industry.

The unexpected evolution of Sabre is, I believe, the most impressive planning achievement of all for Bob Crandall and American, precisely because no one could have expected it. Yet at every stage, the management team allowed it to evolve naturally, not trying to control it or make it a slave to their airline. As the picture of what it could become emerged, they worked harder to encourage its growth and independence. It is in this sense that the leadership at American Airlines were truly master Playmakers.

Playmaking in Action: Creating a Problem Chain

Pick an important problem or opportunity you're facing now, and then work out what the next three problems or opportunities will be that you'll be likely to face after you finish this one. Write them down in sequence as your "forward chain" of problems. Now do a little bit of history: Write down the three problems in sequence that people faced before they came to the one you're working on. This is your "backward chain." Now take a look at your problem chain. Is there anything that can be learned from the past that could help you today that you don't already know? Is there anything you can be doing now to prepare for the future that you're not doing?

LEAD THE WAY

From Planning to Leadership

As for the best leaders, the people do not notice their existence.
The next best, the people honor and praise.
The next, the people fear; and the next, the people hate.

– LAO-TZU (600–550 B.C.)

In the early stages of a problem solving journey, a Playmaker selects problems, strategizes, and plans. But eventually, someone has to lead the way. Leadership is at the heart of playmaking. It often means being the lonely one out in front, forging into unknown territory. But is also means guiding the larger effort once it's begun–leading from behind. Leading from behind involves learning and applying the lessons troops discover in the trenches. Ultimately, it means creating new leaders.

There's more to leadership as more people become capable of leadership. With a variety of styles in the workplace and horizontal organizations that push decision making downward and outward toward the customer, the very nature of leadership is changing, as leaders strive harder to create and nurture other leaders than to remain visibly at the helm. The best leaders create and guide teams that operate almost completely on their own but are susceptible to very subtle influences.

As one of America's best known leaders, Colin Powell has operated at the highest professional level as a problem solver, going from defense, to authorship, and now to the nonprofit world with America's Promise/The Alliance for Youth.

Colin Powell and the Keeping of America's Promise

At the U.S. Chamber of Commerce's meeting in February 1998, during an afternoon session on the workforce, Colin Powell issued a call-to-arms. "He challenged us . . . to really step up, become mentors, to get involved in local communities," recalled Leslie Hortum, former senior vice president at the U.S. Chamber. A huge drive was organized to get summer jobs for kids who'd never been exposed to a business or been taught a skill, who might otherwise just spend their summer hanging out on the street. Local chambers hired kids as summer interns, and businesses were encouraged to do the same. "Literally thousands and thousands of kids got jobs and were hired because Colin Powell challenged the chambers to aggressively do this," said Hortum.

Powell, the charismatic former chairman of the Joint Chiefs of Staff, has a way of getting folks to do what he wants. In just three years, Powell has turned America's Promise into a huge success. Even under the shadow of recent investigations that question whether the organization may have inflated its results, there is little doubt they have made a difference in the lives of millions of at-risk youths. In fact, the questions of exactly how much and who gets the credit (which appeared to be behind the small furor) are the kind of difficulties faced by any leader trying to create large-scale change. From the tiniest of contributions made by mom-and-pop businesses to million-dollar donations from the titans of industry, the money coming in shows how many want to be part of Powell's mission. "When the general asks you to do something, you say, 'Yes sir, what time?'" joked Hortum.

"Powell is bigger than life, obviously," says Hortum, "but when you hear him talk about what he believes in, it's so sincere and so true and so honest, that I think people find it absolutely inspiring and they want to be a part of it. And they want to help him succeed." Maybe so much that they would stretch the truth rather than disappoint him. Still, that sincerity is a hallmark of leadership, because in presenting themselves so, leaders place themselves on the same level and in the same place as everyone else whom they are leading. The followers sense this, embrace it, and want to follow the example.

Most problems and opportunities need a leader to get things started and generate momentum. It is nearly always harder to get something going than to steer it once some movement has been achieved.

When you're out in front as a leader, you take on the burden of generating momentum. There are no excuses. You either make it or you don't. You are the one figuring out where to go, what to do, and how to get there. You are the one who risks failure by launching out in a new direction. In many problem solving situations, where dramatic change and high risks are involved, nothing except leading from in front will get things moving. You are the one people look to when mistakes are made, for the standards and values that will be reaffirmed as those errors are transcended.

Powell is out front for America's Promise, giving speeches and urging corporations and other groups to get involved. Using phrases like "national crusade" and "rescue mission," he implores Americans to give every kid these five promises: a caring adult; safe places; a healthy start; a marketable skill; and a chance to give back to the community. "It isn't brain surgery, and we don't need any more studies," Powell says to business, civic, and community leaders. "I don't want to talk to more psychologists. We need to take these at-risk kids and make them children of promise." Or this, another favorite saying: "It's time to stop building jails and get back to building our children."

Powell gently needles big shots to do more than "just show up at a black tie dinner, give an oversize check and get your picture in the New York Times." "There's nothing wrong with that," he told a group of New Yorkers once, "but it's not enough. I want your talent. I want your time and I want you personally involved. I want you to make this a part of your corporate responsibility and not just something you have to do once a year."

Leaders recognize that even though they are out in front and may have to make the biggest decisions, there are many ideas, lessons and decisions that can be made–often best–without them. In other words, part of good leadership is sharing it, giving it up, and augmenting it by following the instincts, judgments, and initiatives of your best people and showing the entire organization that they are leaders.

Much of what Powell does is listening and learning or "following other people's cues," said Wofford. When America's Promise started, Powell and his small staff at national headquarters in Alexandria, Virginia, sweated and struggled to come up with a workable structure to be a clearinghouse. But they found that governors and mayors were returning to their states and cities and coming up with their own structures. So Powell looked to them for guidance and ideas to be used in the overall program and cross-fertilized around the country.

Great leaders have the wisdom to follow the stream of events when it sweeps them along, rather than always having to determine which direction the current is heading in. This is the art of following and yielding when other leaders naturally emerge, not crushing and dominating them. They sense and nurture the best ideas and directions from within a group so that the whole group grows and generates new energy and forward movement.

"There's a great deal of sharing leadership that Powell is doing. He picks up things that he learns when he goes to a corporation," said Wofford, noting that when Powell called on corporations to get involved, Allstate informed Powell he'd be speaking by satellite to its employees worldwide. Then the manager of the Allstate's southern region got motivated, and 150 employees in Florida became team leaders for a service day in the state. The Allstate manager said it was the best morale-booster that had ever happened in the company. "Well, Powell didn't think of that," said Wofford. "Allstate thought of that."

Traditionally, the notion of leadership incorporates choosing a successor and handing leadership on to the next generation. Modern leadership is about creating more leaders from the day you begin to exercise a leadership position. This creation of new leaders happens not just by singling them out, but by watching them, following them, and then giving them a turn at leading. Good leadership always shifts. It shifts from one person to another, as individuals with different skills take a natural lead in different aspects of a problem solving effort. It also shifts from one generation to another, as leaders emerge and are groomed and cultivated to gain the experience they need to move into leading roles and new responsibilities.

Colin Powell is creating new leaders every day, both among the kids his group reaches and the groups that are keeping the promises. This notion of service, of leading for a purpose, is a cornerstone of enlightened leaders. His fifth promise is all about letting kids give back to their community. "A chance to give back teaches a child the joy of service to others, and the self-respect that comes from knowing that one has a contribution to make to the world," Powell has written. The crusade is about the future, Powell likes to say. "We have no more important task before us than to save the next generation of American leaders."

Playmaking in Action: Leaders Creating Leaders

Choose a problem solving situation that is important to you where you play some kind of leadership role. Create your own short list of the best leaders in the organization. Then concentrate all your effort for a period of time, a day, a week or even longer, solely on giving leadership away, recognizing it in others, encouraging it, and celebrating it. Work on being the voice of leadership in the effort, the one person who can lead the process of generating leadership. Now make the short list again, and see if it's changed. The second list will help you focus on creating an enduring next generation of leaders–the ultimate in leadership.

CHARACTERISTICS OF
A PLAYMAKER

General characteristics and purpose: Playmakers emphasize a particular problem or opportunity. Their goal is working on the right problems, for the right reasons, at the right time. Playmakers are interested in change, in movement, and above all in the coordinated action of people and capability over time to accomplish an objective. They are adventurous and understand the mastery of complex aspects of strategies and power that it takes to create and/or respond to change. They value leadership, vision, and adventure. They tend to focus on goals, strategies, routes, planning and scenarios. Deep learning, profound innovation, or the intricacies of relationships are less important.

Strengths: Playmakers are at their best in responding to a crisis, a major threat, or in leading the approach to a big opportunity. They can help a group coalesce on a common vision, conceptualize the key steps in the path along the way, and

---

Skill Levels of Playmaking TABLE 4.1

Level 1   Ability to organize a group of people for some purpose.
Level 2   Ability to organize a group and actually accomplish something meaningful.
Level 3   Ability to attract people consistently to new and different projects or purposes.
Level 4   Ability to accomplish larger scale changes with sizable groups.
Level 5   Ability to accomplish either very difficult or very large scale changes or both.
Level 6   Ability to accomplish difficult, large scale change repeatably and well.
Level 7   Catalyzes historic changes by leading millions of people to grasp problems or opportunities.

convince others that the journey can be made. In the difficult periods, they are able to help lead and motivate in a way that allows the journey to continue and not degrade or fall apart.

Weaknesses: Playmakers' focus on change can make them ignorant of the value of traditions. They are not usually the ones with enough patience or creativity to build knowledge or push the limits of what is conceivable. When difficulties emerge with human relationships or in gathering knowledge, they can be liable to focus on getting past it without appropriate attention.

Interactions with other types of problem solvers: Playmakers tend to interact constructively with all the other types because their role is defined by the ability to bring them all together to create change. Their goals and strategies spark the creation of communities and bring them to life in a way that Communicators thrive on. Those same destinations and directions create a clear need for both Creators, who will develop solutions to make the journeys possible, and Performers, who are necessary to make them happen. That said, they probably have the most difficulty with Innovators and Discoverers, whose culture and pace are the most different. The relationship between deep knowledge of a territory and one particular journey is not always transparent, which can lead to misperception on both sides that Playmakers and Discoverers don't have much to learn from one another. Because Playmakers tend to be more directed and less inherently curious, there are also problems in communication between the two that mirror the miscues between practitioners and academics. As for Innovators, Playmakers tend to occupy positions of authority, and Innovators often see their role as one of challenging and breaking down authority, a potential source of conflict.

Typical mishandling: Playmakers are mishandled when they conceive of themselves or are fashioned info domineering leaders rather than catalyzers and facilitators. They are diminished when they are not encouraged to let others lead, choosing always to lead themselves and creating personality cults. This constrains the ability of the organization to build other Playmakers.

Guidance for Playmaking

Guiding Principles: Rules and Laws That Bear on Playmaking

- Choose the right problems, then the right tasks.
- If everything's important, nothing is.
- A diversified portfolio reduces risk and increase opportunity.
- Define your destination, your benchmark, then your success.
- The 80/20 rule: Focus on 80 percent, not 100 percent resolution of your problem in goal setting.
- Understand your critical path.
- Think two or three problems ahead.

- If you don't know whether time is against you, it usually is.
- Spot the long lead times.
- It's harder to get something started than it is to steer it.
- The best leadership multiplies itself.

Diagnostics: How Well Are You Managing Your Problem-Solving Journeys?

- Have you oriented yourself in a way that you really know what most of the big problems and opportunities are? How much do you know about them? Do you know what your portfolio is? Are you spending time on the right things? Have you defined the problems in the best possible way? How have you prioritized them and by what criteria?
- For your biggest problems, do you have a clear destination in mind? A direction to head in? Why have you chosen it? How many other alternatives did you consider? How many people agree with you? How do you know? How committed are they to going there? What's your strategy for moving ahead?
- Have you defined success and failure? How specifically? Compared to what? How will you know when and if you get there? What measures have you chosen? By what process? Who has been involved? What measurement systems have you put in place? Can they be independently verified?
- Have you planned for the future? Do you know what's happening just up ahead as well as far down the road? Are you prepared? Are you forecasting the future today? How far out ahead? By what means? Are you tracking your assumptions? How are your current actions shaped by these forecasts?
- Do you have the right leadership to resolve your problems? Are there many leaders or few? Is leadership shared? Do you know today who your next generation of leaders are? How are they going to develop? When are they going to get the chance? Are you listening to the leadership directions from everyone in your organization? Are you signaling the leadership direction, not commanding it?

Syndromes: Diseases That Can Plague Your Ability to Manage Journeys

- "Spread too thin"—Trying to solve too many problems with too little
- "Taskaholism"—Prioritizing tasks and time, but not problems
- "One-at-a-time"—Only able to focus on a single project, not a portfolio
- "Everything's important"—Unable or unwilling to set priorities
- "Muddling through"—Vague, disconnected goals rather than a clear vision and goal ladder

- "Fantasy land"—Concentrating on the vision and not on success, or strategies to make it happen.
- "See no evil, hear no evil"—Success-oriented planning that doesn't account for the possibility of failure and the tough but hidden problems
- "Selling yourself short"—Overestimating what you can accomplish in the short term, underestimating the possibilities in the long term
- "Too few leaders"—Over reliance on one leader and therefore being vulnerable to that leader's inevitable deficiencies

Going Further

Selected resources for further study on playmaking. (See also sources and notes for Part 4 on page 270.)

Books

Bennis, Warren. On Becoming a Leader. Boston: Addison-Wesley, 1989.

Bennis, Warren, ed. *Leaders on Leadership*. Cambridge: Harvard Business Review, 1992.

Bennis, Warren, and Burt Nanus. *Leaders*. New York: Harper Perennial, 1985.

Bryson, John. *Strategic Planning for Public and Nonprofit Organizations*. San Francisco: Jossey Bass, 1991.

Burns, James MacGregor. *Leadership*. New York: Harper & Row, 1979.

Dixit, Avinash, and Barry Nalehuff. *Thinking Strategically*. New York: Norton, 1991.

Gardner, Howard. *Leading Minds*. New York: Basic Books, 1995.

Geldens, Max. *Strategy from Pooh's Corner*. Amsterdam: McKinsey & Co, 1985.

Harvard Business Review, *Global Strategies*. Boston: HBS Press, 1994.

Heifetz, Ronald. *Leadership Without Easy Answers*. Cambridge: Harvard University Press, 1994.

Hickman, Craig. *Mind of a Manager, Soul of a Leader*. New York: Wiley & Sons, 1990.

Kotter, John. *Leading Change*. Cambridge, MA: HBS Press, 1996.

Kouzes, James, and Barry Posner. *Credibility*. San Francisco: Jossey-Bass, 1993.

Luttwak, Edward. *Strategy*. Cambridge: Harvard University Press, 1987.

Ohmae, Kenichi. *The Mind of the Strategist*. Penguin Books, 1982.

Paret, Peter. *Makers of Modern Strategy*. Princeton: Princeton University Press, 1986.

Philips, Donald. *Lincoln on Leadership*. New York: Warner Books, 1992.

Philips, Donald. *The Founding Fathers on Leadership*. New York: Warner Books, 1997.

Roberts, Wess. *Leadership Secrets of Attila the Hun*. New York: Warner Books, 1990.

Rosen, Robert. *Leading People.* Penguin Books, 1996.

Tichy, Noel, with Eli Cohen. *The Leadership Engine.* New York: Harper Business, 1997.

Useem, Michael. *The Leadership Moment.* New York: Times Business, 1998.

Websites

Strategic planning:
  www.iftf.org
Goalsetting:
  www.goalsetting.com
Strategy and business:
  www.strategy-business.com
Performance:
  www.balancedscoredcard.org
  www.cpsciences.com
Benchmarking:
  www.benchnet.com
Business forecasting:
  www.ibforecast.com
Leadership:
  www.wharton.upenn.edu
  www.ccl.org
Community leadership:
  www.communityleaderhip.org

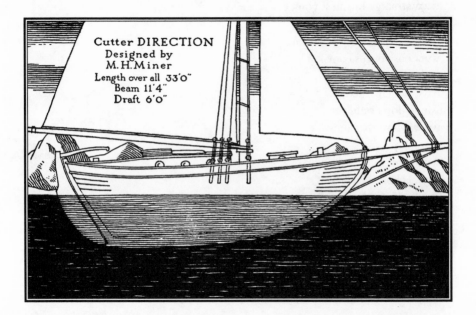

Cutter DIRECTION
Designed by
M. H. Miner
Length over all 33'0"
Beam 11'4"
Draft 6'0"

Part Five

⟩⟨ CREATE THE SOLUTIONS ⟩⟨

The Creator

Design, Build, and Maintain
Optimal Solutions

For every problem there is one solution which is simple, neat, and wrong.
—H. L. MENCKEN (1880–1956)

A solution is a means, a vessel. It is what gets you to your destination. It is not a resolution, the destination itself. The bigger and tougher and more competitive your problem is, the more challenging it is to design, build, and evolve solutions that will hold together under pressure and over time. This job is the province of the Creator. Creators draw on the Innovator's idea, the Discoverer's insight, and the Communicator's network to build specific solutions to solve the problems defined and guided by the Playmaker.

Solutions to large problems nearly always involve more than just technology. A complete solution includes people, tools, resources, information, and the flexible coordination of all four to solve a difficult problem or seize an opportunity. A Creator attempts to design and build solutions to achieve goals as cheaply, safely, and accurately as possible, while taking advantage of the most appropriate technologies.

For example, preparing and executing the Normandy invasion—D-Day—was a superhuman effort in the history of human adventure. The Allied war machine was not designed to deliver a few people, to help them arrive at a destination and enjoy the sights. It was created to conduct campaign after campaign, to deliver hundreds of thousands of men, gain ground against deadly resistance, and then capture a territory permanently and keep it under tight control—the sort of control a modern business strives to maintain over market share.

The Allied Landing at Normandy, June 5–6, 1944

It was the largest number of people ever mobilized for a single journey—millions of men and nearly as many machines. And that was only the start of it. They would have to cover many miles over the English Channel, mostly at night, and ultimately prevail against an implacable, well-armed, and experienced enemy, toughened by years of war. Then, there would be a further 2,000 miles to go, step by step, bridge by bridge, battle by battle until they reached—if they were successful—the enemy capital of Berlin.

It took George Marshall five years to build this solution to the problem of German aggression almost from the ground up. Dwight Eisenhower planned the implementation and guided it to victory. It was Marshall's facility in methodically building the military capability that executed the Normandy invasion, along with so many other campaigns, that won the Second World War. He was peerless as a Creator, someone who could put a combination of men, machines, rules and regulations, command and control systems together on a massive scale that would do what needed to be done, adapt, evolve and do it again.

The approaches Marshall used are ones that would be recognized by any of the great Creators of our era, whether they are attacking a competitor in the marketplace or creating a new enterprise, constructing a skyscraper or forming a grassroots political movement. Their essence is the ability to design, test, and build a functioning capability that can operate in the required territory and make it through the journeys that have been laid out before it.

Marshall chose the best talent to do the most important tasks required, whether it was developing research or building weapons systems. He created a system that produced the tools necessary to do the job, mobilizing the entire U.S. economy to a war footing and directing it. He targeted and managed scarce resources, from rubber for tires to chemicals for weapons. He created intelligence systems and organizations that got the right information to the right people at the right time. He put together institutions that had the autonomy to take independent action but the ability to coordinate if necessary. And he managed to create a continuous balance of power in favor of his direction that helped unify the President, the Congress, and the American people in troubled times.

Creating solutions is the fifth essential problem solving skill. It is also the one most affected by the evolution of technology. The essence of what a Creator does is bend and mold technology into the capability necessary to solve a problem, while recognizing that the underlying technologies may also apply to many different types of issues.

One of the Creator's constant challenges is scale. It's one thing to put together one small-scale solution to make an explorer's journey. It's another completely different enterprise to assemble a large-scale solution that has global reach. Most tough business problems today can more easily be compared to the solution Marshall and Eisenhower developed for the journey to Berlin that started on D-Day.

The powers of the mind and heart may dominate the challenge of Playmakers in directing a problem solving effort. But it is a talent for designing and working with tangible resources and assets, raw materials and machines, that drives Creators. Creators struggle with the tension between elegant, sophisticated solutions and ones that are quick and dirty. They grapple with the point at which a solution is "good enough." And they worry about reusing solutions whenever possible to save resources.

Designing and building solutions in the knowledge age is becoming everyday "rocket science." To incorporate new technological possibilities but still maintain operating tempo, Creators are being challenged to produce ever greater harmonies between people, work processes, information, and machines. While driving at top speed, businesses have to become adept at changing tires and replacing engine parts to upgrade capability so they don't fall behind their competitors. Product designers are expected to continuously evolve workable solutions that can keep and grow market share.

Maintaining control over that complexity and still keeping up with the rate of change is only possible with a disciplined approach to the design and creation of solutions—one which focuses on complete end-to-end solutions that are also smart, flexible, modular and evolvable.

The Creator's Central Idea: The Best Solutions Come from Complete and Evolvable Designs

At a high level, the architecture of a complete solution is the same in almost any field. It includes the components that make up a solution, such as people, processes, technology, and intelligence. It also includes the characteristics or attributes that its design must accomplish, such as efficiency and effectiveness. (See Figure 5.1.) Creators take both of these elements into account as they try to build an appropriately complete solution for any problem.

Among the worst hindrances to problem solvers are solutions either unsuited to the problem they are solving, incomplete, "gold-plated," or so cumbersome, inflexible, or wasteful that they are not only inefficient but are an anchor that can't adapt to changing conditions. To get the best solution, Creators can't afford to fall in love with particular technologies. They must consider multiple alternatives (both components and characteristics) and rigorously evaluate their relative costs, benefits, and risks.

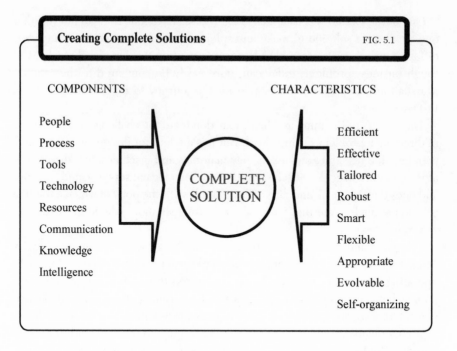

Creating Complete Solutions   FIG. 5.1

COMPONENTS   CHARACTERISTICS

People

Process   Efficient

Tools   Effective

Technology   COMPLETE   Tailored

Resources   SOLUTION   Robust

Communication   Smart

Knowledge   Flexible

Intelligence   Appropriate

                                                 Evolvable

                                                 Self-organizing

The bottom line is that smart Creators are always aware of both the possibilities and the dangerous allure of technology. They recognize the difference between technologies being developed in the lab and tools that can work in the real world, as well as the difference between a robust tool and a "throwaway" one. They know that tools are rarely complete solutions. They think creatively about how to use new technologies and tools. But when it comes time to really spend resources and energy, they focus on the problem and how the solution can resolve it. They concentrate on results before technical elegance. They understand that sometimes the solution is the focus, but most of the time, the focus is the problem that needs to be solved.

Creators in Action: Academic Systems Corporation and Education in the Knowledge Age

If the Creator's central idea is designing and building complete and evolvable solutions, then how does it work in practice? The following story of Academic Systems Corporation and their solution to the problem of education shows Creators in action. With their contribution, a problem solver can build on an Innovator's ideas, a Discoverer's knowledge, a Communicator's relationships, and a Playmaker's leadership to create an inspired, intelligent, living community with both a sense of direction and the actual capability to move it there.

Of some 15 million undergraduate students in America, nearly half go to community colleges. And at a typical community college, 80 percent of the entering freshman class is unprepared in the basics of mathematics and writing. They can't do simple fractions or decimals or write a complete sentence. Eight of ten students flunk at least one of the two basic placement tests and have to take "developmental" courses. And it's not just community colleges where remedial classes are a must. In California, the biggest public school system in the nation, half the students entering the California State University (CSU) system—which includes twenty-three campuses—flunk their mathematics or writing test. And these are presumably among California's best and brightest—by state law, students must be in the top third of their high school class to be admitted at a CSU campus.

Academic Systems Corp. set out to create a new solution to this problem in the form of next-generation interactive instructional software. Instructional software has been tried in the past, but the technology was primitive, and teachers resisted what they perceived as an attempt to replace them with machines. Academic Systems thought they could design a solution that would assist teachers in solving the problem of achieving basic proficiency for the full range of entering college students. "It's easy to point to your very best students, and say 'Look how great this person has done,'" says Edward Landesman, a vice president at Academic Systems Corp. and a former mathematics professor, who helped in the original development of the courses. "But there are many, many students who are right on the edge of learning mathematics well enough to help them in their work and future professions. And many of them get forgotten. Because they don't get that extra help they're locked out of professions and they can't enter certain occupations because they didn't have some of these basic courses. That's a great challenge."

Landesman, the recipient of numerous awards for distinguished university teaching, designed much of the instructional software based on a research and best practice model developed by company founder Bernard Gifford, the "original visionary" as Academic Systems CEO John Brandon puts it. As a former Apple Computer Executive, former dean of the Graduate School of Education at the University of California at Berkeley, and a Ph.D. in Biophysics, Gifford had the background to bring together the combination of people, instructional processes, technology, resources, and money to create a complete solution that would help teach underserved college students mathematics and writing in a new way.

To create this solution, Academic Systems had to find the right people for the job. It recruited the best educators in mathematics and writing across the country, in an advisory role, to help design the best instructional methods possible given available technology. Landesman is fond of saying he spent more time in his first year at Academic Systems thinking about pedagogy and teaching than he did over a twenty-eight-year career of teaching. He and his colleagues identified the hundreds of expert teachers who contributed knowledge, which was then distilled, organized, and engineered into the software—ninety hours of development time for every hour of classroom time created.

Finding the right tools for the job was critical. So much of technology-assisted learning is "power point slides dressed up," said Brandon. "That's not going to cut it." Academic Systems thought through not only how they were going to teach a concept, but how would it be presented and in what sequence, all delivered in a form that would be fun and exciting for the students. "There's a real art to that so it enhances the learning," says Brandon.

For example, one of the algebra lessons describes a female character who makes painted denim jackets in her home and must make two decisions: how many to sell to realize a profit, and whether a distribution deal that a department store has offered her is profitable. Audio and video are used to show her at home as she explains the situation and the equations she must use. Students can try the problem, using graphs and equations, learn what they did right and wrong and then get advice from the computer on what concepts to review based on how they did. Finally, the computer prepares a detailed report on the performance of students that used it.

"We use a lot of multimedia to enhance the reality factor," Brandon says from the company's Silicon Valley headquarters. "The nice thing about the software is we incorporated the best teaching practices we could find for multiple learning styles. It's a very valuable knowledge asset. So if you really need practical application, we'll teach it that way. If you didn't understand it the first way, we'll have the software teach it to you a different way."

Many of the students using Academic Systems courses aren't the typical eighteen-year-old entering college—they may be twenty-eight or even forty-eight, having long forgotten what normally would be middle-school math. The company recognized that it couldn't make assumptions about what knowledge base students would start from, or how fast they'd be able to learn. Their solution had to be robust. The software was designed to help students set a starting point and move at their own pace. The software checks their progress as they move along. "If you don't get it right, the system will come back and say, 'No, that's not right. Do you want a hint before you try again?'" says Brandon. "If you still don't get it right, we will show you the correct way to do it. We've tried to incorporate all this wonderful one-on-one instruction. It can't possibly happen in the typical lecture setting."

The Academic Systems approach was built around a recognition of the scarcest and most valuable resource in the classroom—the teacher's attention and time. "When you teach in a classroom, often you're sort of a sage on the stage," said Landesman. "While many faculty want that and do not wish to give that up, others find the ideal environment is a combination, where they can also get to know each student's strengths and vulnerabilities to give help on an individual basis." What was really needed was a new capability to leverage a teacher's time and skills—the computer equivalent of a teaching assistant, in a sense. In a lecture class, the teacher's time is mostly taken up at the front of the room, explaining the main ideas.

With the Academic Systems approach, teachers are able to get just the right balance with a tool that operates largely on its own, in a limited role. They let the software take the lead and spend more of their time helping the students who need assistance most, as well as motivating and inspiring the students—teaching—rather than preparing lesson plans.

Another important tool was designing the software so that a management information system resides within it to deliver key information when required. The teacher is automatically told not only how a student does at the end of the daily quiz, but also how much time a student spends on each individual task. Because the quizzes are graded within the system, "We take a lot of the busy work away from the teacher," says Brandon.

Even so, teachers were often skeptical at first, and afraid of software that seemed poised to replace them. Academic Systems needed to get information to teachers in a form that the teachers would accept, and just as urgently, they needed feedback from teachers about the frontline successes and failures of the software. They created what they called the Interactive Mathematics and Interactive English Roundtables, using Listserv technology, to let teachers tell Academic Systems—and more importantly, each other—what worked and what didn't.

The same approach was taken on a larger scale to ensure the "evolvability" of the software. First, and most importantly, the software was designed with a specific, high-level methodology that can be adjusted over time. Furthermore, every spring, Academic Systems holds a series of regional "continuous improvement meetings." Faculty members who teach the courses can recommend changes, and then the instructors vote by ballot on what's working and what needs improvement. Then the software is changed. "There's not a textbook company in the world that can afford to do that or that will do that," says Brandon. "It's been a competitive advantage, but it's also a wonderful thing about our software."

Perhaps as a result of inviting so much communication and interaction with teachers, Academic Systems has managed to shift the balance of power within the schools and the educational materials industry in its favor. By making teachers part of their solution, they have been able to shift the old division of power—teachers versus threatening, encroaching machines—to a new alliance between software that depends on the presence of teachers and teachers who depend on their software. Now, with rigorous research and assessment, four basic benefits of the Academic Systems solution are emerging: more effective instructional materials (as shown in increased passing rates), better use of an instructor's time (decreased time spent on organizing materials by 50 percent), greater learner productivity, and greater flexibility in course design.

Academic Systems courses have spread rapidly around the country since being developed in the early 1990s, and are now offered at more than 270 college campuses in 35 states, where they have served hundreds of thousands of students. If its mathematics courses were books, Academic Systems would have the hottest texts on the market.

Teachers, once skeptical, are now giving the coursework positive reviews, according to Landesman. One provost and VP for academic affairs is quoted as saying, "It's an exquisitely fine tool to allow the instructor to intervene just at the right time and just at the right place. It's the best example of what instructional technology is supposed to do, which is to make the instructor a better teacher."

And no single professor could reach the volume of students that Academic Systems does. "This year alone, over 100,000 students will be using it," Landesman says proudly. "When I think back on a whole career, I bet I didn't see more than five or six thousand students. To know that you could be helping hundreds of thousands of students every year—it's a very satisfying endeavor."

In summary, Academic Systems illustrates the secret of effective Creators. They design and build complete solutions that are such a tightly interwoven mix of people, process, technology, information, and knowledge that they not only fit a problem or opportunity, but can evolve over time. In a world where product cycles are a matter of months and competition is global, creating differentiable and sustainable solutions requires this combination of complete and evolvable design.

The rest of this part covers in more depth and detail how the best Creators develop solutions and solve problems. You can either skip to the next part, "Deliver the Results" on page 203, or proceed. Each of the following chapters in turn explains how Creators start with the right people and ultimately progress to powerful, complete solutions.

- "Find the Right People for the Right Work: From Void to a Team" examines how to build a team with the right people and work process in place to set up a complete solution. The story of Microsoft Corporation, renowned for its human resources strategies and large-scale production capability, shows how the combination of recruiting and workflow contributes to their success.
- "Get the Tools to Do the Job: From a Team to Capability" illustrates how a Creator builds effective tools to support a team problem solving effort. NASA's long-term mission to Mars forms the backdrop for a discussion of the issues one faces in working with leading-edge technologies to design practical tools.

- "Target and Conserve Scarce Resources: From Capability to Resources" pinpoints how a Creator empowers a solution with the required resources. John Sawhill at the Nature Conservancy, one of the world's leading resource managers, tells about how he manages the ultimate resource—the wide diversity of species on the planet.
- "Get the Right Information to the Right People: From Resouces to Intelligence" explains how to create smart solutions by buttressing them with information. Dr. Kenneth Castro, the head of the Tuberculosis Division at The Centers for Disease Control, helps bring out what it takes to operate a system of informed professionals on a global scale to fight the battle against TB.
- "Design Solutions That Evolve: From Intelligence to Evolution" takes a cue from Nature as it shows how Creators move from smart solutions to living solutions that can easily adapt and evolve over time. Nobel Laureate Dr. Eric Wieschaus explains how the cells of an embryo construct themselves and why the secret underlying this natural process is at the heart of life itself.
- "Shift the Balance of Power: From Evolution to Power" culminates this part by chronicling the creation of a dominant solution in a competitive environment. The story of Microsoft and the Department of Justice illustrates not only what it takes to build powerful solutions but the limits to such power as well.

FIND THE RIGHT PEOPLE FOR THE RIGHT WORK

From a Void to a Team

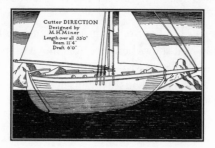

The work of a business, of a government, of most forms of human activity, is something pursued not by individuals but by teams.

—ANDREW GROVE

Creating a solution for any problem starts with finding a team of the right people to do the right work. Few solutions are successful or useful if they don't take into account the human abilities needed to use and manage the processes and tools involved. True push-button solutions are rare. Good solution design matches functional specifications with overall objectives, strategies, and key performance requirements. Creators then proceed to define the processes, recruit the people who will operate them, and choose the tools that will help them most. Some of the biggest and most costly mistakes in problem solving are made by concentrating too early or too exclusively on the technical elements of solutions, rather than on the needed talent and the structure of work.

Creators see people and their work in the context of a specific problem. Then and only then can the combination of effective tools, good processes, and great people make an unbeatable solution. Getting good people may be the hardest part. The ability to assess required skills, attract and retain talent, and divide labor to build a strong, interdependent team is one of the rarest and most sought-after of abilities. Do it right, and you can gradually assemble and tune a well-oiled machine. Do it poorly, and you'll be fighting a constant battle just to keep things in working order, much less solve problems and reach your goals.

Building and structuring a team or organization of any size must be done so that roles and responsibilities match talents and incentives that in turn match work requirements. As the largest and most successful software company on the planet, Microsoft's recruiting strategies are legendary, and their supporting tactics and systems have continued to mature and evolve into a highly refined machine for software production.

Microsoft Corporation's Recruiting and Production Machine

Few organizations have been as successful at this combination of great people and good processes as Microsoft. Their combination of skill acquisition and workflow design has built a formidable production capability. In any field, getting outstanding talent enriches the capability mix and creates a self-sustaining image as a center for the best. The right workflow and clear roles and responsibilities allow people to place themselves effectively in the midst of a dynamic work process and know how they relate to one another.

Fielding the right talent starts with having a clear idea of what you're looking for. This means a combination of general ability and expertise to fit specific positions. Good players need to be "t-shaped," with some mix of general and specialized skills. The best organizations tend to focus on the general skills, counting on them to drive career development and the learning and relearning of evolving specialties over time. Bill Gates's focus has been overall intelligence, ambition, business judgment, and technical expertise—with overall intelligence being the most important.

Once you know what you're looking for, you've then got to know where and how to find it. There is no substitute for knowing all you can about the top talent in your field. This means knowing who works for competitors and who's coming up in the ranks. It means having scouts who work hard to pinpoint the most interesting and potentially valuable candidates.

Microsoft's approach to recruiting is focused, aggressive, and selective. They target the best campuses and winnow 120,000 resumes per year down to a handful of "brilliant" hires (approximately 2 out of every 100 who apply). But they also proactively scour the world for the qualities of mind and problem solving ability unique to the production of high quality computer code. A recruiting Strike Force Team cold-calls those who work for competitors, as well as highly successful and intelligent people in a variety of professions.

Attracting interest is one thing, making good choices and getting people in the door is another. Evaluating a good fit between employee and company needs intensive work, combined with genuine opportunities for both parties to become familiar with each other. Microsoft increases their chances of getting a good fit in their hiring process by accepting only those they believe can be easily adapted to their way of doing business. The key is to let the teams solving the problems choose any new players and to have a rigorous selection process where everybody gets to participate in the decision but which doesn't sink to a lowest common denominator. Tests and problem solving situations are used in addition to dialogue in interviews. The Microsoft interview process is legendary for posing challenging problems and then evaluating not whether the answer is correct, but what strategies, methods, and approaches were employed.

When the right people have passed the test, then their challenge is to work well together. But what's the right work? It's the least number of coordinated actions that will create and constitute the solution. Anything else is waste. The right work is always a process, rather than a single job. The process, or workflow, is a set of actions, undertaken by people and/or machines, to solve a problem. It answers the question what needs to be done, how much, when, in what order, and by whom? For a company like Microsoft that produces computer software, it has several basic steps: planning, developing, and then stabilizing and shipping products.

Often, when a fresh problem presents itself and needs quick resolution, a team plunges in either without a process or with an outdated one that doesn't fit the problem. Still more often, roles and responsibilities are defined on an organizational chart without a workflow. Authorities and accountability may seem clear, but will inevitably become confused when it comes time to act. When workflow is addressed first, it can mean the difference between remaining paralyzed and getting a good start, or between getting a good start and generating real momentum.

Microsoft handles workflow with their Solutions Framework. The Framework is a combination of key roles (marketing, development, program management, testing, training, and logistics) mapped against a defined software development process (which has three steps—planning, development, and stabilization/shipping.) Both are used by all teams to produce all products. Every new project team gets a member, part-time or full-time, who fulfills one or more of these roles. Then the work process of creating computer software, moving from planning, needs assessment, and requirements definition, to design, coding, and testing, is mapped against those six roles. In this way, every phase is covered by multiple team members whose job is to collaborate and move problem resolution along.

Through this combination of people and processes that produce employees and software products, Microsoft has developed a complete solution to the problem of rapid manufacture of consumer software. Defining the right work and the right people so systematically virtually guarantees that—if given the right information and tools—its people are successful in creating the solutions Microsoft's customers need, over and over again.

Creation in Action: Build Your Own Farm System

Whether it's for your team or your company, take a moment to map out your farm system as if you were a major league baseball manager. Identify your big sources of talent, the specifications of people you are always on the lookout for. Determine who your scouts are that will spot and attract talent, figure out your selling points, and then your process for developing your hires once they become part of your organization (i.e., the major leagues). Then, start writing out the names of your key generations, from the ones that will be moving into retirement soon and those in their prime, to the rookies and the up-and-comers you've got your eye on but who aren't ready for the call. Your farm system is your process for managing human capital.

GET THE TOOLS TO DO THE JOB
From a Team to Capability

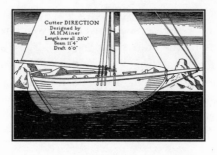

Factory work must be adapted to people, not people to machines.
—PEHR GYLLENHAMMAR

A team of good people need the right systems and tools to do the job. People plus tools equals capability. Creators must decide if existing tools will get the job done, if they can be customized, or if the novelty of the problem requires entirely new technologies and tools. Unnecessary new tools are often created when old ones will do just fine. Conversely, new opportunities to develop better tools are sometimes ignored because it has always been done a certain way before. When facing problems that have never been solved before, Creators usually end up working with a larger portion of "bleeding-edge" technologies that need to be handled with special care and discipline.

To get the right tools for a particular problem, Creators define clear requirements for what tools need to do and distill those into detailed, robust design specifications that can be built to. They proceed to evaluate technical alternatives, choose the most appropriate, and then meet those specifications with the most mainstream technologies possible. A Creator does not want to use a sports utility vehicle for the Indy 500, or a drag racer for an off-road trip.

About the only place lonelier than and as dangerous as the beach at Omaha, Utah, or Gold that George Marshall's troops landed on in 1944 would be the surface of Mars in 2020—which is the first possible date of a manned mission to that planet. NASA, which is currently in the lead in terms of both unmanned and any potential manned mission to Mars, has to think carefully about the tools required for man to make a historic journey to that new beachhead in the universe.

NASA and the Mars Expedition

Any mission to Mars will depend on a wide variety of tools to be successful. Developing these has proven a very difficult job indeed, with many mistakes as well as successes in the long journey of learning how to travel to the red planet. The moon is only three days away; it will probably take six months to get to Mars. Most of the tools help address the issue of how to keep astronauts alive and safe for the almost three-year duration of a mission. Instead of the three ships used for the Apollo moon landing, for example, the current "Mars Direct" plan (only one of several alternatives being considered) will need at least five. One to get into orbit, one to deliver cargo to the surface, one to fly the crew to Mars, one to land on the planet and one to get off it and come home. Once on the planet, the mission will need more robotic tools—like the rover Sojourner we came to know and love from the Mars Pathfinder expedition—to collect information on geology and atmosphere, perform experiments, and support the crew.

The range of technologies behind these tools is dizzying: from special propulsion systems to devices that can create fuel propellant from the Martian atmosphere; from sophisticated telecommunications to biotechnology for maintaining the astronaut's health. "We've talked about a chip in their ear that will be able to constantly take an astronaut's temperature, look at his blood count, and monitor his health throughout the two- or three-year voyage," says Lori Garver, NASA's associate administrator for policy and planning.

Before getting to these technologies and before any manned mission can take place, however, NASA has to get good enough at creating workable unmanned solutions that make a manned mission feasible. The record has been mixed so far, with at least one notable success—the Pathfinder expedition—and many notable failures, from the Mars Observer to the last several failed missions that forced a full stop in the Mars program earlier this year until the problems can be worked out.

NASA spends hundreds of millions of dollars on research, developing technologies that can produce just the right tools for the problems they expect to face. As Garver puts it, "You push at a lot of different ends—materials, propulsion, optics—and as those breakthroughs come, you put a program together based on a schedule that NASA sets out in its strategic plan to achieve overall scientific goals. We don't have a goal of a next generation telescope or spacecraft. We have a goal of seeing farther out into the universe, or exploring the solar system. And then the technology is driven by the goal." Just as with workflow design, it's the problem to be solved which comes first. The mission then drives the tools.

Out of the broader technological potential being developed, specific tools emerge to meet the objectives of any one particular mission. Take the hugely successful Pathfinder expedition, for example. It had two objectives—test a mobile rover that would get data on the planet's atmosphere and surface, and create a low-cost delivery system to transport it there. Everything developed for the mission had to meet requirements that would in turn achieve those objectives. Twenty-five completely new technologies were used to create the Pathfinder tool. Yet the project, led by engineer Tony Spear, hit its targets for almost one-tenth the cost of the Mars Viking expeditions two decades ago and in half the time, while delivering four times the expected amount of data. The members of the team accomplished this with better technology and highly disciplined problem solving that was based on clear, specific mission requirements and limited resources.

For instance, the Pathfinder team rigorously evaluated multiple solutions as it put together the complete mission package. To solve the problem of how to land the spacecraft safely, they considered two alternatives—a parachute that would slow it down or a retro-rocket that would put the brakes on and soften its landing. Then a creative engineer—Scott Hubbard—came up with the idea of airbags to cushion the impact. They now had three alternatives. As it turned out, the airbags could only work if Pathfinder was traveling less than 60 mph, and they calculated it would be moving at almost 140. No matter how they worked the numbers, no one solution would do the trick. In the end, they needed a combination of all three, which worked perfectly. This was a more complete solution they might not have arrived at had they not pushed hard at a variety of possible tools to solve the problem.

But there was another factor behind Pathfinder's success—robust design. (See Figure 5.2.) In the real world of Creators, tools have to be designed with lots of room for error. Performance is subpar. Predicted conditions change. Equipment breaks. And if tools break in the wrong place, where help is far away, then you better either be a good repairman, with easily substitutable components, and/ or have a spare. Engineers have a term for solutions that can handle all these challenges—robust. Robust solutions have reliable technology, redundant systems, liberal tolerances, multiple backups, and any components are tested, tested, and then tested again.

Finally, you can have the right tool and a creative and robust solution, but if your tool can't easily plug in to a variety of other tools, then it's of much less use to you. Tools today need to be designed for use in the "collective toolkits" that are building up around value chains and information networks. Outside the rarified world of space exploration, there is ever less room for unique, proprietary technologies. The level of technology interconnectedness—what some call the great convergence—demands that most new tools or technologies be thought of simultaneously from two perspectives: what they can do; and how they can work with an evolving, integrated global network of smart tools and machines.

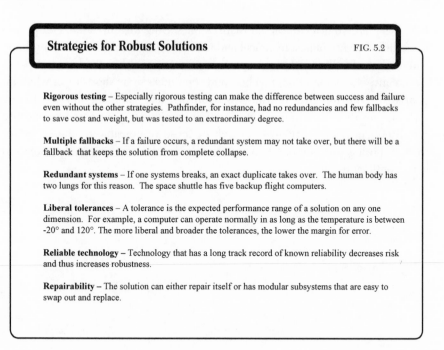

Strategies for Robust Solutions FIG. 5.2

Rigorous testing – Especially rigorous testing can make the difference between success and failure even without the other strategies. Pathfinder, for instance, had no redundancies and few fallbacks to save cost and weight, but was tested to an extraordinary degree.

Multiple fallbacks – If a failure occurs, a redundant system may not take over, but there will be a fallback that keeps the solution from complete collapse.

Redundant systems – If one systems breaks, an exact duplicate takes over. The human body has two lungs for this reason. The space shuttle has five backup flight computers.

Liberal tolerances – A tolerance is the expected performance range of a solution on any one dimension. For example, a computer can operate normally in as long as the temperature is between -20° and 120°. The more liberal and broader the tolerances, the lower the margin for error.

Reliable technology – Technology that has a long track record of known reliability decreases risk and thus increases robustness.

Repairability – The solution can either repair itself or has modular subsystems that are easy to swap out and replace.

Naturally, plug-in tools are much more viable once a technology has started to mature, because at the beginning, everyone's trying to figure out what tools are possible, not how they are going to fit together. As a result, plug-ins are hard for NASA to find; nevertheless, the same principle applies to tools that have to work together on a particular mission or set of missions. Every tool designer contributing to the Mars Mission has to think and plan for how his tool will work with others. Does it just need to interconnect? Is it serving as a fallback? Is it a redundant backup? Is it a bottleneck? Is it a single-point-of-failure, a highly vulnerable component on which the entire life of the system depends?

If a manned mission to Mars ever takes place, there will be an entire community of tools working with each other and with the astronauts to form a complete solution to the problem of traveling to the red planet. Behind those tools will be a wave of developing technology that will not only enable our first interplanetary journey, but, if history is any guide, will also transform our own planet in many unpredictable ways.

Creators in Action: Analyzing Alternative Technologies Before Picking Tools

Choose a problem or opportunity that is very important to you, and then spend several hours—if not a few days—getting a variety of points of view on one question: What are your technical alternatives for solving this problem? Get people from different disciplines, technical and nontechnical, familiar with the problem and totally unfamiliar. Get both experts and novices. Look at the broadest possible creative spectrum of approaches, and then make your short list of what appear to be the top five alternatives. Contrast and compare those with the technologies that were under consideration previous to your exercise, and use the discrepancies to challenge yourself or those responsible to choose better tools and bring your solution to a new level. Consider combining alternatives to get an optimal result.

TARGET AND CONSERVE
SCARCE RESOURCES
From Capability to Resources

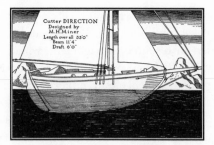

*Mere parsimony is not economy. Expense, and great expense,
may be an essential part of true economy. Economy is a
distributive virtue, and consists not in saving but selection.
Parsimony requires no providence, no sagacity, no powers of
combination, no comparison, no judgment.*

—EDMUND BURKE (1729–1797)

A capable team that lacks resources has no true action potential. Creators and their
solutions use time, energy, and materials (whether natural or man-made). Money
can help buy any or all of these, but it is merely a secondary claim on one of these
basic resources. Supplies are not always easily accessible or sufficient to meet a project's demand. And prices may vary significantly across suppliers and over time. As a
result, a competent Creator needs to master resource management—targeting, controlling, and conserving the scarce resources that are needed to get a job done. In a
competitive environment, with other individuals and firms trying to obtain the same
resources, this task takes on an added dimension of importance and complexity.

Creators ask: Which resources are the most important to the goal? Just how
scarce are they? Who else is competing for them? What is the state of supply and
demand? Is enough available at the right price?

The Nature Conservancy has spent many decades trying to conserve scarce natural resources both for and from the problem solving energies of mankind. Their highly successful, market-oriented methods blend the best thinking of nonprofit and private-sector minds. Because land is the source of so much energy and material, and therefore the primary fount of resources on the planet, the organizations that are experts at managing and conserving land have special lessons to teach in resource management.

John Sawhill, The Nature Conservancy and Sustaining Biodiversity

John Sawhill was the president of a major university, a senior cabinet official, and a leading partner in a global consulting firm. Throughout his career he had been a world-renowned expert in resource management, whether that resource was knowledge or energy. As CEO and president of the The Nature Conservancy (TNC) he faced his greatest challenge ever, protecting species to maintain biodiversity on our planet. For the last forty years, The Nature Conservancy has been one of the best examples of a nonprofit institution using profit-oriented strategies, management techniques, and a market orientation to achieve public goals with private-sector means. Over those forty years, by either purchasing or receiving gifts of land, TNC has protected over 12 million acres, in 1,600 separate preserves—the largest system of private sanctuaries in the world—managed from over 350 offices around the world and with $2.3 billion in assets. Their mission has always been to preserve plants and animals that represent the diversity of life. Sawhill called it the "Noah's Ark" strategy: "Like Noah, we were building an ark—or, more accurately, a lot of little arks." Their vision has been to protect as many endangered species as possible by acquiring the land on which they live.

As an organization, the Conservancy's greatest resources are its assets and its people, but after Sawhill had been there a few years, he couldn't help noticing that these critical resources weren't producing enough of the right results—protecting endangered species. Suspicions emerged when the bog turtle population in Schenob Brook in Massachusetts started declining, even though the land was protected. Scientific studies showed that activities in water resources outside of the boundaries of the preserve were affecting the health of the species. Soon, they realized the same problem was happening elsewhere. They couldn't just fence off a small piece of land and expect it to protect all the species that lived there. They had been focusing on one key asset, not all the critical resources. In the past, it had been easy to measure their success. All they had to do was look at the number of acres that had been protected and pat themselves on the back.

The Nature Conservancy's portfolio of land was increasing, but the more the scientists looked, the more clear it became that they needed to look at other resources beyond just land, such as water. But water is not a resource you can buy or control, like the land that had been the focus for decades of the Conservancy's activities. It is wider ranging, with complicated relationships between the many parties, upstream and downstream, who use and own rights to the water. It was a whole different ball game.

The Conservancy needed to develop an entirely new corporate strategy designed to target scarce resources, including land, water and air, and influence the behavior of those who used them. Their change in strategy for targeting and conserving scarce resources is a model for how to use scientific knowledge to improve problem solving effectiveness. They called their new strategy the "Last Great Places" program, and it focused on much larger ecosystems or tracts of land and water that—if they were managed effectively—could realistically be expected to affect the biodiversity of the area. The true scarce resource, they reaffirmed, is the species, not the water or the land alone. A more complete solution was needed to resolve their problem.

The primary lesson Sawhill learned from his career in managing resources was, he said, "You need to have a crystal clear vision of where you are going and what problem you are trying to solve. Don't hang onto extraneous assets or resources." The problem you are solving will determine what levels and types of resources you need, if you can only understand it well enough to discover the true implications for resource management.

In a short digression, Sawhill told a story about targeting and leveraging scarce resources that occurred when he became president of New York University (NYU), long before the Nature Conservancy. Here was the situation. There were many plans in the works at NYU and so much that needed to be done, but the coffers were bare. There was literally no money. So, he realized his tenure would not make much of an impact unless he could find some resources.

He started with the simplest idea of all, take an inventory of what you've got. And when he did this, he found out the university owned a company called Muller Macaroni. Far from being a resource itself, the company was actually a net drain, largely because of taxes that were being paid on dividends from operations. So here was a nonperforming asset, with value, that could be sold—with the proceeds to be used to create a tax-free endowment that would earn interest, which could be applied to other purposes directly associated with the university's mission.

He put the company on the auction block, and his eyes twinkled when he described the final sale. "I had brought a piece of paper in my front pocket with the highest possible price I thought I could sell it for. But at the last minute, I decided to ask for more, $115 million, and he agreed right away. The piece of paper had $85 million written on it."

When he got to the Conservancy, Sawhill followed his own advice and not only took an inventory of assets but commissioned a study to advise him on the strategic use of assets. The main question was, should The Nature Conservancy go global and broaden its impact or try to make better use of the resources and as-

---

Strategies for Using Resouces More Effectively   FIG. 5.3

Conservation – The simplest and easiest way is simply to use less. Determine how much you absolutely need to use .

Substitutes – Many resources have substitutes, which can perform the same function in a cheaper, less wasteful way.

Sourcing – This option involves letting someone else who is an expert at managing the resource take control as a supplier.

Reuse – Reusing partial or previous solutions to problems saves time and energy, and in areas like knowledge management and software development, is proving a potent strategy.

Recycling – Recycling differs from reuse in that it refers directly to resource usage rather than to solutions. Recycling can effectively increase the availability of resources.

Efficiency – Improving efficiency simply means wasting less. Improved processes and technologies can often help improve efficiency.

Sharing (collusion) and Scaling – Finally, sharing resources for multiple uses or in order to benefit from economies of scale can also increase resource yields.

Selling—Switching control of an asset or resource to someone who will get more value out of it than you can.

---

sets it had? The answer turned out to be the second. This decision was one input into the new conservation strategy discussed above. It made more sense to figure out how to use existing assets, through new strategies, to get better mission results, and to worry later about how broadly the new strategy, if it was successful, could be applied.

There are a variety of ways to get the most out of your resource base. (See Figure 5.3.) If you are regularly evaluating all these options and really looking for ways to increase the yield on your scarce resources, you will get better results. The Nature Conservancy's results have consequences for all of us—the protection of the most priceless resources in existence—diverse forms of life.

Creators in Action: Take Stock

Make a list of what you believe to be your scarcest resources and assets, and why. Then take a complete inventory of them and see what you've actually got. Now, with your inventory in hand, write down the list of the three most important problems and opportunities you face in the next one to two years. Then answer these questions: What are the scarce resources that are critical to solving those problems? Do you have the scarce resources you need? Do you have extraneous resources that could be offloaded to provide you more of what's lacking? Now, make a plan to reallocate your stock of resources and assets to align them with the real problems you're facing.

GET THE RIGHT INFORMATION
TO THE RIGHT PEOPLE

From Resources to Intelligence

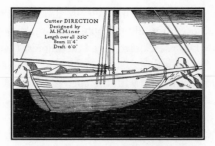

> *"A man's judgment cannot be better than the information on which he has based it. Give him no news, or present him only with distorted and incomplete data, with ignorant, sloppy, or biased reporting, with propaganda and deliberate falsehoods, and you destroy his whole reasoning process . . . "*
>
> **–ARTHUR SULZBERGER (1891–1968)**

Smart solutions incorporate intelligence, experience, and decisionmaking. Good decisionmaking demands the best available information. Every solution needs an information system, whether simple or complex, to get the right information to the right people in a form they can use.

One of the most demanding challenges for Creators in information age problem solving is building information systems that create, store, and deliver the right information, keeping it safe, accurate, and up-to-date and then making it available when needed. The best information systems derive their power from a clear understanding of who needs to know what, when, and why, which then serves as a basis for sophisticated automation.

One of the most apparently successful solutions of the last half century to the problem of infectious disease has been antibiotic drugs. They have addressed a host of mortal afflictions and alleviated much suffering. Yet as we are now discovering, because the solution was incomplete and not very "smart" (i.e., physicians and patients did not understand how damaging incomplete dosages were), it has created an even larger problem—drug-resistant strains of bacteria that nothing can kill.

The CDC and the Crusade Against Tuberculosis

At the forefront of trying to resolve this issue are the Centers for Disease Control (CDC). When a disease with epidemic potential breaks out somewhere in the world, the Centers for Disease Control need the highest quality and reliability of information exchange to fight their battles against an often unknown and unseen biological enemy. Such is the case with the current worldwide resurgence of the killer bacteria tuberculosis (TB)—just one of the many diseases that may be resurgent due to ineffective use of antibiotics.

TB still kills some 2 million people around the globe each year—with AIDS its only rival as the deadliest infectious disease. In fact, the World Health Organization declared TB a global emergency in 1993. With a smaller world, TB—a disease of the lungs that is spread when an infected person coughs into the air—is a threat to anyone. It can now spread around the world in twenty-four hours, if one infected person coughs into an airliner cabin full of passengers. With such highly communicable diseases, prevention, reaction, and treatment are all important.

For the CDC and other health organizations waging a global war on TB, much of their work revolves around getting the right information to the right people at the right time. It's imperative for three reasons—prevention, reaction, and elimination (i.e., preventing the problem in the first place, reacting quickly to a problem to get a solution in place, and coordinating strategies to make solutions work and resolve a problem completely).

First, the right information can prevent an outbreak. For instance, doctors believe the frightening new strains of drug-resistant TB are caused when sick people are given the wrong medicine or don't take the drugs for a long enough period. In other words, many doctors and patients simply misuse the available drugs because they are poorly educated or misinformed. Better information on a complete solution (i.e., how to use available drugs) could stop new strains from developing in the first place.

Second, after an outbreak of a new strain or a reemergence of an old one, early information gives the detectives at the CDC a head start in understanding and curtailing the spread of the disease. In the age of biological weapons, early warning has a particularly important but depressing use: to determine as quickly as possible whether a new outbreak is likely to be a military attack by a foreign power.

Third, in the process of eliminating a disease, information helps the CDC and its network of public health organizations around the world in their attempts to get complete, effective solutions in place by determining the pattern of the spread of the disease and the effectiveness of treatments.

Developing an information capability doesn't start with a new computer. It starts with the people who need to be informed. What problems are they trying to solve? What decisions do they need to make? What responsibilities do they have for communication with one another and outside customers or stakeholders? These questions help identify the key players and their information needs.

For many years, the CDC, as an American agency, regarded tuberculosis as an American problem, and the key players as American physicians, nurses, and public health officials. But with the explosion of travel to and from these shores, the United States has become far more vulnerable to the global health environment.

Now the CDC has shifted to a global view of the disease. The key players are still doctors, health care workers, and public health officials, but from all over the world. Physicians and nurses are the eyes and ears of the CDC as they make decisions about patients affected with disease, yet they may have only limited knowledge of TB and its treatment and prevention. Public health officials must marshal public resources to aid in the massive campaigns necessary—such as vaccination programs—to prevent a disease or to eliminate one. But in countries with no history of combating TB effectively, such campaigns may seem a waste of resources.

Identifying the key decisionmakers, what they need, and how to engage them in an information system that supports a complete solution is only a first step. People can be very peculiar about how they give and receive information. On the giving end, if they do not trust that it will be put to good use, they will not make an effort to deliver it effectively. On the receiving end, if it is not offered in a meaningful format, with adequate assurance of the quality or in a way that is insensitive to culture or style issues, it will be rejected. Inattention to these principles can destroy the usefulness of an entire information system—no matter how accurate and valuable the information may be or how good the automation behind it is.

Much of the value of information depends on the presentation, whether that means a speaker presenting himself effectively or creating just the right chart to display a data set. In some places, the CDC and global health officials have to take special care with how they shape and deliver information. In Russia, for instance, Americans can't just stampede in with the new methods, says Castro, even though the country has an alarming TB crisis in its prison system. An estimated 100,000 of Russia's one million inmates already have TB, and another 30,000 were expected to catch it in 1999. The filthy and overcrowded jails have been described as incubators for the bacteria. The rate of TB infection in Russia's jails is about sixty times what the WHO considers an epidemic.

But some Russian public health officials and physicians find it hard to let go of their old ways. "The approach to TB in many parts of Russia is not unlike our approach a few decades ago, where we relied very heavily on doing surgery, on sanatoria, and less so on outpatient treatment with a drug regime, " says Castro.

"There has been, as a result of the years of Cold War, relative isolation, where many of the Russian professionals were not exposed to the western approach to TB," says Castro. "As a result they're not immediately wanting to abandon what they've learned in favor of something they haven't seen in practice. To get our information across, there's some convincing, a buy-in, that needs to take place, not by having them look at the U.S. reality, but look at it in their own environment." This means presenting CDC approaches with a sensitivity to and understanding of how Russian physicians view their patients, their medical philosophy, their scientific approach, and their cultural norms.

Good information has to be in acceptable form and has to arrive in a timely fashion to drive effective solutions. Information is useless if it's stuck away in a file cabinet or a database and not available when needed for decisionmaking. Making information available appropriately is especially difficult when situations are complex and changing rapidly, as in the outbreak of a major disease.

When New York City suffered a TB outbreak in the 1990s, state and federal officials raced to contain it—eventually building a modernized isolation ward at Rikers Island and closing down the biggest homeless shelters. Health workers had to make rounds at crack houses, subway stations, and parks to make sure the sick—many of them homeless and drug addicts—were taking their medication. "We had to deploy new resources," says Castro. "We hired new staff, new outreach workers, many who came from that community, so they could gain access to a homeless individual under the bridge to make sure they completed their treatment."

Although observing a patient's ingestion of drugs to ensure a complete solution was the goal, Castro says, he thinks it worked so well because the health workers looked at information on all of the patient's problems and were able to respond and assist in a timely fashion. They helped refer them to drug rehab programs or, if they were homeless, helped them gain access to HUD-sponsored single-room occupancy hotels. By addressing the patient's overall health, and not just the particular disease, health care workers gave patients more reason to stick with the months-long program. This new approach wove the patient into the CDC solution and both offered and yielded new types of information at a time when the patient needed it. Consequently, it created an incentive for a higher level of involvement and participation in the solution.

So, what can the CDC tell us about where we stand in the battle against TB? The truth is, news from the front is mixed. Castro's division refers to TB "elimination" rather than "eradication." Elimination is defined as bringing down TB to one case per million people by the year 2010. Eradication would mean getting rid of it altogether, like small pox. Does that mean eradication is even possible? "Not with the tools that we have in hand," says Castro. "You probably would need a very good vaccine. With a good vaccine we could talk about eradication of TB, but not with what we have in hand." In 1996, the Director of the CDC went even further, saying "We know we will never conquer infectious diseases. The questions is whether we can control these organisms so we can coexist."

If there is a field where we have created a misleading aura of confidence in tools and those who use them to solve our problems, it is medicine. The most dangerous attitude for any problem solver to adopt, especially when facing a major challenge, is that simply getting the right tool will resolve it. Getting the right tool is nearly always more complicated than it appears. In trying to solve the problem of infectious diseases, we've gotten some good tools, but they cure rather than prevent, the physicians haven't guided their use effectively, patients haven't used them well, and we haven't focused on a complete solution until it's almost too late. As drug-resistant bacteria begin to outpace our ability to create new pharmaceutical tools to deal with them, it remains to be seen who is the better problem solver, our species or theirs.

Creators in Action: Pinpointing Information Needs

Pick a key problem or opportunity and the corresponding solution you have developed, and then make a short list of the most important decisionmakers who are part of the solution. Go to each of these individuals and ask them these questions: What are the most important decisions you make? Why? What type of information do you need, in what form and at what time to make those decisions in the best possible fashion? Are you getting that now? If not, what are the most important pieces you are missing? Use their responses to these questions to improve your ability to put together an information system that will fully support your solution.

DESIGN SOLUTIONS
THAT EVOLVE
From Intelligence to Evolution

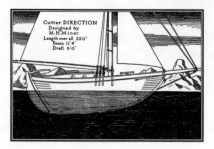

As with most media from which things are built,
whether the thing is a cathedral, a bacterium, a sonnet,
a fugue or a word processor, architecture dominates material.

—ALAN KAY

The best-designed solution is not just one that works well, nor one that is easy and economical to repair, nor even one that works well with other solutions if necessary. The best-designed solution can evolve and be upgraded in design and functionality as it learns to perform in changing environments.

To achieve evolvability, Creators must serve two conflicting demands. The first, integration, simply requires that all the components of a solution work well with one another. But evolvability and flexibility, the second, means that the solution can respond quickly and fluidly to changes in the environment. To achieve that kind of flexibility, Creators must see to it that different pieces of a solution have autonomy and adaptability. As the plug-and-play information economy picks up pace, solutions are simultaneously getting smarter, more autonomous, and more interdependent—whether it be a nano-tool, a piece of smart material, or a software agent.

If a species is a solution to the problem of life surviving in a particular ecological niche, the most complex solution we know of is the human body, and the Nobel prize winners who discovered how it builds itself from a single cell to the embryo stage, Dr. Eric Weischaus and Dr. Christiane Nusslein-Volhard, explain the natural principles that guide that process in a way that suggests how Creators can design robust, evolvable solutions.

Dr. Eric Wieschaus on the Design and Growth of Embryos

Wieschaus and Nusslein-Volhard shared the Nobel Prize in medicine or physiology with Edward B. Lewis in 1995 for their work illuminating how a cluster of cells, in the first few hours and days after fertilization, lays down a "body plan," or architecture, for an organism. This design will integrate the way billions of independent cells work together to build the organism. For both scientists, the fascination is with patterns and relationships, how things fit together, yet remain separate and autonomous. "It occurred to us," Nusslein-Volhard explained once of her experiments, "that you can't really know what a gene does without knowing how it fits in with other genes. Is it unique or one of many? How many? What is its place in the hierarchy? It seemed essential to find out how complicated the system was." "How does something so complex develop out of something so simple?" she asked herself time and again.

Part of the answer is the remarkable ability of cells to be both specialists and generalists as they develop into a complex organism. If you want optimal performance for one particular problem, then an intricately assembled combination of hand-picked specialists is the right way to go. If you want a solution that will evolve fastest and most flexibly over a longer period of time, then you want a better mix of general and specialized capability. This latter turns out to be exactly how embryos are designed. "The basic idea is that all of the cells have most of the machinery to do everything," Wieschaus explained.

There is an analogy here to the "mass customization" approach that has replaced the traditional assembly line at Volvo and other manufacturing organizations. On the new, team-oriented assembly line, the workers, like embryonic cells, are generalists: Any one of them has the cross-training to do any of the necessary jobs. Having this general capability clearly makes it less necessary that specific workers—or specific cells—arrange themselves in perfect physical relationship to one another. Instead they can communicate with one another, make choices, and then become one thing or another for each particular engine.

As cells grow, a particular gene "turns on," thereby deciding whether to become skin or muscle, join the head or some other part of the body. "What's ultimately a hundredfold difference in growth, or a hundredfold difference in whether you're going to be muscle or whether you're going to be skin, comes down to what was initially just a subtle little difference," Wieschaus explained.

"Because genes respond in a decisive, binary switch kind of way—turn on or turn off—they can make decisions. And they make decisions based on what are essentially environmental cues or signals or graded distributions of chemicals that are kind of murky themselves. Genes are made in a way that they can respond and make these choices and come on or not. And these choices add up."

Wieschaus sees an analogy to a team of house cleaners who arrive in a dirty home and assign themselves different tasks. "It's as though the house cleaners come into your house and there are cues, different grades of dirtiness, and they each have thresholds," Wieschaus said. "And so one of them picks the dirtiest area and one of them picks the less dirty area and without talking at all to each other they assign themselves tasks. That would be how individual genes respond to a gradient of dirtiness in your house. You could see how the cleaners would gravitate and assign themselves different tasks without ever talking to each other because it's the situation that defines how the division of labor is created for each household solution."

The difficulty lies in those gray areas where the room is somewhat dirty, Wieschaus said, and there are potentially overlapping responsibilities. "Cells have a mechanism to talk with each other and make sure, if it's important that only one cell does a particular job, they have a way of saying, 'Well, if you're going to do it, then I won't do it.' When a cell makes a decision, it communicates to the other cells something that essentially precludes them from making that same choice."

The process is called "lateral inhibition." "You inhibit your neighbors, the people who are lateral to you, from making the same choices that you make," Wieschaus said. "And that insures (if it's important) that if one cell makes this choice the other cells have to make another choice." In a similar way, when one line worker in a production team at Volvo steps up to perform a particular task, the other workers recognize that they are free to do other work. So the first step, Wieschaus said, is that "somebody makes the decision. The second step is how the cells respond, how you keep anybody else from making that same decision."

Communication between cells alters and adapts over time as the organism grows and develops to scale. A cell "changes how hard it sticks to other cells, it changes where it is, it changes the types of proteins that it makes and that it sends out to other cells. So the communication between cells is constantly changing and constantly reflects the state of growth that the cell is in at that time. That's useful information to all the other cells, of course, because what they do and what's available for them to do depends on the presence of and messages from other cells."

In other words, the embryo builds itself through constant and sensitive communication between components that have a mixture of general and specialized abilities. Those abilities themselves evolve toward ever more specialized roles as the building process continues. Ultimately, once the organism (solution) is completed, no more learning is necessary. Then, to change the physical architecture of the organism and continue life, starting a new generation through reproduction is required.

Like cells, workers need to create a solution and then go on to create another, and another. Human problem solvers are more sophisticated than embryonic cells—they don't have to wait for the next generation of problem solvers to be born, only for the next problem solving assignment. Still, the flexibility of cells provides another guideline for the organization of human problem solving teams.

Wieschaus says his greatest finding is that genes operate the same, whether they're in fruit flies or humans: "It didn't take any new decisionmaking strategies or any new gene products to make it human versus make a fly. Those fundamental strategies for cell planning, communication, and decisionmaking evolved, arose in the primitive ancestor of both flies and humans."

"That general framework for how to build solutions, if you will, is at the core of all life on Earth. Once that had evolved, then the original organism was set to suddenly diversify, to spread out and radiate and form all the different types of animals and plants that exist today in the world," explained Wieschaus. "Because what that organism had was its fundamental decisionmaking ability and a fundamental duty to communicate those decisions between cells and set up patterns."

Here is the wisdom which nature offers us for solution design and construction. The more flexible and evolvable you want your solutions, the more important it is to develop and refine your metaprocesses of problem solving, decisionmaking, and communication among the Creators who build them. To guarantee solutions that can evolve, creative teams must be self-organizing according to a universal process and set of principles. This way, they too can evolve by reorganizing to suit each new problem solving challenge.

Creators in Action: Designing a Solution Architecture

Pick the solution you're involved with that is the most complex and also the most repetitive—meaning it's something you build over and over again. Now imagine the individual workers as cells, and the process of solution as a growing embryo. How can you apply the lessons of nature to improve your process of construction? For instance, how can you increase the cross-training of your employees to cover broader ground and simultaneously intensify communication and teamwork between them? Most importantly, map out at the very highest level a "constitution" or solution architecture of principles that drive how decisions are made and problems are solved in your organization. This document will be the core of your evolutionary ability.

SHIFT THE BALANCE OF POWER
From Evolution to Power

*The power of a man is his present means to
obtain some future apparent good.*

—THOMAS HOBBES (1588–1679)

Solutions don't work if people don't want them. And whether they want a solution, or want someone else to have it, depends on how key players in a territory view their interests. In any organization, industry, or political entity, there are people with goals the same as yours, similar to yours, and in conflict with yours. There are people without goals and those who don't know what a goal is. There are those who will shift their goals at a moment's notice and others who will stubbornly stick to a given path no matter what happens around them. Building and designing complete solutions has to encompass how to win the competitive battles that are inevitable between your solutions and others. Shifting the balance of power in your favor is ultimately what will allow your solution to begin to work the way you've designed it to.

History shows that, whether in politics, nature, economics, or military affairs, great imbalances of power are destructive. Too little power, or power that is too fragmented, is more likely to produce chaos and disorganization than innovation. Too much concentrated power, as in the case of a monopolist, can favor one set of solutions in the marketplace so overwhelmingly that it stifles innovation. (See Figure 5.4.) The principle of both gaining and balancing power is thus an essential one for any problem solver. And what better example of the danger of ignoring this principle than Microsoft's ability to grow such a successful company and yet go too far and bring on the antitrust case brought by the U.S. government against it? Whether you belong to a competitive workgroup, company, or community, the same laws of gaining and balancing power that apply to Microsoft will apply to you as well.

Microsoft and the Department of Justice Antitrust Case

When a Microsoft executive threatened to cut off the "air supply" of a competitor who didn't bow to the company's wishes, the memo's fighting words came to exemplify the federal government's case that the computer giant had crossed the line. In its extraordinary antitrust case against Microsoft, the federal government charged the company with using illegal tactics to bully or stamp out competitors, to the detriment of consumers.

It had been a long road for Gates and company from 1975, when they first entered the market for operating systems software, to the Department of Justice decision to prosecute the organization. For decades, Microsoft had been first admired, then feared, as it executed a series of effective strategic and tactical moves to acquire power.

Whether you're powerless and trying to gain power or powerful and trying to protect or balance power, first you have to assess things as they are. How many

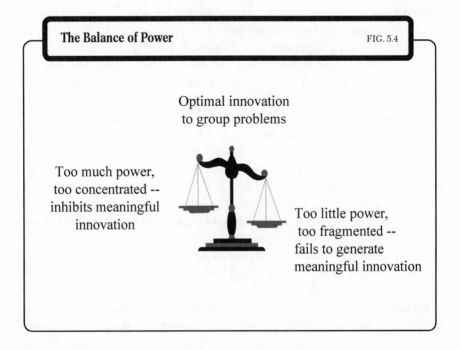

The Balance of Power   FIG. 5.4

Optimal innovation
to group problems

Too much power,
too concentrated --
inhibits meaningful
innovation

Too little power,
too fragmented --
fails to generate
meaningful innovation

players are there? What is their relative power? Are new players emerging regularly and rapidly or infrequently and slowly? Who is gaining or losing power?
How fast? And perhaps most importantly, what are the players using their power
for? Is it temporary or lasting in its effects? Will power in the system balance itself out or is intervention necessary?

On Microsoft's way to gaining power during the late '70s and early '80s, Gates
made a series of strategic judgments about the balance of power in the computer
industry that set the stage for his ultimate success. First was the judgment behind the focus on software. He judged the power of hardware providers was already in decline. "I thought we should only do software. When you have the
microprocessor doubling in power every two years, in a sense you can think of
computer power as almost free. So you ask, why be in the business of making
something that's almost free? What is the scarce resource? What is it that limits
being able to get value out of that infinite computing power? Software." Second,
he focused on the operating system, the most fundamental component of the
computer, rather than on any particular application. This focus would create
power by taking the critical intervening position between the machine and the
user. Third was his assessment of his dual customer base—the ultimate users of
software, but even more importantly the developers of applications software.
Developers were the focus of the powerful intellectual capital that would have to
be marshaled and controlled to dominate software markets.

Once you've assessed a balance and determined that it is in your interest to
change it, then you need to plan a new balance. Will you simply take a small toehold? Are you going to fight for a majority share? Or are you going to overthrow
the dominant player? Plotting a new balance is a nontrivial task. One has to understand the existing alignments and interests of the players to figure out how
they can be rearranged. But one way or another, a reconfiguration of power always comes down to building new capability, constraining capability, or allying to
realign the balance of power. Either one or all three of those options are the
means by which you can shape a new balance of power—whether it is in your office, your neighborhood, your company, or your industry.

In its rise to power, Microsoft pursued all of these strategies to create a new
balance of power in the software industry. It built a powerful internal capability,
by attracting high-quality talent and driving that talent with a fierce desire to succeed. It created alliances with developers, hardware providers, and anyone connected to the operating system of a computer, that would protect the Microsoft
solution at the expense of other competitors. Finally, it constrained the capability
of those competitors. And it is at this last step that it ran into trouble. Those constraints were what created the potential harm to consumers specifically and innovation in general.

Reshaping a balance of power means creating winners and losers. Everyone
fights and jockeys for position. Energy and resources are expended. Injuries are

part of the game. Gloating in victory and suffering in defeat go with the territory. Reshaping power relationships takes unrelenting pressure and determination, the ability to cut deals, reassess strategies, and maneuver oneself into a position of power through sheer persistence and skill. Microsoft demonstrated all of these skills in creating its massive power base from scratch.

But that same fierce persistence to reshape the balance of power is where Microsoft went too far, according to David Boies, the attorney hired by the Justice Department to make the government's case. Microsoft cofounder Bill Gates knew in May 1995 that a new competitor was on the horizon, writing in a memo that Netscape could hurt Windows. He wanted to negotiate with Netscape, proposing that the upstart be paid off or Microsoft buy a chunk of it. "What you have here is," Boies argued at trial, "in and of itself an attempt at monopolization" and "restraint of trade." Boies, known for his mastery of detail in the courtroom—he played bridge professionally before his wife made him get a real job—would go on to charge that one of Gates's assistants threatened to "choke Netscape's air supply" if it didn't go along.

Microsoft had a hold over companies like Netscape, Boies argued, because such companies had to know Microsoft's Application Program Interfaces, or APIs, to connect to Windows. And for three months, Microsoft withheld APIs that Netscape needed to be compatible with Windows. Boies said that Microsoft then put in place a "predatory pricing campaign" that gave its browser away, bundling it with Windows, whereas Netscape was trying to sell its browsers.

As further evidence of Microsoft's predatory ways, Boies argued that Gates had tried to coerce America Online into dumping Netscape's browser and promoting Microsoft's Internet Explorer. Boies offered up a January 1996 e-mail in which an executive from America Online paraphrased a conversation with Gates: "Gates delivered a characteristically blunt query: how much do we need to pay you to screw Netscape?" Microsoft was also searching for ways, Boies argued, to make it harder for PC manufacturers to reconfigure screens displaying the Windows icon. It was a manipulation of technology, Boies contended, not for innovation or to help customers, but to strangle the competition.

In the government's bid to restrain the software maker's power, the Microsoft trial presents an interesting challenge: to shape a new balance of power in cyberspace. The eventual solution—whether it is negotiated or imposed by the courts—is also likely to contain all three elements needed to shift power: Allowing new capability to thrive might involve damage awards that would fuel enhanced competitiveness. Constraining capability would mean limits put on Microsoft's ability to participate in certain types of markets and products. And realigning the balance of power would involve some kind of breakup of the giant corporation.

The process of reshaping a balance of power can be likened to turning a diamond formation into a wing formation in football. (See Figure 5.5.) You need to

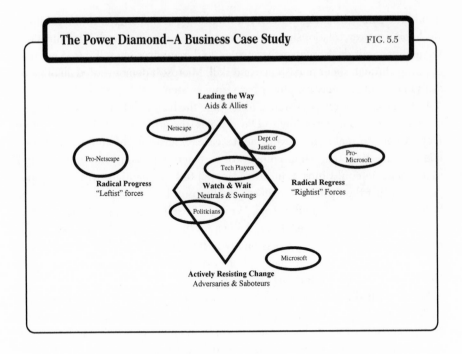

The Power Diamond–A Business Case Study   FIG. 5.5

Leading the Way
Aids & Allies

Netscape

Dept of
Justice

Pro-Netscape

Pro-
Microsoft

Tech Players

Radical Progress   **Watch & Wait**   **Radical Regress**
"Leftist" forces   Neutrals & Swings   "Rightist" Forces

Politicians

Microsoft

Actively Resisting Change
Adversaries & Saboteurs

lop off the bottom of the diamond (the players who are working against you), shape and steer it in a favorable direction, and extend the body of the diamond itself, spreading its wings by recruiting, attracting, and converting those players to your effort. This "flying wing" shape has more than symbolic significance, because it is with this type of configuration that you can actually take off and get your solution moving, concentrating on implementation and steering the formation successfully toward your targeted destination.

Before the judge even ruled, one thing was clear: If the Justice Department wanted to even the playing field in the technology world, it had some impact. Microsoft had been chastened, analysts said, and computer manufacturers were beginning to feel emboldened to sell personal computers that carried the systems of Microsoft rivals. Red Hat software had taken on the Microsoft operating system monopoly. Transmeta had taken on the Intel microchip position, which often cooperated with Microsoft in the "Wintel" dynasty, so named by those who saw Windows and Intel as in effect a cartel. The balance of power was changing, just the way the government hoped it would. The diamond was already reshaping itself in the massive computer industry, with AOL taking the place of Netscape in competing with Microsoft for the next generation interface of the global computer.

That is a message likely to resonate for some time throughout the high technology industry and may extend into the content and programming industries as well, with the advent of huge deals like that of AOL and Time-Warner. The cries are already starting that such concentrations of power mean doom for consumer choice and the freedom of speech and information in a twenty-first century democracy. Only time will tell, but the Microsoft case has clearly shown that no matter how sophisticated our technologies, the laws of acquiring and balancing power haven't changed a bit. As Shakespeare wrote, "O! it is excellent / to have a giant's strength, but it is tyrannous / to use it like a giant."

Creators in Action: Shape Your Own Flying Wing

Pick a situation you're in where you're either currently or potentially vulnerable to outside forces. It could be someone after your job, another team after your project, or a competitor after your clients. Map out your own political diamond, with the forces against, for, neutral, to the right and to the left. Actually write down the names of key players on the diamond. Now formulate a strategy for making it into a flying wing. First, figure out how to neutralize adversaries. Second, work out how to convert neutrals. Third, energize your own constituency. If you can execute this, your troubles and sense of vulnerability may soon be behind you.

CHARACTERISTICS OF
A CREATOR

General characteristics and purpose: Creators emphasize solutions that are technically elegant or that have the capability to solve multiple problems. Their goal is designing end-to-end, complete, evolvable solutions. Creators enjoy all the aspects of creating something tangible. They may focus on design rather than construction, or enjoy both. But their passion involves creating things that live or have some sort of lasting character—whether it be a form of life, a sculpture, or a machine. They value quality, precision, efficiency, skill, and technology. For most Creators, relationships, general knowledge, and creative ideas are less important.

Strengths: Creators build the solutions necessary to solve problems on a continuous basis. They conceptualize design, formulate specifications, help create

---

Skill Levels of Creation   TABLE 5.1

Level 1   Shows ability and aptitude for making things.
Level 2   Can make things of some reasonable complexity that are also useful.
Level 3   Show repeatable ability to improve on a design and evolve it through multiple iterations.
Level 4   Able to achieve necessary discipline and skill to build large scale devices in the field.
Level 5   Able to build difficult and/or large scale devices, as appropriate, that are extremely successful.
Level 6   Able to build successful solutions consistently and repeatably.
Level 7   Conceives, creates and builds a lasting solution series that changes human capabilities.

construction budgets, and produce the solutions at the right time in the right form—to the best of their knowledge. They are instinctively concerned about developing technologies and techniques to solve more than one type of problem.

Weaknesses: The most important weakness of Creators is their infatuation with technology and building irrespective of the nature of the problem. When something needs to get done on time and on budget, engineers and designers are frequently the last to compromise on an 80 percent solution, preferring something more perfect and elegant than workable. In a project context, as opposed to R&D, this refusal to compromise can be a serious liability.

Interactions with other types of problem solvers: Creators have a strong affinity for Performers, the people who will live in or use their contraptions. The Creator's solution will not resolve the problem unless the Performer uses and applies it well. And a Performer who needs to get to a particular destination won't make it without a viable solution. Moreover, because more and more solution creation takes place in iterative fashion according to the spiral method, Creators and Performers are typically working in very close concert with one another. Creators can also have natural alliances with Innovators if their plans and points of view are well aligned. But mix a practical Creator who needs to get a solution built on time with an Innovator who wants to bring a great deal of style and form to add to function, and it will be a volatile mix. Similarly, Creators need Communicators, and they appreciate them as long as they are practical and not too touchy-feely. For most Creators, Playmakers are a necessary evil, the ones who tend to be in the spotlight and get credit as leaders. That relationship works well when there is a deep amount of mutual respect for differing talents and the Playmaker makes an extra effort to give a Creator credit. Creators have a natural affinity with Discoverers, whose knowledge can be tremendously useful to an intelligent Creator, by offering not only new technical alternatives but also helpful design inputs.

Typical mishandling: Creators get into the most trouble when they are left in limbo—neither the focus of a specific problem solving effort nor the focus of an R&D effort. This kind of situation usually means they are expected to constantly meet unpredictable and changing demands for solutions outside an organized problem solving process.

Guidance for Creation

Vital Principles: Rules and Laws That Bear on Creation

- The best people often are the biggest part of a solution.
- Time spent up front on good design is harvested on the back end in easier execution.

- Specifications without requirements will create a solution but not solve a problem.
- Pursue alternatives: There are nearly always multiple solutions to a problem.
- Imitation is the sincerest form of flattery, and its faster, easier, and cheaper.
- One and done: Get the right information the first time.
- Always have a mix of specialists and generalists.
- Solutions to large-scale problems differ substantially from solutions to smaller-scale problems.
- Architecture and process drive evolvability.
- Tit for tat: Play fair until the hardball starts, then play hard.

Diagnostics: How Well Are You Creating the Solutions to Your Problems?

- Do you have the people you need, organized with the right roles and responsibilities? Is their work process efficient and do they work together well?
- Do they have the tools they need and can they use them well? Are they the best tools available? Do they have the help they need, and is it the right help? Are the tools defining the problem or is the problem defining the tools? Are your solutions robust? Are they working together or against one another? Do you have an architecture that defines the component solutions and how the pieces of the puzzle fit together?
- Do you know what your scarcest resources are? Can you distinguish them from your assets? How are your scarce resources critical to solving your problem or opportunity? What are your sources? What is your return on them? Are your supplies under control? How well are you allocating your scarce resources?
- What are the biggest, most frequent decisions being made? Who makes them, and what information do those people need, in what form, when? How well informed are they now? How can you get them the right information at the right time?
- Do you know the current state of power in your environment? Who are the major and minor players? How much power do they really have? How much do you have? How much do you want? How much can you realistically get? Who would be on your side? Who would be against you? What deal structures would allow you to get the power you decide to go for? How long might it take?

Syndromes: Diseases That Can Plague
Your Ability to Create the Best Solutions

- "Who's on First?"—Poor division of labor and responsibility, leading to confusion
- "If it doesn't fit, force it"—Forcing old workflow on a new problem
- "Hammers looking for nails"—Solutions looking for problems
- "Create a new problem"—Poorly designed solution, creating more problems than it solves
- "Fly by the seat of your pants"—Designing on the fly without a disciplined process
- "Waste and underinvestment"—Failure to take into account the full cost of waste created by a solution, thereby miscalculating the potential for new investments
- "Imperfect market"—Allocation of resources without good information or other assumptions underlying a healthy market
- "Box canyon"—Trapped with a proprietary technology or custom design that doesn't work with anyone else's
- "Grand design"—Grand architecture for a solution, which eventually collapses due to overwhelming complexity
- "Archipelago"—Islands of assets that are separated and not shared because of organization structure or professional myopia

Going Further

Resources for further study. (See also sources and notes for Part 5 on page 272.)

Books

Ball, Philip. *Made to Measure.* Princeton: Princeton University Press, 1997.
Barrett, Krome. *Logic and Design.* Westfield, NJ: Eastview Editions, 1980.
Bates, Kenneth. *Basic Design.* New York: Funk & Wagnalls, 1975.
Bolt, Brian. *Mathematics Meets Technology.* Cambridge: Cambridge University Press, 1991.
Booher, Harold, ed. *Manprint.* New York: Van Nostrand Reinhold, 1990.
Ching, Francis. *Architecture.* New York: Van Nostrand Reinhold, 1979.
Darwin, Charles. *The Origin of Species.* 1859. Reprint, New York: Random House, 1993.
De Duve, Christian. *Vital Dust.* New York: Basic Books, 1995.
Deming, W. Edwards. *Out of the Crisis.* Cambridge, MA: MIT Press, 1986.
Garrison, Ervan. *A History of Engineering and Technology.* Boston: CRC Press, 1991.

Gause, Donald, and Gerald Weinberg. *Exploring Requirements.* New York: Dorset House, 1998.

Hammer, Michael, and James Champy. *Reengineering the Corporation.* New York: Harper, 1993

Hawken, Paul. *The Ecology of Commerce.* New York: Harper Business,1993.

Hoffherr, Glenn, et al. *Breakthrough Thinking.* New York: Prentice-Hall, 1994.

Imai, Masaaki. *Kaizen.* New York: McGraw-Hill, 1976.

Juran, J. M. *Juran on Planning Quality.* New York: The Free Press, 1988.

Katzenbach, Jon, and Doug Smith. *The Wisdom of Teams.* Boston: HBS Press, 1993

Lowenstein, Werner. *The Touchstone of Life.* New York: Oxford University Press, 1999.

Machiavelli, Niccolo. *The Prince.* 1513. Reprint, New York: Penguin Books, 1983.

Matthews, Christopher. *Hardball.* New York: Summit Books, 1988

McCarthy, Jim. *Dynamics of Software Development.* Redmond, WA: Microsoft Press, 1995.

Moore, Geoffrey. *The Gorilla Game.* New York: Harper Business, 1998.

Morgan, Gareth. *Images of Organization.* London: Sage Publications, 1986.

National Research Council, *Enhancing Organizational Performance.* Washington, DC: National Academy Press, 1997.

National Research Council. *The Changing Nature of Work.* Washington, DC: National Academy Press, 1999.

Norman, Donald. *The Design of Everyday Things.* New York: Doubleday, 1988.

Norman, Donald. *Things That Make Us Smart.* Boston: Addison-Wesley, 1993.

Parker, Glenn. *Team Players and Teamwork.* San Francisco: Jossey-Bass, 1990.

Penzias, Arno. *Ideas and Information.* New York: Simon & Schuster, 1989.

Rochlin, Gene. *Trapped in the Net.* Princeton: Princeton University Press, 1997.

Shrage, Michael. *Shared Minds.* New York: Random House, 1990.

Winograd, Terry. *Bringing Design to Software.* Boston: Addison Wesley, 1996.

Websites

Recruiting:
   www.monster.com, www.hotjobs.com
Human resources management:
   www.shrm.org
Human resources guide:
   www.hr-guide.com

Business processes:
  www.prosci.com
Change management:
  www.change-management.org
Teambuilding:
  www.accel-team.com
Business cases:
  www.solutionmatrix.com
Information technology:
  www.ccic.gov
MIT Media Lab:
  www.media.mit.edu
Xerox PARC:
  www.parc.xerox.com
Bell Labs:
  www.belllabs.com
Information systems:
  www.cio.com, www.informationweek.com
Design:
  www.fastcompany.com/online/resources/(choose theme)

Part Six

❧Deliver the Results❧

The Performer

Practice Intuitive, Disciplined Execution

There is no substitute for hard work.
Genius is 1 percent inspiration and 99 percent perspiration.
— THOMAS EDISON (1847–1931)

Delivering results is the last essential of problem solving excellence. Here we are not talking about new goals or journeys, or revolutionary capabilities, but rather the capacity to execute a plan, with a given solution, in demanding conditions and usually against competition. This final element of problem solving excellence is often assumed, overlooked, or underemphasized. The number of problem solving frameworks or methods that simply leave a blank space for "implementation" is legion.

On any successful expedition, there is someone known as a Performer. Performers take the Creator's solutions, the Innovator's ideas, the Discoverer's knowledge, the Communicator's people, and pull it all together to reach a full resolution of the problem or opportunity defined by the Playmaker. Performers are the hard-bitten, practical characters who are always willing to get their hands dirty to make things happen. Inspiring visions from the Innovator or Playmaker, which are so necessary to capture the imagination of the crew, usually ignore painful realities. Theories of the Discoverer must be put into practice. Blueprints and designs of the Creator usually leave out something critical. Performers are typically left to take up the slack.

The best Performers turn plans into progress and deliver results over and above expectations. They maneuver through challenges to generate and maintain momentum. They make solutions work for customers and capture unanticipated opportunities. Delivering results means making progress, avoiding obstacles, staying on course, and clearing a smooth path. It is the ability to close the gap, consistently, between ideal and reality, between plan and accomplishment.

Reinhold Messner's Solo Ascent of Mount Everest, August 15–20, 1980

It was the twenty-ninth of May, 1953, when Sir Edmund Hillary and Tenzing Norgay first reached the summit of this mountain. The ultimate destination on Earth. The top of the world. The third pole. Everest. This most remote of places has subsequently been reached by massive teams from dozens of countries ranging from Japan to Germany, England to the United States. They took months and launched huge assault-style missions, burdened with technology from oxygen tanks to navigational gear, in their attempts to gain the summit. Few, if any, believed it could be done alone and without oxygen. The unknown was not whether the journey was possible, but how well—how perfectly in many alpinists' minds—it could be executed.

That was where Reinhold Messner came in. It was the summer of 1980, in the middle of monsoon season, when he attempted a route from the north that had never been tried. He prepared for the ascent alone and made it unaided by any technology more complicated than boots, ropes, storm gear, and a backpack. By the time he had finished, he had become the first man ever to scale Everest solo and without oxygen. In doing so, Messner set a historic standard for willpower, endurance, and execution.

How did he do it? This was not just a simple question of talent. Messner's ability to execute a dramatic plan perfectly was a result of discipline and focus, flexibility and maneuverability, resourcefulness and anticipation of difficulty—all under pressure of time, cold, and raw fear. In his journals of the expedition, he tells how the fear was so great that he turned back three times on his first solo attempt of another mountain—Kanga Parmak—made in preparation for the Everest trip.

Messner exemplifies world class execution because he utilized the full range of practices and approaches that make the difference in getting things done. He simplified his goal and his means—no scientific observation, no companions, minimal equipment. He set the right pace and charted the best routes to the top. He tested himself rigorously in preparing for the final summit attempt to be sure as little was left to chance as possible. He made the right decisions at the right time, when critical choices were needed on weather patterns, routing, and material. He maximized his pursuit of the goal while minimizing risks. And he maintained the kind of edge that allowed him to endure when conditions surpassed the difficulty of even his carefully planned scenarios.

In a world where complexity is pervasive, competition is fierce, and information overload is a common disease, the ability to execute consistently is highly prized. The best Performers refine a sense, developed over decades of hard-won experience, of what will work under certain conditions and what just won't hold up. They also follow an ordered, systematic approach to protecting their team and opportunistically take advantage of any chance that comes along to gain a leg up. Intuition tells them there will be a setback somewhere along the way to counterbalance it. They have the presence of mind and professionalism to rigorously and continually test tools, strategies, and approaches. This way, when a situation occurs with no margin of error, the kinks have been worked out and the weaknesses exposed and corrected for. If implementation is done poorly, surprises become a way of doing business, and an organization or individual becomes reactive, succumbing eventually to a sense of being out of control or a cascading set of failures. If it is done well, problems are highlighted early, resources are mobilized to resolve them, goals are adjusted for new possibilities, and antennae are sensitized for unanticipated risks.

Performers also recognize that there is an important interrelationship between creating solutions and implementing them. In some cases, a solution may be designed so well, and in such a predictable environment, that execution is straightforward—as in operating a building once it's been constructed. In other cases, no matter how well the solution has been designed, the chaotic and challenging nature of the environment puts the premium on implementation skills—not unlike the situation with business managers in today's global economy. The example of delivering results that appears in this part's overview section—the story of a peerless competitor in the world's toughest solo round-the-globe sailing races—is a textbook case of the latter situation. In this endeavor, everyone's got a peerless solution, but the difference between life and death, success and failure, is in how well the solution is executed.

The Performer's Central Idea–The Best Progress Comes from Combining Intuition and Discipline

Performers know the inherent paradox of implementation: you must be highly disciplined to make a solution work according to plan, but you must be very intuitive to ensure that the actions and decisions you take are the right ones given the environment you are in. Actors may spend hundreds of hours learning lines and studying character, but it is their intuition about that character and their intuitive responses to the audience and to their fellow performers on stage that make the difference between a dry recitation and a standing ovation. A construction manager may spend thousands of hours managing budgets, schedules, and adhering to regulations and construction disciplines, from cost control to safety. But it is only his intuition about people, bureaucrats, materials, weather, and other imponderables that will make his decisions savvy ones.

Great Performers know that implementation of a solution is best driven by strong intuitions that are constantly balanced with discipline. (See Figure 6.1.) If Performers honor their strong intuitions, then they take advantage of the capacity of the human mind and heart to recognize complex patterns. If they ignore those intuitions, they miss opportunities, and subtle indications of risk go unseen. Intuition helps make possible the ideal customization of a plan and solution to the actual conditions encountered during implementation.

Yet, if intuition dominates, then a performance, especially if it involves multiple players solving a large scale problem, will quickly go off track. Regular disciplines are required to check progress against plans, meet promised milestones, and to keep solutions working well with preventive maintenance so they don't break down at critical moments. Performers at the top of their game are those who can go back and forth between gut instinct and formal analysis, the inspired quick fix and the planned architecture, the opportunistic sprint and the planned pit stop.

Performers in Action: Isabelle Autissier and Sailing Solo Around the World

If the Performer's central idea is that the best progress comes from balancing intuition and discipline, then how does that apply in practice? How do Performers

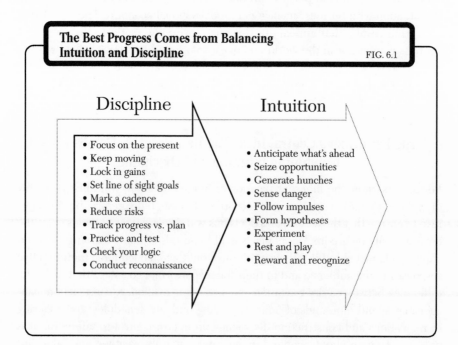

The Best Progress Comes from Balancing Intuition and Discipline   FIG. 6.1

Discipline

- Focus on the present
- Keep moving
- Lock in gains
- Set line of sight goals
- Mark a cadence
- Reduce risks
- Track progress vs. plan
- Practice and test
- Check your logic
- Conduct reconnaissance

Intuition

- Anticipate what's ahead
- Seize opportunities
- Generate hunches
- Sense danger
- Follow impulses
- Form hypotheses
- Experiment
- Rest and play
- Reward and recognize

manage risks and take advantage of opportunities to consistently exceed expectations and deliver valuable results? The following story of Isabelle Autissier—the great French sailor—and her solo racing around the world shows a Performer in action. With the contribution of a Performer, a problem solver can build on an Innovator's ideas, a Discoverer's knowledge, a Communicator's relationships, a Playmaker's leadership, and a Creator's solutions to create an inspired, intelligent, living community with a sense of direction and a powerful capability that makes things happen.

There are no other athletic competitions in the world exactly like racing alone around the world. Every year only a few are held, with small fields of daring athletes fighting to make the grade. The magnitude of the problems to be solved and the heroism of the sailors' solo performances are breathtaking. One of these races is called the Vendée Globe. Start from the town of Vendée in France in the springtime. Then sail around the globe as fast as possible, alone, and return—alive if you can—to where you started up to six months and 27,000 miles later. Without stopping. To get around the globe as fast as possible means going straight towards Antarctica, to what is called the Southern Ocean, where a boat can circumnavigate by covering the shortest possible distance. The climate is deadly. The combination of winds over 120 km per hour and sixty- to eighty-foot waves is so consistent that the author of a recent book on the race entitled it *Godforsaken Seas.*

Here are all the challenges a Performer faces in problem solving execution exhibited in high relief. Each sailor is using nearly equivalent navigational and sailing equipment. Many of the boats are designed by the same company. A better solution won't win you this race. The difference between the best and the worst is the difference in the technical skill of execution—and in some cases either very good or very bad luck. Nearly every year, a sailor dies. For most of the competitors, survival is the first goal, with winning an almost secondary consideration.

Isabelle Autissier, a Frenchwoman who has raced in this and the globe's other extreme sailing competitions many times, is an archetypal Performer and has become an icon in the current annals of women's sports. She set the New York to San Francisco world speed record around Cape Horn, was the first woman to complete a single-handed around-the-world race, and is the first woman to enter the elite of the world's sailing community. With her technical training, her quiet, reserved demeanor, her legendary persistence, and her tactical ingenuity, she has played at the forefront of what was typically a male game for many years now.

One of the more extraordinary aspects of the execution skills of sailors like Autissier is their ability to find simple, effective resolutions to the problems they face along the way. They start out with perfect, well-tuned machines, but by the time they've completed one-third of the journey, they may have lost an entire mast, a sail, a key piece of communications equipment. As a result, they are experts at dreaming up repair schemes that are viable enough to allow them to complete the race. In one situation, Autissier was completely dismasted in a vicious storm. To keep the collapsed rigging and broken machinery from destroying the boat required cutting through it with power tools, knives, anything available. Then came hours spent jury-rigging a new sail that would allow her to limp along in an unbalanced but survivable fashion.

If they can avoid the most deadly accidents, captains like Autissier still have to pilot a course through massive swirling low pressure systems that move across the oceans at twenty to thirty miles per hour. The best sailors pick just the right course to take advantage of high winds pointed in the right direction, but avoid the most damaging weather, and at the same time maneuver through the wave fronts that confront them in dizzying variety.

Because the Vendée Globe is very long, pacing is critical. In a recent race, one of Autissier's competitors, and the eventual winner, Christophe Auguin, spent the first few weeks behind the rest of the fleet. He used the initial legs of the race to test and tune his boat to hone it to the highest levels of performance. After Auguin's initial warm-up trailing behind the others, he then pushed himself to a steady pace all through the dangerous lower degrees of latitude, never making the mistake of trying to gain too much of an edge too fast. He knew that pushing the edge too far in such an unforgiving environment might just be the last mistake he ever made. As Autissier comments respectfully, "You try to push yourself as hard as you can and you try to push your boat. But you must not push too hard, because if you push too hard you will break something. It's very important to know the balance." At the end of the race, even though Auguin had steadily taken over the lead and was ahead of Autissier by a good distance, he continued pacing himself, actually stopping overnight close to the finish line to rest himself and his systems. He didn't want to risk losing the race at the last minute from a human or mechanical malfunction.

In addition to resourcefulness and good pacing, Autissier and the other skippers are excellent decisionmakers. Every problem is, at its root, a chain of hundreds or thousands of decisions that get you from point A to point B. Whether you make most of those decisions well, and keep from making one very poorly, determines if you come home in one piece or not at all.

Autissier once saved her own life with her decisiveness. In the round-the-globe-race formerly called the BOC challenge, a malfunctioning autopilot led to a complete capsize of her craft 1,900 miles offshore of Cape Horn. The danger of her predicament and her resourcefulness produced a global media event. She was decisive enough to close the cabin door as she felt the boat flip over, to prevent water from flooding the interior. In systematic sequence, she then tried, working by flashlight, to right the boat using her hydraulically-controlled pivoting keel. This failed. Then she made a satellite telephone call to her team headquarters, crying "I'm upside down!" just before it ran out of power. She activated an emergency beacon and waited, until within a short time her electricity disappeared.

Things continued to get worse, fast. A hatch door ripped off and let seawater pour into her tiny compartment. She sealed it quickly and moved heavy objects to the stern as ballast. Her next move, still decisively working her way through the problem, was to activate two more emergency beacon systems. Then to fight hypothermia, she struggled into her survival suit. Finally, she rescued flares, a radar transponder, fresh water, a gas stove, and fresh food to wait it out. Fortunately, a fellow competitor was able to get close enough to rescue her. As she recounts it, "When you are in a situation where your very life is involved, you do not have time to be frightened. You switch in your mind to being very determined. You know you must stay alive and keep your boat alive and you do not think about anything else. I know the dangers are very close, but I don't think about it. I do not think about death. I think about life and staying alive."

In a place like the Southern Ocean where just about anything can kill you—a wave sweeps you overboard, your boat pitchpoles surfing down an eighty-foot swell, you collide at night with an unseen freighter or iceberg—managing risks is perhaps the most important execution skill of all. The successful Performers in this drama are ones who are constantly preventing failures by keeping the ship in good repair as well as keeping on the lookout for treacherous weather conditions that might possibly be avoided—even if it is at the cost of a few days. The details of risk management range from covering one's hands with cream several times a day, as one man does, to make sure they are always functioning as well as possible to keeping extensive spares and well-stocked repair kits.

But sailors must also recognize when a risk becomes an opportunity. Winning often means taking risks. Weather fronts have the potential to kill you or help you win the race, if you can choose the right route to take. In another one of her races, which she both survived and won, Autissier studied the weather patterns around the first leg for more than a year beforehand. When the starting gun went off, she headed east while everyone else headed north. It was the trickiest of four legs, going from Charleston, South Carolina, to Cape Town, South Africa. As one observer put it, "Sailors must skirt the high pressure weather system around Bermuda, tack upwind against the Atlantic trade winds, cross the treacherous doldrums, avoid the calms near St. Helena and try to roar home on the heavy winds of the South Atlantic." Autissier's innovative course won her the leg by two days. The others averaged three to four knots, she averaged nine. They were caught for four days in Bermuda, she was there only twelve hours.

Autissier's deep character emerges when she talks about her life and career, and how by pursuing gradually increasing tests and challenges over the years, she has built her tremendous skill and confidence in execution. This is definitely a professional who knows what it means to work systematically to build skills on small-scale problems while working up to the biggest ones. She says, "If I trust myself for what I do on the water, it is because I have advanced step-by-step and have always tried to balance and understand the growing difficulty of whatever task I was undertaking." In other words, like other great Performers, she is intensely aware of how experience and skill must compensate for the increasing scale of a problem and its degree of difficulty. She continues, "It took me more than 20 years to do the single-handed circumnavigation I was planning at age 12. This required patience, which our societies often disapprove of, but it gives me the necessary perspective to feel confident in myself."

Because of such determination and competitive instincts, sailors like Autissier drive the designers of their boats to invest in new technologies and new designs that seek any possible performance edge. When she sailed her first major around-the-world race years ago, she recalls contemplating all the possible performance improvements that could be made for the next race. Afterwards, she sat down with her naval architect to push the performance envelope of the boat by customizing it to her style. These improvements started by making the boat simpler and lighter. The list of changes got too long very quickly. As she put it, "Making a list of innovations is easy; choosing those which would be realistic, performance-oriented and within the budget took more time. Our primary innovation, a pivoting keel, is not a completely new idea. But its potential was very attractive. Even so, placing the bet was daring, a little risky. But I was keen on it."

Finally, Autissier sums up just what it takes to make it as a Performer at this level. "To be a good sailor, you try to understand the sea and the wind, not to combat or master them. To be a good single-hander, you have to succeed in understanding yourself, in knowing your strong and weak points as well as your boat's. Only then can you combine them as harmoniously as possible and push ahead toward your objectives. To be a good racer, you must be able to give everything and invest your heart and mind totally. In solo racing, everything is underscored, there's no room for errors, no limit to the joys. Emotions are intensified to a degree that they will never reach on land."

In summary, Autissier and her fellow solo racers demonstrate what's behind great Performers. They combine discipline and intuition in their pacing and piloting to generate and keep momentum while taking advantage of local conditions. They are decisive and constantly balance risks and returns as they confront new dangers and possibilities. Moreover, they recognize what it takes to conquer large-scale or very difficult challenges and are always working to maintain their performance edge through feedback that engenders new strategies, technologies, or techniques.

The rest of this part covers in more depth and detail how the best Performers use their tactical execution skills to consistently deliver results. You can either skip to the next part, the "Guide to the Guide," on page 245; go back to any of the other parts to pursue them in depth; or proceed. Each of the following chapters in turn outlines how Performers start with simple, focused action and ultimately progress to maintaining a continuous competitive edge.

- "Simplify and Specify: From Drift to Action" takes the first step by showing how a Performer gets started and keeps focused even in the midst of great technical complexity. Ron Ponder, the man who built the Federal Express package-tracking and delivery system, shows how to concentrate on achievable line-of-sight goals.
- "Set the Pace and Pilot a Course: From Action to Rhythm" illustrates how Performers establish a rhythm and pace for a long journey while navigating a course that is sensitive to tactical considerations. Lou Gerstner, at the helm of the IBM turnaround, speaks about what it takes to set a clear heading, to pace and pilot a successful course in business.
- "Make the Right Decisions at the Right Time: From Rhythm to Momentum" emphasizes the decisionmaking cycles that sustain momentum in a problem solving effort. Kathleen Sullivan—the Dean of Stanford Law School—enlightens us about key principles of decision making in the political and judicial systems.
- "Optimize Risk and Return: From Momentum to Value" identifies how Performers assess dangers and possibilities to deliver maximum value for minimum resources and risks. CEO Jeff Skilling of Enron Corporation tells how that leading organization manages risks (i.e., downside) and creates new potential returns (i.e., upside).
- "Fail Small and Early to Win Big Later: From Value to Scale" pinpoints how a Performer moves a problem solving effort from small-scale to very large-scale implementation. Dominic Fonti, a leading construction project manager, explains how these principles apply in building a skyscraper from start to finish in the midst of Manhattan.
- "Maintain an Edge: From Scale to Advantage" shows how Performers keep a competitive edge over time. Paul Kaminski, the man who guided the Air Force's Stealth program from inception to maturity, tells how he managed to define and then work successfully at the "bleeding edge" of space-age technology.

SIMPLIFY AND SPECIFY
From Drift to Action

*Beauty of style and harmony and grace and
good rhythm depend on simplicity.*

–PLATO (C. 428–348 B.C.)

Executing solutions to tough, complex problems requires the ability to constantly
simplify and specify goals and priorities in order to move from plans to action.
This must be done even while maintaining an appreciation for subtlety and an in-
depth understanding of the stakes and the many variables involved in determining an outcome. Such mental focus helps Performers spend time and energy on
appropriate aspects of the problem at hand, not extraneous details.

Learning how to focus on the right angle of attack, the critical paths, and the
essential solutions that will ultimately determine success or failure is vital to effective implementation. But when you're under time pressure, facing daunting
technical or political complexity and concerned with producing quality results,
choosing the right things to focus on is not an easy task. The answer is usually to
choose a succession of compromise solutions, that are both feasible and within
line of sight, while keeping your eye on the ultimate result.

When building the FedEx package-tracking and delivery system, Ron Ponder—their chief information officer, who was nicknamed the Professor because
of his low-key style—faced hundreds of decisions where simplifying the com-

plexity the engineers wanted to introduce was the difference between success and failure. He and his team also faced the most intense time and competitive pressure imaginable.

Ron Ponder and the Federal Express Package Tracking System

A decade ago, FedEx faced the most intense competition from the United Parcel Service (UPS). This rivalry was far beyond Army versus Navy or Harvard versus Yale. It was much more like Microsoft versus Netscape, where the mutual antipathy was so great that each one literally wanted to neutralize the other. The challenge for each was to create value and efficiency in the transportation system to gain competitive advantage. The question was who would get the next big leg up first.

Package tracking was one of the biggest unexploited opportunities. To build customer trust and reliability into the delivery system required keeping constant tabs on packages throughout their average seventeen-hour journey. The first goal CEO Fred Smith set was to know the status of a package, at any given time, within thirty minutes. The first to build such a system would not only gain a critical competitive advantage in measuring quality and satisfying customers, but also make history. FedEx needed to solve it quickly and well, or UPS might solve it first.

When FedEx began tackling this problem, one part of the solution—the dispatch system to move data from central control to the delivery van—was already in place. But a tracking system required two-way communication. They needed a data stream from the van back to central control as well.

This was a simple concept, but very difficult to execute. Packages had to be marked with bar codes. Readers had to scan this information reliably and be operated by delivery personnel. For Ponder and his team of engineers, logisticians, operations researchers, and programmers, there was long debate. But the clock was ticking. Ponder saw that his planners were getting bogged down in the debates and the fascination with a perfect solution. They needed to simplify.

As he put it, "Most people try to solve a problem by creating a war machine. They charge up the hill, and they are overcome by the complexity, the inability to marshal the people and understand what they're doing, and it all caves in on itself. Instead, you have to break the problems up into pieces and choose a small enough piece to simplify. Create the simple themes and ideas, a very small number. And yet, someone has to know enough about the problem to understand all the aspects and lead the decomposition into logical pieces. Today, most people still don't understand this."

The FedEx team broke the problem down into four pieces: how to get the data from the package itself (a handheld scanner), how to get it back to the central computer (a truck-based computer), how to represent and manage the data once it was there (building the database), and how to access and interact with the data (the customer interface).

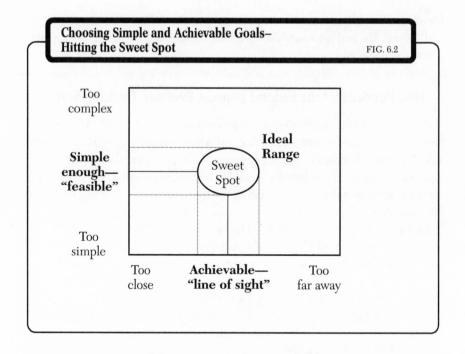

Once you understand the components of a solution, then the challenge is to set your objectives so that they are "line of sight." (See Figure 6.2.) This means they are achievable enough that you can envision them directly ahead, like an upcoming landmark visible from where you are on the trail, rather than so far off you'll have to navigate around lots of hills and valleys to get there. This visibility of the objective creates more focus and energy on execution as opposed to navigation, improving the odds of making progress. Small line-of-sight journeys keep you on a viable path, or at least near it, so that you can make progress while continuing to strive for flawless execution. With persistence—in other words, if you stay the course—the overall problem gradually becomes tractable.

The real implementation difficulties started with the second problem component—a truck-based computer. They had a scanner to get the data from the package. And there was a device—called DADS—on the vans that could get the data back to the central computer. But a missing link existed. There was no way to get the data from the scanner into the DADS device. It had been designed and installed before they decided to create a package-tracking system. As a result, the technologies didn't fit together. FedEx seemed to be faced with the need to rebuild the whole system from scratch to make these two pieces fit. The more they talked about it, the more complex the proposed resolutions became. The entire implementation process started to get out of control.

Ponder's simple resolution was to make a clumsy but straightforward modification to the DADS system in the vans—a docking station for the scanner. They developed a little black device called "the shoe." It was oblong, and had a makeshift connection to its communication lines for data transfer. It was homely looking. Like a shoe for one's foot, it had a snug little place for the handheld scanner to slide into and feed its data into the system—hence the name. This was their first step down the road to a tracking system, the moment when it all started to come together.

The shoe didn't look good. It wasn't elegantly designed. But it was fast, and it worked. It hit the "sweet spot" of simplicity and achievability and was the missing link that made the system two-way for the first time. They designed it in their own labs and had it out to the field in a matter of months.

Decisions like "the shoe" are great events, according to Ponder, where you feel the breakthrough and momentum that results. He says, "Once the shoe was accomplished, people could see how we were going to get from that crude means of data transfer, to a more refined one later on as the system evolved towards ever higher levels of sophistication. They were on their way."

Somehow, with that "sense of direction," one is able to make better decisions, even if all the information isn't available. As Ponder puts it, "With that approach, you can make better decisions on the fly because you have simplified the whole picture. You are not as wrong as often. Even if you don't have all the information you need. With the tracking system, many difficult decisions lay ahead of us, and we made them better with our experience from that first leg of the journey. Eventually, it evolved to the web-based personal tracking system that is so well known today."

The value of thinking about complex issues in simple terms—as in a clear destination, a roadmap, and line-of-sight goals—is priceless, according to Ponder. As he says, "If you are lucky enough to have an enormously complex problem, and you have been able to organize it in such a way that you can see the different pieces and have made it simple for everybody, that simplicity has a way of becoming reality."

Performers in Action: Setting Line-of-Sight Goals

Choose a problem solving effort you're involved in that has either just begun or still has a long way to go, one where you feel the complexity may be getting a bit out of control. Take five minutes and describe exactly where you are, today, in the effort. Then describe the ultimate goal at the end of the project. Now, take another five minutes and describe the next feasible line-of-sight goal that you could see the team accomplishing. And finally, try to fill up the space between that first line-of-sight goal and your ultimate destination with a chain of goals that seem realistic. You may have just figured out the high-level path through the confusion you are sensing.

SET THE PACE, AND PILOT A COURSE

From Action to Rhythm

Press On. Nothing in the world can take the place of persistence.
Talent will not; nothing is more common than unsuccessful men with talent.
Genius will not; unrewarded genius is almost a proverb.
Education will not; the world of education is full of derelicts.
Persistence and determination alone are omnipotent.

—**HARRY S. TRUMAN (1884–1972)**

Most difficult problems will not yield quickly, no matter how good a Performer you are. Moving too fast creates unnecessary stress and burnout, whereas moving too slow, with little sense of urgency, makes it difficult to maintain motivation. Moving too steadily might ignore opportunities to get ahead with a sprint here or there. Moving too erratically can make tactical anticipation and navigation impossible. By setting an appropriate pace, closely monitoring progress, adjusting to conditions, and increasing the resilience of the crew, you can find the right balance in steering toward a challenging resolution. Pacing requires a sense of limits and deep knowledge of your capability. It also requires the ability to be tolerant of short- or long-term setbacks, while still retaining a focus on the objective you set out to achieve. If you set a good pace and work to find your way, steady progress will often get you to your destination.

Beyond pacing, implementation requires avoiding unexpected obstacles and navigating necessary detours to make consistent progress and go from simple focus to an ongoing rhythm of forward movement. That progress consists of an accumulated set of actions and tactics to move things forward, step-by-step, to build speed and momentum. Then piloting based on effective navigation ensures that the progress you're making is in the right direction.

In his effort to turn around IBM, Lou Gerstner has made pacing and good piloting his touchstones. He has refused to let the market or stakeholders push him faster than he thinks it is possible to go. Yet he has moved with alacrity and made changes that increase the organization's flexibility and adaptability. His deliberate, methodical approach has led to an IBM turnaround that may eventually be judged one of the greatest corporate comebacks of the century.

Lou Gerstner and the IBM Turnaround

On April Fool's Day, 1993, when Lou Gerstner decided to take over the job no one wanted, turning IBM around, he started from a dismal place. In his own words, "It just looked like it was going into a death spiral. I wasn't convinced it was solvable." The stock was at an all-time low, one-fourth of its high seven years earlier. Its work force was being cut drastically. Write-offs were to the tune of $20 billion. The company had been crushed by the desktop computer revolution. A bunker mentality had set in, and those in charge were making preparations to split it up and spin off the pieces in a protracted death waltz.

When Gerstner came on board he first took the helm and established a clear heading. He made his most critical decision—to keep IBM whole—within ninety days. In that same ninety days, he made the basic decisions about key solutions— to continue focusing on mainframes, to retain a role as technology partner to oversized corporate America, to cut debt, to energize the workforce, and to step up marketing efforts across the board. And he decided to keep a focus on integrated solutions, disavowing the idea that businesses would rather build their own systems from scratch. "This technology stuff is hard," he explained. "And if I'm a company, what I really want is somebody who can help me implement it."

After setting a clear heading, he worked to stabilize his ship. Stop the leakage, assess the crew, and then worry about the long haul. "Transforming IBM is not something we can do in one or two years," he said eighteen months into the job. "The better we are at fixing some of the short-term things, the more time we have to deal with the long-term issues. You can't really start addressing the long-term issues unless you've got a stabilization."

Shortly thereafter, Gerstner announced, first to employees and then at a Manhattan news conference, that 35,000 IBM jobs would be cut. He believed in cuts by guillotine rather than slow death. "We need to get behind us this Chinese water torture we have been going through," he said. In his memo to employees, Gerstner said the austerity moves had kept him awake at night, but swift action was critical. "Making reductions slice by slice, quarter by quarter, as we have over the past couple of years is unfair and debilitating. It creates anxiety for you and uncertainty among our customers," Gerstner wrote.

Gerstner then refined his course further and set four goals for his first year: paring IBM to make it more efficient; developing a strategy to crystallize which business IBM would focus on; decentralizing decisionmaking; and nurturing IBM's relationship with customers. He returned the emphasis to customers and solutions—and as a result IBM's services section began growing rapidly.

Yet despite the importance of these course corrections, much of Gerstner's challenge at IBM was also about pacing. Wall Street was clamoring for a quick fix. Yet, although the CEO had instilled a sense of urgency, he wasn't going to be bullied into making bad decisions. IBM had its own built-in performance envelope and thus limits to how fast it could change. "He took his time strategically," said Steve Milunovic, an analyst and long-time IBM watcher at Merrill Lynch, "but he put a tourniquet on the company's finances pretty quickly."

At that first shareholders meeting, less than a month into the job, Gerstner warned stockholders—who'd seen IBM stock plummet to $45 a share, down from $175 six years earlier—not to expect "quick fixes." "The steps we will take will not be pussyfooting but bold strides," he promised. "We will try as hard as we can to get this company right-sized for this competitive industry we are in."

Most people tend to overestimate what they can do in the short term and underestimate what they can do in the long term. This is part of why pacing, and ultimately patience, can be so vital in solving problems—especially large and complex ones that take months or years to crack.

Endurance is a function of pace, capability, and conditioning. Whether it involves machines or people, everything has a capacity for change that it will tolerate without a stress overload. If you push too hard too fast—past these limits—friction or strain builds up, components degrade and fail, stress increases, and failure looms. If you push too slowly, however, you may either not reach your goals or cause equal amounts of frustration among those who are anxious and enthusiastic to get to the targeted destination. Getting the right balance and rhythm is vital from the very beginning of a problem solving effort. For if you start out too quickly and burn yourself out, the rest of the race will, at a minimum, be agonizing, and most likely will never come to fruition.

IBM has had its setbacks, sometimes moving two steps ahead and one step back. Its PC and hardware business, long its heritage, now is probably the weakest part of the business, said Milunovic.

But Gerstner tolerates the setbacks with a will to go on. He originally signed on for five years, then agreed to another five—saying he'd turned the company around, but now it was time to march ahead and take a lead. "This is the year we've got to make it happen," Gerstner told employees in 1998, declaring the company had to start gaining market share. "None of us at IBM is here, certainly not me, because we want to work on a perpetual turnaround. We're finished with the turnaround." "He's not a patient guy," Milunovic said, "but he does understand strategic implications and how it takes time to do things. The first five years was the turnaround, the second five years is getting growth up and becoming the leader again. So far so good."

It hasn't been easy for Gerstner and his team, but they've come a long way with a combination of bold strategic moves and continual tactical progress. Each year, IBM achieved a particular business milestone, methodically but quickly moving to ratchet up the pace of change but not faster than the people he wanted to stay could handle. He has kept clearly on course with the goals he set originally and has added billions of new value to the market capitalization of the company.

He opened his annual stockholders meeting in 1999 with a report that dividend payments had jumped 92 percent in three years. In his address to stockholders, he noted that services had been growing 20 percent a year, and that again IBM had been awarded more U.S. patents than any other company on the planet—its sixth straight year with the title.

Gerstner told shareholders in 1999 that his team at IBM was proud of the turnaround, but unfulfilled: "Unfulfilled—because we recognize that all we've done so far just gets us in position, just gives us the platform from which to launch our bid for leadership."

Performers in Action: Pacing Yourself

Choose a problem or an opportunity that you're currently deeply involved in. Now step back, close your eyes, and try to sense the rhythm and the pace of the project to date. How stable or erratic has it been? Has it been too slow or too fast? Is anyone consciously managing the pace? Have there been too many sprints? Not enough? Is everyone getting enough rest? Now think about what's likely to be coming up in the next six months. Given the way the pace has been managed so far and what you're likely to face, what are the implications? Jot down your insights on pacing, test them with your colleagues, and find a way to bring them to the next leg of your journey.

MAKE THE RIGHT DECISIONS
AT THE RIGHT TIME
From Rhythm to Momentum

*Nothing is more difficult, and therefore more precious,
than to be able to decide.*

—NAPOLEON I (1769–1821)

Decisions drive change. Making the right decisions at the right time, while involving the appropriate people, is a crux of any Performer's capability. It moves a
problem solving effort from building a rhythm to generating real momentum.
Perhaps the most important aspect of this practice is knowing the difference between the big decisions, in which you can't afford a mistake, and the small ones,
in which deciding quickly is more important than deciding perfectly. The right
decisions can build momentum. The wrong ones can break it quickly.

Naturally, timing is also crucial. Good decisions are of little use at the wrong
time. Performers don't just decide whether to decide early or late, they decide
whether to decide at all—they sense the "ripeness" of a decision. Although this
sounds simple, all too often this principle goes unconsidered or is given only the
most cursory treatment. We often feel pressured into making decisions before
they are ripe, or procrastinate until after a moment of opportunity has past.

Kathleen Sullivan and the Dilemmas of Free Speech in Paradise

Ultimately, the best decisionmaking, whether it's on the front line dealing with clients, on the factory floor, or in the executive suite, is a mix of accurate information, clearheaded analysis, trusted counsel, and gut instinct. Kathleen Sullivan, now the Dean of Stanford Law School, has mastered the art of shaping major decisions in the legal system. Her approach illuminates key factors that influence successful decisionmaking.

It was a political standoff one wouldn't expect on Waikiki Beach in Honolulu. This most famous of all beaches constitutes sixty acres of property, cut off from the city by a canal, that is probably the most valuable oceanfront in the world. Normally, luxury commerce proceeds apace on this well-appointed strip, but in this case the city government had a front-page conflict on its hands. The conflict was threatening to become a full-blown community crisis.

On one side were a group of unlikely troublemakers, T-shirt salesmen, with rickety folding tables and fringed grass aprons. They sold colorful island shirts, emblazoned with multiple tropical reds, blues, and greens. The shirts were basically indistinguishable from any other flowered shirt, except that they were imprinted with small messages, such as "Hang Loose Hawaii," some of which could be interpreted as covertly political.

The problem was, they had set up their folding tables on one of the more profitable hotel strips in the city, an elite neighborhood catering to some of the most exclusive tourists arriving from Europe, the Americas, and Asia. Traffic flow was inhibited, and safety was an issue. Moreover, the city had just finished a massive investment effort, having laid beautiful tiles and constructed hardwood benches to make the location even more refined and exotic. The idea was to make Kalakaua Highway the Champs Elysées of Honolulu. From the perspective of civic leaders, the T-shirt salesmen were a flea-market pimple on the most beautiful commercial face of the island.

Opposing the T-shirt salesmen was the city government of Honolulu, consisting of the mayor and the city council, the commercial interests, and the attorney for the city government, Kathleen Sullivan, a former professor at Harvard who had studied under the eminent constitutional lawyer Laurence Tribe and is frequently mentioned as a potential candidate for future slots on the Supreme Court.

The city's primary offensive weapon was legislation that would forbid the vendors to occupy their choice spot on the beachwalk. But the T-shirt vendors had their own weapon, the U.S. Constitution. They were claiming protection under the banner of free speech, and threatening a lawsuit if the government interfered.

But did selling T-shirts constitute speech? And was it a protected right to sell T-shirts on a busy commercial beachfront? When Sullivan, as a constitutional expert, arrived to advise her client on decisions related to these issues, the political temperature had already risen significantly.

The city had several alternatives to decide on. They had an ordinance from 1967 on peddling, prohibiting peddlers on the streets of Waikiki Beach and five other historic spots. But if they enforced an existing law, the vendors would sue. And cities in general are very vulnerable to damages, without the protections that the federal or state governments have. "As a result," Sullivan said, "the city was very risk-averse about violating constitutional rights—really bending over backwards. To solve this, the council wanted to pursue a second option, to pass a new law. So when I arrived I said 'Stop! Don't just do something, stand there!' Passing a new law would make the city even more vulnerable against a charge of 'viewpoint' discrimination, being singled out for treatment by a lawgiving body."

The mayor, a Pearl Harbor veteran, was very frustrated. "He was a decisive, action-oriented mayor, dressed in a workman's jumpsuit and always ready to jump on a fire truck and solve problems," Sullivan recalled. The need for patience and deliberation was not an easy message to get across to him. He got so impatient, he dreamed up a third option. He had the Parks department deliver huge potted palms, in the middle of the night, in a vain attempt to forestall the vendors from selling their wares. This, of course, had just the opposite effect of what was intended. It not only didn't stop the vendors, it emboldened them further. Moreover, it added a new problem, because now the city was even more vulnerable to being sued by the vendors for the mayor's action of singling them out.

Sullivan had to convince the city's decisionmakers to step back and delay decisions until they had formulated a more thoughtful course of action. Her first principle in situations like this, where complex legal issues are at play, is to first do no harm, to make sure the client doesn't do anything to irrevocably harm their position. The temptation in crisis is to act, especially in these hurried days of the information age. But in certain types of problems, such hasty decisions can foreclose options and do more harm than good. More information needed to be gathered, and more knowledge shared, before the decision would be ripe.

First she focused on the most important unresolved question that she believed the courts would have to grapple with, whether the regulation of speech was the issue or whether regulation of the sale of speech was the issue. In her view, the answer was sales, not speech.

Second, she tried to get some comfort from other people who had made similar decisions about the right direction to go in. Sullivan immediately called key contacts in other city corporation counsel offices and the federal government. She grilled them and tried to gain whatever knowledge she could. Their advice confirmed her instincts and her analysis.

Third, she had to decide how to frame the choice for the courts. To do this, she began a process of moving toward what she calls a "reflective equilibrium." This requires thinking backward through all that has happened to date and forward through all the potential paths that are open to the client—just as a chess player would calculate moves in a chess game. It also involves thinking up and down, from the individual participant's point of view, through the lower court perspectives up to the appeals level and even the Supreme Court.

"If this case was framed as poor beleaguered voices being suffocated, then we would have lost," said Sullivan. "If it was framed as greedy mass marketers of T-shirts seeking profits and displacing the people from their own public spaces, when they have lots of other place to go, then we would win." The court's decision should be made about how commercial business was to be done in the city and should be on that basis, not the higher ground of the constitutional issue of free speech.

Sullivan actually anticipated that on the substance of sales versus speech, she would probably lose. But by framing it that way, when they ended up on the First Amendment issue, she would be positioned to emphasize that this was not a cardinal First Amendment sin, and that the government should have a lot of leeway to regulate where speech takes place. She wanted her opponents to look like what they were, in her view, individuals out for commercial gain using the First Amendment as a fig leaf and thereby sullying it in the process.

Viewed in these terms, the law that was already on the books "was a beautiful ordinance," says Sullivan. "It was general. It was not directed at speech. So the decision I advised the city to make was, 'Let's start citing them under this ordinance, and if they sue you, I'll defend you because I think your case is foolproof.'"

The decision was made. The police issued citations under the law. The vendors immediately filed a lawsuit, and the issue began to percolate through the courts. By avoiding a new legislative process and prosecuting based on existing law, they set themselves up for a decision on the right grounds in the courts. As Sullivan explains, "A great deal of what good legal problem solvers do is prediction. We try to predict what a court will do, and in particular, we try to predict the scope of a ruling—what will it include. Will it be narrow or broad?" This foresight becomes an important element in good decisionmaking. (See Figure 6.3.)

So how did the Waikiki story end? It was a two-year adventure in the courts, and the journey started in District Court. The judges ruled that the peddling ordinance could be used to clear the main street but not the side streets.

Sullivan commented, "This is one way to make a decision—split the difference. There's something right on both sides. There's free speech here on the part of the vendors, but there are also legitimate safety and aesthetic issues on the side of the government. Therefore, split the difference and let them sell on the side streets."

From the city's perspective, though, this decision was terrible. Congestion and safety problems on the narrow side streets would actually be worse than on the larger main street. So the City appealed. In the final decision, the appellate

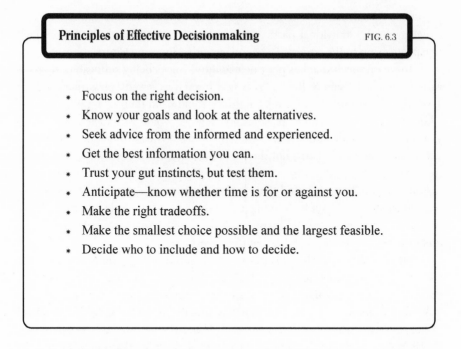

Principles of Effective Decisionmaking   FIG. 6.3

* Focus on the right decision.
* Know your goals and look at the alternatives.
* Seek advice from the informed and experienced.
* Get the best information you can.
* Trust your gut instincts, but test them.
* Anticipate—know whether time is for or against you.
* Make the right tradeoffs.
* Make the smallest choice possible and the largest feasible.
* Decide who to include and how to decide.

judges held that the city did not have to prove its case on a block-by-block basis and that it was reasonable to ask the vendors to sell in another part of the city. The Waikiki beachfront returned to its pristine state. The vendors continued making money on T-shirts, somewhere else. And most importantly, a precedent was reinforced that protected a long tradition of both allowing free speech in public places and being reasonable about how to implement that in a community with practical considerations in managing itself.

Performers in Action: Guiding Your Decisionmaking Process

On your next major decision, force yourself to answer three questions: When is the right time to decide? How should I decide? And how can I tell if I've made a good decision? Ask and answer them at the beginning and all during the decisionmaking process, reaffirming or changing your answers as the situation dictates. In addition, choose three independent individuals who have knowledge of the situation and ask their advice on the same questions, from beginning to end. You'll be surprised how much perspective and wisdom this can generate.

OPTIMIZE RISK AND RETURN

From Momentum to Value

*Where the probability of advantage exceeds not that of loss,
wisdom never adventures.*

—WILLIAM PENN (1644–1718)

Generating momentum through intelligent, well-timed decisions is one thing, but arriving successfully at the destination to deliver something of value is another. In any problem solving effort, there are countless opportunities at every step of the way to optimize returns and risks of the venture. Performers must continually work to consolidate gains, protect against potential threats, and push the benefits that can be achieved to the limit. Most organizations are being challenged by their customers, employees, and stakeholders to exceed expectations at almost every turn.

From the moment they engage in a new project, skilled Performers look relentlessly for ways to reduce risks and increase potential benefits. Early on, they define what will be the minimum required for success and try to achieve it early, thus breaking the back of the problem. They also keep their eyes open for small, unanticipated tactical advantages that will give them a leg up—a piece of information here, a relationship there, or an opening created by an opponent that can be exploited.

In the last decade, the combination of globalized financial markets, mathematical sophistication, computing power, and software innovation has made risk management a science and a competitive advantage for many firms. Enron Corporation has made a specialty of creating new businesses that deal with risk and opportunity in innovative new ways. Their approach illustrates how a systematic and disciplined approach to risk and opportunity can produce tremendous success.

Jeff Skilling and Enron Corporation's Approach Toward Risk

Jeffrey K. Skilling spent one day in Las Vegas twenty years ago, and he didn't like it much. The slots, blackjack tables, and roulette wheel held no thrill for him. And he's not a poker player. "I don't like to gamble," he says from Enron Corp.'s Houston headquarters. "Because when you gamble the outcome is random and the house has the advantage. I'd much rather be in a situation where I understand the risks and I'm able to hire people and build an organization to properly manage that risk. Then I'm the house. And then I'm not really gambling. That's a business."

Skilling is president and chief operating officer at Enron, the energy giant that has grown so much over the past decade that it's now the world's largest marketer of natural gas and electricity. From 1988 to 1995, total returns to Enron shareholders increased on average 27 percent. The company was ranked as the most admired company in its industry in a recent *Fortune Magazine* poll. It's also a pioneer in the hedge business—using its financial expertise and risk management tools to make financial deals in the energy industry and other commodity businesses. What's the key to Enron's success in the volatile energy sector? It knows how to manage risk, to minimize its liability, and maximize returns.

The first rule in managing risk is to explicitly state your risks, their relative priority in terms of potential damage, and what you know about them and need to know. (See Figure 6.4.) "It's Economics 101, the way businesses make money is they take on risks," explains Skilling. "What we're trying to do is to ensure that the risks we take on are risks that we can handle." Managing risk depends heavily on quality information and analysis. Before any investment or business transaction, Enron goes through a detailed evaluation and dissection of the risks that are involved.

For example, early on, Enron recognized that clients buying gas on the spot markets (i.e., the daily markets, where prices can fluctuate significantly) hated the price volatility. The difference in prices from one day to the next could vary by as much as 20 percent to 30 percent. It was too great a risk to purchase early and too much effort to purchase episodically. By using computer risk modeling and financial derivatives, Enron developed three separate products that allow customers to get guaranteed preagreed prices for their gas. The "Gas Bank" guarantees a fixed volume at a fixed price. The "Index" also fixes volume, but allows price to fluctuate in proportion to a natural gas index. And the "Gas Cap"

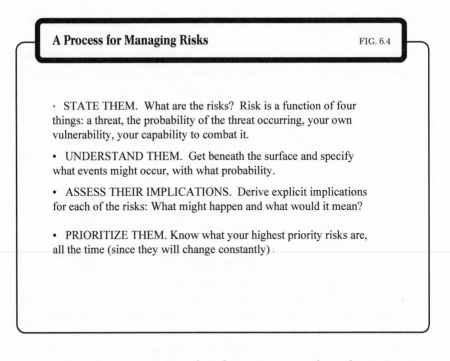

A Process for Managing Risks FIG. 6.4

- STATE THEM. What are the risks? Risk is a function of four things: a threat, the probability of the threat occurring, your own vulnerability, your capability to combat it.

- UNDERSTAND THEM. Get beneath the surface and specify what events might occur, with what probability.

- ASSESS THEIR IMPLICATIONS. Derive explicit implications for each of the risks: What might happen and what would it mean?

- PRIORITIZE THEM. Know what your highest priority risks are, all the time (since they will change constantly)

sets a preagreed maximum price but determines no volume limitation. Customers now have all the options they need. They spend moderate amounts to protect against the risks of fluctuating prices, thereby improving the predictability of their own businesses.

"Any risks that we're not good at managing, we hive off and we sell to other people," Skilling says. Cold weather—which can hurt Enron's gas supplies and economics—is an area where Enron has sought out someone else to buy the risk. Who would want it? Manufacturers of snowmobiles, for one, or owners of ski resorts. "We're worried about it getting really cold. Snowmobilers are worried about it getting warm. So we go to them and say, 'Hey look. If it's really warm we'll pay you. If it's really cold, you pay us.' By doing that they're happy because if it's real cold they have a lot of money to pay. If it's really cold we need the money to ensure that we can purchase the gas supplies to meet our customers' needs."

Enron tries to dump what Skilling calls "systematic risks," things like underlying commodity prices or weather. Risk factors that are systematic and part of the structure of an underlying environment—like the weather—are very hard to control. Whereas those that are non-systematic—such as on-time delivery—can be influenced and managed, a critical distinction for anyone managing risks in problem solving implementation.

Enron likes to keep nonsystematic risks. "For example, when you're selling a long-term gas contract to a customer, the thing that we're really good at is making sure that we can get the gas from where it's being produced to that customer.

And so we've created a whole network of infrastructure, pipelines, and switches in the system that allow us to have a good logistics system to deliver that gas. If we have a broad enough system with enough interconnects and switches, you're reducing the nonsystematic risks in that transaction. If a pipeline blows up somewhere in the network, Enron knows it's got other paths it can use."

Enron has the help of $1 billion worth of sophisticated computer equipment to help it sort out risks. They calculate how much gas demand will vary by what the temperatures are. "So we can mathematically determine how much exposure we have to cold weather. And so we sell that amount of exposure to offset that risk in our portfolio."

In an interesting contrast to the focus on risk, Skilling has aggressively nurtured the entrepreneurial spirit. To manage a giant portfolio effectively, he says, decisionmaking has to be decentralized. After the computers identify risks and break them into individual components, or "buckets of risks," a person is put in charge of each bucket. There are about 1,200 such buckets at Enron—and the people running them are "basically entrepreneurs," says Skilling. "We say to them, 'Hey, look. We've got this risk in our portfolio that we don't think is good for us to hold. Can you find someone that has an interest in holding that risk that we can make a market with?'"

Simultaneously reducing downside and increasing upside like this is exactly what the best Performers do. The Performers at Enron take what other companies view as downside—the risk of losing customers, the costs of pollution—and see it as a new upside. Just as a farmer's weed is only a plant no one wants to buy, risk is only downside until there's a customer for it. For this reason, Enron recruiters don't just seek to hire engineers. "We want people who have commercial savvy, or people who are interested in developing a business," says Skilling. "They may be an engineer or a history major, I don't care. If they're interested in creating a business, we want them working here."

Under Skilling, Enron is the type of place where trying and failing is worth more than not trying at all. "Somebody that's gone out and tried something that hasn't worked, they are more valuable to us because they've learned something," says Skilling. "If you went out and shot everybody that tried an idea that didn't work, you're basically shooting the people that have the most value to you longer term." Of course, entrepreneurs are only given so much rope. For each bucket of risk that the systems have identified, Skilling gets a report—every single day— that shows how the corporation has fared that day in that risk component.

Professional environments like Enron, which have a healthy approach to risk, encourage controlled and calculated risk taking as a way of learning and pushing the limits. They recognize the need for positive, mutual support primarily because the default human attitude is so biased against risk. There is no neutral posture. You either actively support risk taking and create environments where people's fear of failure is reduced, or your environment will be biased against innovation and leaning backward rather than forward.

The net result of Skilling's approach is optimization. Optimizing means getting the most for the least. It is a mathematical and economic term for squeezing the most you can out of a solution—recognizing that in the real world, we operate under constraints and come up against tradeoffs. With a balanced view of risks and possibilities, costs and returns, a Performer is ready to optimize problem resolution, getting the most for least.

Because the real world of implementation is complex and throws many potential threats and options at us, seeking optimization is no small task. There are many alternative tactics that assist in creating beneficial options for progress while avoiding harmful disasters. The difference between "ideal", "great," and "good enough" performance comes down to making regular judgments about the biggest and most important risks and opportunities you face and keeping focused on the highest priority ones. By keeping both risks and opportunities in mind together, and prioritizing them on the same "radar screen" (see Figure 6.5), you can move toward an optimal approach to managing downside and creating upside. Working with Figure 6.5, as you will be in the exercise that follows this section, gives you a concrete way to prioritize risks and returns together, so that you

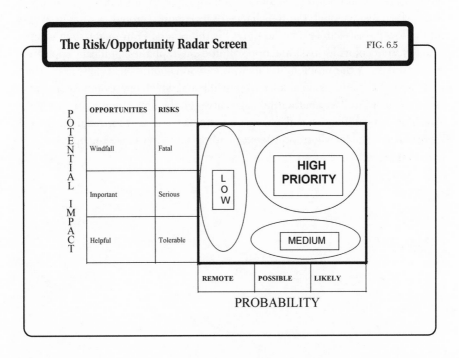

The Risk/Opportunity Radar Screen   FIG. 6.5

can become more adept at understanding their interrelationships and how to get the best balance between them.

"We have the most disciplined, buttoned-down risk management systems of any company in the world today, period," says Skilling. "If you do that right and you can identify the risks that you're taking on, you're much more comfortable taking on risks that other people don't understand. So I think, to the outside world, we look like buccaneers. But I can tell you we have the most disciplined, sophisticated risk management architecture of any company in the world. Bar none. It's the combination of disciplined risk management and rampant opportunism that makes it so dynamic here."

Performers in Action: Prioritizing Risks and Opportunities

First look at Figure 6.5. Notice that the vertical axis maps the potential impact of an event and the horizontal axis maps the probability that the event will occur. This structure allows you to map any potential opportunity or risk on the graph. Now take a sheet of paper. Give yourself five minutes to write down the major risks that you face in a problem solving situation you're currently involved in. Underneath, take another five minutes to write down the major opportunities you have. Now, using the radar screen, assess at least two significant risks and two opportunities. If it's an opportunity, would realizing it be a windfall, important, or just helpful? How probable is it that the opportunity can be realized? If it would be a real windfall, but the chance of its coming through is remote, it goes in the low priority circle. Do the same for the others. (You might even want to use different colors for risks and opportunities.) Graph the significant opportunities and risks of the problem in this way, and you'll get a clear picture of which risks need to be addressed as soon as possible and which opportunities cry out to be pursued, as well as whether the risks outweigh the opportunities or vice versa. You'll have a good basis for deciding how to move ahead. Your radar screen will help you see exactly where your focus needs to be to maximize the opportunities and minimize the risks.

FAIL SMALL AND EARLY TO WIN BIG LATER

From Value to Scale

On s'engage et puis on voit!
(One jumps into the fray, then figures out what to do next.)
—NAPOLEON BONAPARTE

Value is easy to deliver on a small scale, but not on a large one. In the real world of moving to scale, the unexpected often overcomes your plans. This is true whether you're building software or bringing products to market, starting a business or planning a promotion campaign. On the one hand, scarce resources and intensifying time pressure demand that you make choices and move expeditiously from start to finish. On the other, demanding customers and increasing competition require exploring creative options and paths that take time and effort. The pressure is to get it all done on time, to specification, and on budget, and that pressure can lead to increased risks, ballooning costs, and even project failures.

To learn quickly about the biggest potential flaws in your execution, especially in tackling problems that are large scale or have a high degree of difficulty, you must fail small and early to win big later on. In other words, test your solution first, then scale it up as the kinks are worked out. Performers using this strategy essentially swing back and forth between solution building and implementation in a regular fashion, constantly making corrections in design for what was shown to be lacking in the real world.

This method results in many small-scale failures early on in a project, with resulting lessons that prevent larger-scale failures later on. In building the man-made peaks we know as skyscrapers, Dominic Fonti, a leading construction manager in Manhattan, used this basic technique to make certain that the designed solution would actually be completed successfully.

Dominic Fonti and the Construction of Skyscrapers

From where they were sitting, almost a thousand feet in the air, people seemed like ants. A few months earlier, at another construction site down the street, an 8-foot piece of wood had fallen from this height and decapitated a pedestrian. The top of the Empire State building and airplanes landing in La Guardia were almost at eye level. Perched atop a massive skyscraper in the center of midtown Manhattan, fifty men prepared to spend the next several months putting the roof on one of the largest office complexes to be built in years—1.6 million square feet in all. The wind was cold, as winter was coming on. Time pressure was high. The project was in danger of being both late and over budget. Thousands of tenants, whose leases were already up, were getting ready to move in.

Later, the team would recall the queasy feeling they'd had in their stomachs as they prepared to haul hundreds of tons of copper plate, glass and steel forty-seven stories up in the air and begin construction on this final piece, the roof. The question in every one of their minds was the same. After all they had gone through in creating this building, was it all going to come together at the very end, or fall apart?

Two years earlier, in 1986, Dominic Fonti, the manager who had daily responsibility for construction (and now runs his own firm, Fonti & Associates, in New York City), had begun an awesome task. He had to build a 770-foot skyscraper—from breaking ground to seeing tenants move in—in three years. For every month that the project was early or late, up to $3 million per month in interest charges plus rent receipts would be gained or lost. His clients were demanding. They wanted to have it all—new, elaborate designs, built cheap and fast, but still safe.

"When I started the job, I had black hair," says Fonti, his friendly face smiling as he runs fingers through his short hair. "By the time I finished it was gray. Three years. For those three years I worked six days a week. I used to talk to myself and say, 'Well, if it was an easy job anybody could do it.' I took it as a challenge. I enjoy challenges."

As in many industries today, the economics of Worldwide Plaza project placed tremendous importance on speed. Time is money. A lot of money. So the Play-makers (i.e., the developers) running the show made a major decision to put this large, long project on a "fast track"—an especially aggressive schedule. This meant that, to save time, design, financing, and construction would proceed in parallel and concurrently rather than stepwise and sequentially. Foundations would be dug and steel structures set up while decisions on items like the roof had not even been made.

"Compressing" the scheduled tasks like this would create a faster project, but at greater risk of mistakes and overspending. The Playmakers believed it would be possible. The truth is, they were taking a large calculated risk that the inevitable problems created by compressing the schedule would be outweighed by the benefits of speed. And they were counting on a good Performer. Fonti was the one who had to make it happen. "Problematic? No," said Fonti of the fast-track process of building and designing simultaneously. "It just creates other challenges. You have to be quick on your feet, more open to incorporating last-minute changes, at the same time not to minimize impact to costs, impact to schedule. That's usually a tough thing to do."

The answer to speedier, large-scale problem solving goes by the name of the "spiral approach." (See Figure 6.6.) It is the basic technique Fonti used to construct Worldwide Plaza. The process is driven by a simple logic: Define a problem, conceive a solution, build a prototype, test it, evaluate it, fix it, redesign until it's stable, and then scale it up step by step until the whole problem is solved. The beginning, or starting place, is your current capability. The destination is a complete solution.

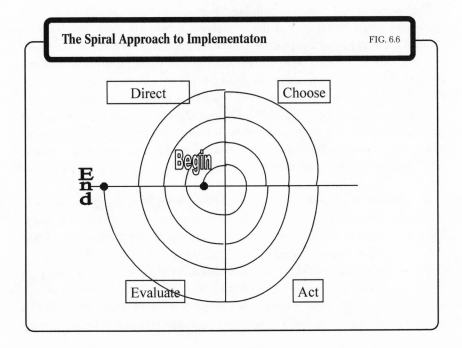

The Spiral Approach to Implementaton FIG. 6.6

In each loop, you **Direct** (set goals and identify alternatives and constraints), **Choose** (decide best alternatives by analyzing costs and risks, benefits and possibilities), **Act** (build a prototype and test the solution), and **Evaluate** (learn from your mistakes). The spiral approach takes you from the starting point to a destination several times. Each time, you'll be closer to a permanent, full-scale answer. It systematically bridges the gaps between initial concept and final completion. It's common sense. Crawl before you walk. Walk before you run.

The overall benefit of the spiral approach is manageable risk and adaptability at speed. It delivers these benefits because of four important advantages: better learning, better solutions, increased confidence levels, and greater adaptability. They derive from its essence, rapid learning by doing: First, it generates faster, more accurate learning. Second, it creates faster, more aggressive, better-defined problems and solutions. Third, it builds confidence and momentum. Fourth, it enables greater flexibility and adaptability to change, especially in the early phases of a project.

Because Fonti used a spiral approach, the design evolved over time. They started with rough drawings, moving on to scale models and more detailed designs at the six-month point. It was these preliminary drawings on which finances and budget estimates depended. At twelve months, a workable, complete design with computerized scale drawings was produced that was good enough to begin farming out tasks to contractors for bidding. This design was the basis for the first simulated prototype, created by modeling the final building using one of the most sophisticated computer-aided design programs in the world.

The computer model for the building was so realistic that the architects could look at the whole building or at the keyholes of a door life size. They could fly through the structure at any possible scale even before the first shovel-full of dirt was dug. Suzanne Smith created the model by translating hand drawings into computerized form and was completely dedicated to maintaining and running it throughout the project. As Suzanne said at the time, "In some cases, when we were asked 'Is this going to fit?' we could look at the computer drawing and say 'yes' or 'no' with very, very great accuracy. If it was just a hand drawing you could never really know whether you can get that piece of stone around that column, whether there's really four inches for the backup structure and the piece of stone or not."

Once a workable, stable design resulted from prototyping, the process of scaling up the solution began as the project continued to move around the spiral. The process demanded constant attention to modeling and testing wherever possible to flush out design problems.

One of the biggest tests of all came in constructing a prototype, or mock-up, of the curtain wall. The curtain wall, or outside skin of the building, is a combination of glass, sealants, steel, concrete, and masonry, often in unique mixtures. Big painful failures can happen if the mixture is not fully tested. A striking example of this kind of failure happened in the early '70s, in connection with the John Hancock building by I. M. Pei in Boston, when many of the windows fell out. The total cost of the problem, which involved replacing all 10,000 panes of glass, was estimated to be more than the cost of the building itself: $95 million. Investigation afterwards seemed to show that the cause of the problem was a combination of chemical reactions between sealants and a new type of coated window that had not been fully tested under the stresses and strains of weather, wind, and sun.

Testing these factors for Worldwide Plaza would mean building a complete section of wall with all the elements and subjecting it to the worst environmental stresses anticipated. The cost was about $40,000. Big, but a pittance in comparison with the risks and total size of the project. It was done at a construction research lab in Miami. None of the work on walls could start until it passed the test. It was a key quality gate that had to be passed through before another journey around the spiral could proceed.

When it was tested, the team found that windows needed to be one half inch shorter, otherwise they literally wouldn't have fit. "With 2,000 windows, even more, if something happens and you have to spend another $1,000 a window, you're talking about a quarter of a million dollars if not more on site," Fonti says of the value of testing. "You better spend $40,000 on the test, find out the bugs and correct them up front before you start actual physical construction."

Every project, no matter how well managed, eventually gets to a crunch period. Budgets inflate, schedules stretch, synchronization between teams starts to fail, design creep threatens, and stress rises relentlessly. By scaling up deliberately in a crunch, with conscious changes and adjustments, the large problems can be prevented and the original concept proven out.

For Dominic Fonti, the crunch occurred two years into the project during testing of the many components of the building, as full-scale construction of the steel skeleton and the masonry outside were proceeding in parallel.

Despite everyone's best efforts, the project was facing a big failure late in the game. The steel frame at the top of the building couldn't hold the machinery to bring up the panels. The frame didn't fit together the way it should have, and the walls were out of alignment. The weather was also a factor. Fonti would ride up the forty-nine stories a couple of times a week, climb the rest and find the highly paid laborers—expensive because of their precarious work—drinking coffee and relaxing. It was sunny on the ground but damp and misty on the roof—making the steel too slippery to work on. Then the contractor went bankrupt. All of the setbacks together cost not only time but more than $100,000—more than had been saved by all the earlier money-saving innovations combined.

Yet even though they had a sizable failure toward the end of the game, many and even more serious failures had been prevented by good spiral implementation techniques. Fonti continued improvising, and he did not let problems with the roof stop other work. "One of the things in implementation is when you come to a problem and you hit a wall, you don't just stop and throw up your hands," says Fonti. "You stop, you assess the situation and ask: What is the problem, what is the cause of the problem? And then you say to yourself, especially on a big project, 'Can I isolate the problem to minimize its impact on the project? Can I go around it, can I go over it, can I go underneath it?' You go around, you try to isolate the problem and not to use that as a crutch. I always tell my guys, 'Don't ever stop. You hit a situation, you analyze it and determine how to best go around it to minimize its impact on the job.'"

In the end the roof was completed, and the skyscraper with it. And although concurrency created losses, the compression of work also created gains—that $3 million in interest charges for every month saved over the original, slow-track schedule. The big win at the end more than compensated for the smaller failures along the way.

Performers in Action: Getting a Prototype Off the Ground

Think of the biggest problem or opportunity you've ever wanted to tackle but somehow just haven't gotten around to. Once you've decided on one, give yourself a week and force yourself to build a prototype. Create a very small-scale version of what you'd like to do. If it's a new office, make a drawing or a model. If it's a new company, create a small version of its first product. Use the experience of making the model to let your imagination go and to let your own motivation form. Once you've done this exercise, you'll know a lot more about whether you really want to do the project or not. And if you do, you'll already have taken the first step.

MAINTAIN AN EDGE

From Scale to Advantage

To improve is to change; to be perfect is to change often.
—WINSTON CHURCHILL (1874–1965)

Once you approach a full-scale solution, today's capability may have you ahead of the competition, but it is never enough to keep you there. Only the struggle to improve constantly, to find ever better ways of doing things, drives the achievement of lasting advantage. The abilities you showed in an early race, allowing you to beat your adversary with room to spare, may not be enough when you face a more able competitor or one determined for a rematch and revenge. Constantly applying what you learn to self-improvement—maintaining an edge—is a practice that pays high dividends in preparing for future challenges and uncovering new possibilities. The end of execution is the beginning of innovation.

But implementing research and development programs that succeed and make a difference, especially if they are truly on the "bleeding edge," is an art in itself. In the arena of national security, responsibility for that crucial edge often rests with unsung heroes developing brand-new technologies, like Paul Kaminski, the program manager of the military's famous Stealth program.

Paul Kaminski and the Department of Defense's Stealth Program

The interesting thing about the birth of the Stealth program in the late '70s is that the first major debate was whether the entire effort might be counterproductive. The logic went as follows. The United States was already the clear military super-power in the world. Now, it was considering a tremendous investment in a new ca-pability, a new edge. Eventually, the concern went, other nations will learn how to develop it, and down the road, the edge may be used against us, maybe sooner than we think. So, why develop the technology in the first place?

In fact, according to Kaminski, there were four different constituencies in-volved in this debate on whether to gain the edge or not. First, there were the "hopeful techies" who were by definition optimistic about both whether it could be done at all and how others might be able to respond. Second, there were the "skeptics," who opposed the techies on both counts. Third, there was the "trade-off" group. They were pretty certain something could be done, but were worried it might not be enough to be worth the money. Fourth, there were the "problem-after-next" group, who were pretty sure the technology was possible, but were more worried about whether we would really live in a safer world if someone else were able to replicate it in the short to medium term.

In the end, the hopeful techies were able to convince enough of the other groups to move ahead. How did they do it? The more they planned the program and learned how much it might cost, the more certain they all became that no ex-isting or future adversary would have the quantity or quality of resources to com-pete with the effort. Thus the likelihood was that, if the United States gained the edge, it would be their edge alone for some time to come. And over the next ten years, this program by itself took nearly 10 percent of the total Air Force budget, over $100 billion dollars.

And how did the Stealth team create this edge? The idea was not to create an airplane that could fly, then figure out how to hide it. They started from the other direction, and went into the project with the goal of making a device that had the smallest possible profile, invisible in fact. Then they would figure out how to make it fly. They were focused on several orders of magnitude of improvement in the reduction of an aircraft's radar signature, making it as close to invisible as humanly and technically possible.

Creating a performance edge is comparable to the thinking that goes into de-signing and constructing a real blade. One wants to sharpen regularly, but not too often; to get a sharp blade, but not too sharp. The most important thing is to cre-ate the shape of your blade in the first place. A narrow blade will be easy to sharpen, but it will blunt or break quickly. A broad blade will be sturdy and less likely to blunt, but it will be harder to sharpen. It's sharpness must be traded off against fragility. The sharper you try to make something, the more likely it is you will either break the blade or get cut in making the attempt.

The analogy with the development of a cutting-edge aircraft technology is clear and transparent. For in the initial phases of creating the edge, there are always mistakes that crop up and failures that can literally either kill the pilots or kill the programs. Learning how to anticipate and then respond to these "edge events" is a critical part of creating a performance edge.

Here's an example of an edge event. The Stealth engineers called it "CnBeta," and it almost killed the $100 billion program and the efforts of the best American scientists and engineers. CnBeta was a coefficient for stability and control in the design of the F–117 Stealth fighter. Specifically, it was the amount of counterforce required to control yaw during flight. They had already started flight testing when they discovered that CnBeta was off by a factor of ten from what they had originally estimated. This was a major blow to the program, and in Kaminski's words, "Most programs would have died as a result of such an error. Ours survived because of professionalism, circumspection, and trust. We dealt with it quickly and quietly."

The engineers used a model of the engagement that precisely allowed them to discover what effect the mistake would have. They put the aircraft through hundreds of simulations, purposely generating angles of attack that would cause high yaw or roll rates, seeking to understand just how limiting this flaw would be, how it would really affect the airplane's functionality. There were some delays. There was fear. There was depression. This was the low point of the entire ten-year program for Kaminski. In the end, having tested sensitivities in a full range of scenarios, they decided that the problem wasn't as large as they originally believed, and that it could be compensated for with the "fly-by-wire" computer software that was so vital to the entire weapon system.

In the world of the Performer, there's a lot of trial and error that is necessary to actually put into practice the extreme ideas that Creators dream up. And it's not all about making the technology work the way it's supposed to. It's also about learning how to get the human beings to adjust and hone their edge in a new way that is appropriate for the new technologies. The iterative process of implementing new technologies that are adapted to the people that will use them, and then adapting the people to the technologies they must use, takes much patience and deliberate effort.

Ultimately, the Stealth testing program allowed Kaminski and his team to work through most of the technical issues. But it also highlighted a set of nontechnical problems that turned out to be even more challenging. It turned out that, no matter what they did with materials or design, they could reduce the radar signature only so much. If pilots flew the plane the way they normally flew other fighters, they could still be picked up on radar because of their jerky, jaunty movements to avoid other aircraft and obstacles in flight. This style, which the pilots called "turn and burn," was at the heart of the pilot culture, with its exhilarating g-forces and heroic feeling.

For the Stealth fighter solution to work effectively, however, the pilots were going to have to learn an entirely new way of engaging with the enemy. Instead of turning and burning at the first sight of an adversary, the pilots had to learn a "careful zig-zag." They had to continue on their zig-zag course irrespective of what aircraft were around them, making the assumption that they had not been targeted or picked up. Not only was this tactic against the pilot's culture, it was both more boring and more frightening. What aviators call the "pucker factor"— a normal anatomical response to extreme terror—was a serious issue.

As a pilot, you had to have a lot of confidence in the technology and maintain a serious psychological edge before you could fly a careful zig-zag route with ene- mies flying close around you, able to blow you out of the sky. And the boredom was a factor on long flights. Several pilots were actually lost in training due to lack of stimulus and the aircraft's unique flight-handling characteristics. So ex- pectations and mental habits, training, and even pilot selection had to be read- justed. This was a new solution, and to gain the edge and hone it required change in behavior, not just technology. Improving the psychological edge had to go along with improving the technological edge.

The peak moment came for Kaminski many years after he had started this rev- olutionary program. All the after-action reporting from the Gulf War and other engagements showed that the aircraft did perform as predicted in all the action planning models. In some ways, the Stealth bomber became the symbol of America's high-tech advantage in this very visible international engagement. For Paul Kaminski, it was a personal triumph, a team effort, and also his contribution to maintaining the security edge required to continue protecting the American democracy in a dangerous age.

Performers in Action: Developing a New Edge

Pick an area of your business where there is an old solution (it should be one that's fairly significant in terms of resources), one that has been designed and im- plemented the same way for a long time. See if you can't find the person who un- derstands it the best and spend half an hour with them getting a short history that brings you up to the current day and includes any future plans. Get a sense of what new competitors may be offering that competes with your solution. Now, see if there isn't an opportunity to be created by taking that solution to a com- pletely new level. Simply think of the edge that, if you had it, would make you unassailable. Once you find the most important edge, you've found a door to the next generation. Now all you have to do is find an Innovator who will develop the idea, a Playmaker who will sponsor it, a Discoverer to research it, a Creator to design it, a Communicator to sell it, a Performer to make it happen, and you're in business.

CHARACTERISTICS OF A PERFORMER

General characteristics and purpose: Performers emphasize results to be achieved in resolving a particular problem. Their goal is implementing solutions effectively in complex, competitive situations. Performers are fascinated by the process of resolving an issue, the journey from here to there. They value engagement, discipline, resourcefulness, and courage. For them, the action and the performance is everything. A Performer spends time on practical steps of execution, protocols, barriers, troubleshooting, adaptation, risk management. Concepts, ideas, play, and more in-depth knowledge are less important.

Strengths: The strength of a Performer lies in focus, action, results, and adaptability to differing conditions that were not originally envisioned in the Playmaker's plans or the Discoverer's models and simulations. Their expert local knowledge of

---

Skill Levels of Performance TABLE 6.1

Level 1   Able to follow instructions clearly and efficiently to solve a problem.
Level 2   Able to solve different types of problems, given the potential solutions.
Level 3   Able to resolve larger scale problems or those with some degree of difficulty.
Level 4   Able to resolve large scale or highly difficult problems with high quality, speed and efficiency.
Level 5   Able to resolve nearly any problem, repeatably, with best in class levels of performance.
Level 6   Able to dominate an entire field, regularly winning top competitions.
Level 7   Able to perform at such high levels of quality that the performance itself transcends the problem.

a particular route or terrain can also be extraordinarily useful for known problems whose solutions are being implemented with some new variation.

Weaknesses: Performers are less likely to define new problems or come up with dramatic solutions. They are at their best not at the beginning of an effort but once it has gained some momentum and definition. Their biggest mistakes come in lending their talents to a poorly defined problem, with little potential impact and inadequate solutions.

Interactions with other types of problem solvers: Performers have the greatest affinity with Communicators and Creators, both of whom they need to sustain the intensity and quality of a problem solving effort. Communicators help sustain identity and reduce conflict through rough spots at the same time that they build confidence and joint commitment during the peak experiences. For most Performers, relationships with Discoverers and Innovators tend to be shallow. Performers tend to see Discoverers and Innovators as curiosities, because even though they are necessary for ideas, resources, and knowledge, they are simply not hands-on types who are used to getting their fingernails dirty. Often, a symbiosis develops between Playmakers who are true leaders and the loyal Performers who are necessary to get a job done but who, without a leader, might find it difficult to set a direction.

Typical mishandling: Great Performers are most severely mishandled when they are expected to make up for bad design, poor problem definition, or weak strategy.

Guidance for Performance

Vital Principles: Rules and Laws That Bear on Delivering Results

- Trust your gut instincts as well as the data.
- Either you're on top of things, or they're on top of you.
- Sweat the risks up-front and set a tempo.
- Avoid slippery slopes and find leverage points.
- Understand your degree of contro—anticipate system delays.
- Close the loops—time equals resource.
- Understand the minimum required for success.
- The best way to predict the future is to invent it.

Diagnostics: How Well Are You Delivering Results?

- Are you able to consistently exceed performance expectations? Are the plans you've made not relating to or reflecting the reality you're confronting? Are you seeing too many new problems that were unanticipated? What are the gaps between goals and actual performance and why? Are you shooting too low? Are you reaching too high?
- Are you on track and on pace? Have you calculated your pace to completion of the journey? Are timing or budgetary milestones being missed? Can

you envision reaching your next milestone soon or does it seem impossibly far off? What is your current level of capacity utilization? What level of resources do you have now or have accessible soon? At what cost? What obstacles and shortcuts exist? What course corrections are needed to compensate for obstacles and take advantage of shortcuts?

- Which are the most important things you need to decide? How and when are you going to make each decision and who will you involve? Is time working for or against you? Have you gotten all the inputs you need? From the right people? Based on the best possible information? Are you deciding before everything is known or waiting until the knowledge is perfect?
- Do you know what your biggest risks and opportunities are? What about their implications and the probabilities associated with them? The costs and values? What events will trigger the risks or possibilities? How are you eliminating the biggest risks and grasping the greatest opportunities?
- How many iterations will it take to get to a full-scale solution? Why is that the right number? Are you using the spiral approach? Are you making enough time for reflection and learning between each step? Once you get to a new level, are you anticipating the possible scaling effects? Do you have a plan to deal with them? If you decide to shortcut the process, do you know what the risks are, and are you prepared for them?
- Have you thought about what edge will be required to stay ahead of your competition in the months or years ahead? Will it be in technology, people, information? What are you investing in now to develop that edge? How long will you be able to maintain your current edge?

Syndromes: Diseases That Can Affect Your Ability to Execute

- "Playing the hero"—Overreliance on heroic execution to make up for poor overall problem solving
- "Idea proliferation"—Not prioritizing a surfeit of suggestions.
- "Perfectionism"—The perfect becoming the enemy of the good
- "Just keep doing it"—Overreliance on action without learning or course corrections
- "Deciding by not deciding"—Procrastination under the guise of consideration
- "Jumping the gun"—Making a decision before you have to, one that makes subsequent decisions even harder
- "Success-based planning"—Focusing only on success and not risk of failure and necessary preparations
- "More, more, more"—Maximizing rather than optimizing behavior
- "The hump"—Failure to account for, test for, and prepare for scaling effects
- "Behind the curve"—Good execution, but just not fast enough

- "Requirements' creep"—Changing your requirements as you implement the solution and in a disorganized fashion
- "Lost in the weeds"—Unable to get beyond details in implementation and to continually reallocate time, resources, and attention to most important issues

Going Further

Resources for further study. (Also see sources and notes for Part 6 on page 274.)

Books

Bernstein, Peter. *Against the Gods: The Remarkable Story of Risk.* New York: Wiley & Sons, 1996.

Brooks, Frederick. *The Mythical Man-Month.* Boston: Addison-Wesley, 1995.

Csikszentmihalyi, Mihaly. *Flow.* New York: Harper Perennial, 1990.

De Bono, Edward. *Six Action Shoes.* New York: Harper Business, 1991.

Dixit, Avinash, and Robert Pindyck. "The Options Approach to Capital Investment." *Harvard Business Review,* May/June 1995.

Goldratt, Elihu. *Critical Chain.* Great Barrington, MA: North River Press, 1991.

Kidder, Rushworth. *How Good People Make Tough Choices.* New York: Simon & Schuster, 1995.

Klein, Gary. *Source of Power: How People Make Decisions.* (1998) Cambridge, MA: MIT Press, 1998.

MacCrimmon, Kenneth, and Donald Wehrung. *Taking Risks, The Management of Uncertainty.* New York: The Free Press, 1985.

Morgan, M. Granger. "Risk Analysis and Management." *Scientific American,* July 1993.

Pelton, Warren, et al. *Tough Choices.* New York: Dow Jones Irwin, 1990.

Schaffer, Robert H. *The Breakthrough Strategy.* New York: Harper & Row, 1988.

"Survey of Corporate Risk Management." *The Economist,* Feb. 10, 1996.

Waterman, Robert. *The Renewal Factor.* New York: Bantam Books, 1987.

Websites

Project Management: www.allpm.com

Project Management: www.pmi.org

Decision Support Resources: www.dssresources.com

Risk management: www.nonprofitrisk.org; www.riskmanagement.com

Decisionmaking: dsi.gsu.edu; www.round.table.com

Rapid prototyping: www-rpl.stanford.edu

Control theory: www.theorem.net

Operations research: www.informs.org

THE GUIDE TO THE GUIDE

Rising to the Challenge

Before we move into the more practical part of the Guide, this seems a good place to reflect on the broader significance of what we've said so far, its place in the world we live in. For the first time in history, the technology now exists so that any separated group of people, anywhere in the world, can carry on a conversation or share any type of information anytime—whether by the Internet, telephone, video conference, or some other communications medium. The question is whether these conversations will be any different than they've always been?

In the year 2000, for the first time, scientists completed an entire map of the human genetic code, arguably the most vital knowledge asset on the planet. The question is, will we use that asset for the best possible purposes, with the widest possible scope?

In the year 2001, according to the Western calendar, we enter a new millennium, with 250 million years of human evolution behind us and our next thousand years ahead of us. The question is, what will we make of that time?

Soon, the technology will be available to store all the knowledge that has ever been generated by the human mind in digital form. The question is, will we progress from managing data and information to enhancing joint learning and striving for collective wisdom?

In the next decade, digital computers will finally acquire the full processing power—though not necessarily the intelligence—of the human mind. The question is, will we be capable of thinking on a new level that allows us to harness this power for worthy ends?

I believe only a new level of thinking and shared knowledge—thinking like problem solvers—will lead to worthy answers to these questions.

The germ of that thinking and knowledge lies within each of us. It simply has yet to be liberated and brought together. Just as we have discovered our genome and its architecture, I believe we have begun to discover this new shared knowledge, this new thinking, with its structure formed around the metaphor of adventure, of movement, of change. Gathering and using this knowledge of problem solving, as Walter Lippman once wrote, is something well worth doing:

> The world is a better place to live in because it contains human beings who will give up ease and security in order to do what they themselves think worth doing. They do the useless, brave, noble, divinely foolish, and the very wisest things that are done by man. And what they prove to themselves and to others is that Man is no mere creature of his habits, no automaton in his routine, but that in the dust of which he is made there is also fire, lighted now and then by great winds from the sky.

Strategic Implications of This Work

Aside from its broader significance, the work represented by this book has a number of potential strategic implications.

First, this framework for how human beings solve problems, together with several existing technologies for decision making and knowledge manipulation, makes it possible to engineer problem solving methods and expertise into computer systems in an entirely new way. This approach is more systematic and formal than human intelligence, but looser and more flexible and generalizable than artificial intelligence. I call it "assisted intelligence," and it will create an entirely new category of Web-based devices called "context" or "solving engines" to complement existing search engines and begin to turn the world wide Web from a place where questions are answered and products are exchanged, to a place where better decisions are made and problems are solved.

Second, the vocabulary, language, and knowledge here is a small fraction of a universal vocabulary and store of collective knowledge on human problem solving. It is the tip of an iceberg. This knowledge has never before been brought together in one place, and it constitutes what I like to think of as a genome of the mind. I am now working with others to start a nonprofit institute and alliance dedicated to the task of involving problem solvers from around the world in the task of conceptualizing, planning, and executing an effort to assemble this knowledge. We are calling it the Exolve Project. It will focus on collecting and conserving strategic knowledge on problem solving, much as The Nature Conservancy protects species, for the benefit of the educational community and the global public.

Third, once the new solving technologies I've mentioned, together with the common store of knowledge, become more mature and available, they have the potential to revolutionize the process of education, a basic cause of many of our social problems and opportunities. The processes of problem solving and learning will become even more tightly linked, as specialized knowledge is absorbed in concert with general knowledge that can be practically applied and is widely applicable. This approach forms the basis for a completely new and original type of core curriculum. The Exolve Project (www.exolve.org) is dedicated to helping to make this change in education possible and to bring it to those who otherwise could not afford it. In other words, we are working to synthesize knowledge assets from the brightest minds on the planet in a form so accessible that it can help anyone in the educational system from early on in their development.

Understanding Your Problem Solving Personality

Each profession has its own unique advantages and disadvantages in terms of problem solving. Over hundreds of years, each one has evolved its own methods, approaches, techniques, standards, and even vocabulary of problem solving. (See Figure A.1.)

The best problem solvers have always known that tackling really tough issues requires a multidisciplinary perspective. So they develop, largely by trial and error, a way of thinking and working that transcends their chosen profession, discipline, industry, or special interest.

There's no time for that process of trial and error any more. Professionals tackling challenging problems and opportunities need a common vocabulary, shared sources of knowledge of techniques, principles, and the awareness of syndromes that can get in the way of good problem solving.

Professional Biases in Problem Solving   FIG. A.1

Profession	Dominant approach	Advantages	Disadvantages
Science	Observation, analysis, theory, problem, solution	Deep analytics, long-term insight	Practical implications
Medicine	Symptom, disease, diagnosis, treatment	Speed and risk-orientation	Inconsistency, reductionism
Engineering	Requirements, design, construction, maintenance	Execution, follow-through	Neglect of human interface
Business	Opportunity, cause and fix, plan, execute, check	Speed, customer focus, bottom-line	Superficial, Short-term
Law	Situation, issue, principle, argument, decision	Complexity, logic and persuasion, risk	Follow-through and fallout
Civics and Politics	Perception, problem, interests, negotiation, solution, action	Human perception, common interests	Superficiality, sub-optimization
Art	Observation, intuition, inspiration, creation	Creativity	Lasting change
Defense	Threat, vulnerability, capability, deployment, engagement	Organized, large-actions, security, R&D	Built to protect or destroy, not to create or change

One way to get the best that all of these professions have to offer, and leave the worst, is to weave them together using the six essential problem solving skills as a general guide.

As I explained in the Introduction, I've identified the professions that tend to show certain strengths in problem solving and mapped them against the six essential problem solving skills, creating a set of six "personalities" that pull together the best from what those professions represent. (Figure A.2 here repeats Figure I.2 in the Introduction.)

Scan over the pages identifying the characteristics of the different personalities and then take stock of where your strengths and vulnerabilities are as a problem solver:

- The Innovator—page 32
- The Discoverer—page 73
- The Communicator—page 114
- The Playmaker—page 153
- The Creator—page 196
- The Performer—page 241

Identify which of the six personality elements fits you best. It doesn't have to be one. It can be a combination of two or three. You may even believe you are just about equal in every category. There are no rigid formulas. The personalities

The Six Problem Solving Personalities FIG. A.2

Problem Solving Essential	"Personalities" (likely professional source of knowledge and skill)
Mindset	**The Innovator** (artist, entrepreneur, visionary, designer, counselor, poet, spiritual leader)
Territory	**The Discoverer** (scientist, historian, researcher, investigator, journalist, teacher, accountant)
Relationships	**The Communicator** (politician, civic leader or civil servant, social work legislator, publicist, agent, salesperson)
Journeys	**The Playmaker** (commander, executive, physician, judge, consultant, coach)
Solutions	**The Creator** (architect, builder, engineer, inventor, investor, trader, author)
Execution	**The Performer** (athlete, attorney, entertainer, nurse, musician, customer representative)

are meant to generate insight and create helpful categorizations, not stereotypes. Whatever your own personality profile, they can help you think more clearly about putting a problem solving team together, one which adds the minimum number of people required to make up for your vulnerabilities while not overlapping too heavily with your strengths.

To clarify the differences between the personalities, please refer to the following Table A.1. It reviews each personality and the role it plays, sums up the essential skill involved, the central idea, and the contribution each has to make to the kind of virtuous cycle a good problem solving team creates. At www.exolve.com, you can also perform a computerized self-assessment of your problem solving personality that will help you develop a personal action plan for improvement.

Putting a Problem Solving Team Together

Great problem solvers know what their strengths and weaknesses are, and they build teams to compensate for them—creating wholes that are equal to or greater than the sum of their parts. Once you have an idea of what your personality is, then you have done the most important part. Now, whatever problem or opportunity you face, look for other people who have complementary strengths to put all the pieces of a complete problem solving capability together. Just make sure you

The Elements of Best Problem Solving			TABLE. A.1
Personality and Role	Problem Solving Essential	Central Idea	Contribution to the Virtuous Cycle
The Innovator			
Identifies alternative problems, strategies, and solutions	Generate the Mindset Develop potent ideas and attitudes	Best Innovation comes from taking alternative points of view	A committed mindset open to the best possibilities
The Discoverer			
Deepens understanding about problems and solutions	Know the Territory Ask the right questions and get good information	Best Insight comes from balancing perspective and immersion	Understanding and insight about the environment
The Communicator			
Connects problem resolution to the needs of people	Build the Relationships Cultivate quality communication and interaction	Best Relationships come from creating and propagating concentric circles	Broader, deeper more cohesive relationships
The Playmaker			
Chooses the problem, defines the goals and how to reach them	Manage the Journeys Choose destinations and set directions	Best Leadership comes from managing problems as journeys	Compelling game plan and specific requirements
The Creator			
Designs and builds concrete solutions	Create the Solutions Design, build, and maintain optimal solutions	Best Solutions come from creating complete and evolvable designs	Powerful, flexible, and resilient capability
The Performer			
Uses the solution to resolve the problem	Deliver the Results Practice intuitive, disciplined execution	Best Progress comes from combining discipline and intuition	Performance that exceeds expectations

know your and your teammates' strengths and weaknesses and how they fit together. It's never a perfect puzzle. Just make sure you've got all six covered somehow and that the overlaps or conflicts aren't too serious. The table of strengths and weaknesses, Table A.2, indicates from a slightly different point of view what each personality can add to, and take away from, a problem solving effort.

Advantages and Disadvantages of Personalities

TABLE. A.2

Personality	Advantages	Disadvantages
The Innovator	Adds creative element that is necessary to deal with ambiguous situations or tough dilemmas	Can be frustratingly divergent when convergent, simple, thinking and action are needed; are often gadflies that add tension.
The Discoverer	Brings to bear specialized knowledge and systematic approach to defining and resolving issues	Can be impractical in expanding knowledge base beyond what is required to make progress; can have difficulty at learning while doing
The Communicator	Becomes the "glue" factor that ties the team together and facilitates maturing of relationships	Can be unreliable when analytical objectivity is required in assessing performance or breaking down a problem
The Playmaker	Serves as the point person for determining direction, course corrections and strategy	Big picture perspective can lack the systematic, blocking and tackling approach necessary to produce results
The Creator	Builds the team, marshals resources and constructs the best possible solutions	Can end up focusing on the technology or the solution and forgetting about the problem itself
The Performer	Installs, operates and pushes the solution and the people to the limits of their performance envelope	Concentration on the route and course can make them inflexible to change and unable to step back and plan next leg of the journey

Although this is anything but an exact science, by using the charts that suggest levels of ability for each of the six personalities or the web diagnostic (Innovator, p. 32, Discoverer, p. 73, Communicator, p. 114, Playmaker, p. 153, Creator, p. 196 and Performer, p. 241), you can put together a rough estimate for yourself of whether any team you may be a part of is complete or not. Figure A.3 shows a complete problem solving team, while Figure A.4 shows a team that is out of balance, lacking strong sills in innovation and execution.

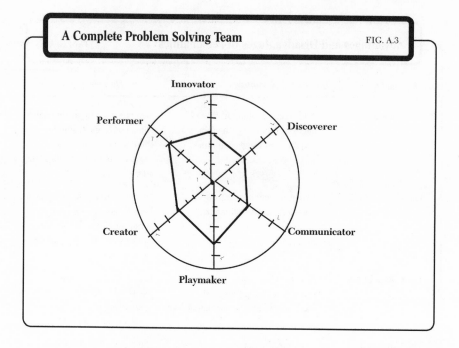

A Complete Problem Solving Team   FIG. A.3

Obviously the unbalanced team is likely to be less creative and less able to deliver on its promises. The more complete your team, the greater your likelihood of success.

Managing Personalities Together over Time: Virtuous and Vicious Cycles

The six essentials are a high-level design for a complete engine of thought. If you can get all six in place, learn how they interrelate, and get them working together, you can eventually problem solve at speeds and go places you never thought possible. Improving your skill in one essential also enhances your ability to execute the others. If all six are being applied together, they can begin to produce a virtuous cycle, or upward spiral of improving performance, feeding off of one another.

However, if you are missing any of the six or if they are seriously out of balance or proportion, the virtuous cycle can become vicious and compound your troubles. One weak essential will degrade the effectiveness of another, which in turn makes another still worse. This results in a downward spiral or, at a minimum, a stagnant, or flat improvement curve.

Great problem solvers create virtuous cycles by working hard to refine and integrate the degree to which they make the six essentials work together. (Figure A.5, which repeats Figure I.4, illustrates how the virtuous cycle works.)

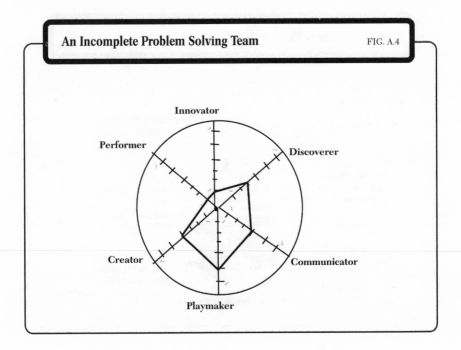

An Incomplete Problem Solving Team　　FIG. A.4

Innovator

Performer

Discoverer

Creator

Communicator

Playmaker

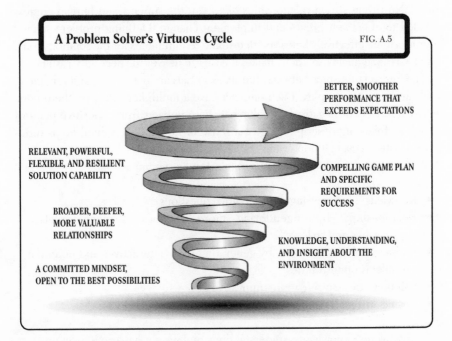

A Problem Solver's Virtuous Cycle　　FIG. A.5

BETTER, SMOOTHER PERFORMANCE THAT EXCEEDS EXPECTATIONS

RELEVANT, POWERFUL, FLEXIBLE, AND RESILIENT SOLUTION CAPABILITY

COMPELLING GAME PLAN AND SPECIFIC REQUIREMENTS FOR SUCCESS

BROADER, DEEPER, MORE VALUABLE RELATIONSHIPS

KNOWLEDGE, UNDERSTANDING, AND INSIGHT ABOUT THE ENVIRONMENT

A COMMITTED MINDSET, OPEN TO THE BEST POSSIBILITIES

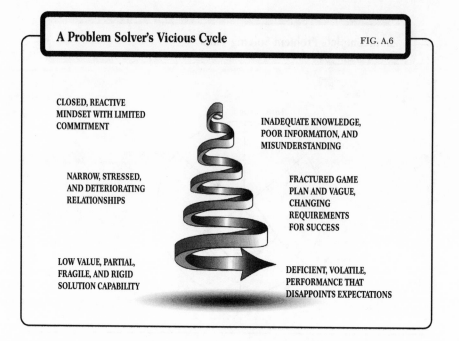

A Problem Solver's Vicious Cycle   FIG. A.6

CLOSED, REACTIVE
MINDSET WITH LIMITED
COMMITMENT

INADEQUATE KNOWLEDGE,
POOR INFORMATION, AND
MISUNDERSTANDING

NARROW, STRESSED,
AND DETERIORATING
RELATIONSHIPS

FRACTURED GAME
PLAN AND VAGUE,
CHANGING
REQUIREMENTS
FOR SUCCESS

LOW VALUE, PARTIAL,
FRAGILE, AND RIGID
SOLUTION CAPABILITY

DEFICIENT, VOLATILE,
PERFORMANCE THAT
DISAPPOINTS EXPECTATIONS

The right mindset drives better judgment and decisionmaking while improving your effectiveness in moving creatively and decisively through a problem solving effort. Gaining knowledge of the territory helps you define problems more effectively. Nurturing strong relationships gives you the support and human context needed to effectively create and implement change. Defining problem solving journeys more effectively helps you determine requirements for the solutions you'll need. Creating quality solutions makes it easier to deliver the necessary results.

The interrelationships between the six essentials are both linear and nonlinear, and can be quite complex. Each one can have a multiplier effect on the others, either positively or negatively. Looking at these impacts from a positive point of view, the following descriptions give a sense of how each essential helps influence a virtuous cycle if done well:

An Innovator's open and committed mindset has an impact on:

- Knowledge, by inspiring more creative questions
- Relationships, by engendering more openness through creative approaches and styles
- Problem-Solving Journeys, by generating more alternatives and potential problems/opportunities
- Solutions, by inspiring more innovative designs
- Results, through more resourceful implementation.

A Discoverer's knowledge, understanding, and insight have an impact on:

- Mindset, through better information that underpins a more informed and balanced mindset
- Relationships, through more insight into character, personality, and potential fit
- Problem-Solving Journeys, by better defined problems and clearer choices between alternative issues
- Solutions, through more informed design of specific and well-suited them
- Results, because better intelligence reduces risk in implementation.

A Communicator's connections and relationships have an impact on:

- Mindset, by creating safe environments that encourage more creative interdisciplinary thinking
- Knowledge, by facilitating faster access to more trustworthy sources
- Problem-Solving Journeys, by offering deeper insights into and better intelligence on problems
- Solutions, through enhancing one's ability to marshal people to build
- Results, by creating more resilience and adaptability in implementation.

A Playmaker's direction-setting and strategy have an impact on:

- Mindset, by focusing creative thinking on the most important issues
- Knowledge, by defining the goals which drive key questions and unknowns
- Relationships, through defining specifically the kind of value that resolution of a problem will add to various relationships
- Solutions, because a better defined problem is easier to fit with the right solution
- Results, since the right strategic navigation increases energy for implementation.

A Creator's intelligent design and construction of solutions has an impact on:

- Mindset, freeing up time and focus for creative execution
- Knowledge, by allowing concentration on the toughest unknowns
- Relationships, through increasing pride of creation and ownership
- Problem-Solving Journeys, by offering technology that addresses more potential issues
- Results, through better quality, easier, faster, less wasteful resolution.

And finally, a Performer's combination of intuition and discipline has an impact on"

- Mindset, through increased confidence and optimism, which generate unbounded ideas
- Knowledge, by allowing time for gathering intelligence and learning, not just acting
- Relationships, by enhancing mutual interdependence and creating group identity
- Problem-Solving Journeys, by generating increased trust and incentive to delegate larger issues
- Solutions, because it results in less wear and tear on solutions and increases their yield.

Once you actually start solving any problem, you will immediately begin to drift towards either a vicious or a virtuous cycle. (To illustrate the vicious cycle, I've repeated Figure I.5 here as Figure A.6.)

In my experience, there are few in-betweens. What may look like just muddling through or moving along slowly is usually just the gradual onset of a vicious cycle. Preventing vicious cycles and enhancing virtuous cycles is the whole ball game for problem solvers.

Managing Problems over Time: Every Problem Is a Journey

Any problem or opportunity in any profession, from the smallest to the largest, the simplest to the most complex, the shortest to the longest, goes through the same phases over time. (Figure A.7, repeating Figure 4.1, lays out the phases of the journey in detail.)

These start from **orientation** in a new environment, when problems and opportunities first present themselves, and finish off with closure and **evaluation** of what was accomplished, what was learned and what it means. Once you understand these essential phases, you can be on top of any problem, no matter how big it is, and gain an ability to navigate through it, knowing where you are at each step of the journey.

In the following chart (Figure A.8) are concrete examples of recognizable classes of problem, which all proceed through these six phases if they are completely solved.

Now you've pulled a whole problem solving team together. You've also gained some sense of the interrelationships between the six essentials. In addition, you can break any problem, no matter how complex, down into the key phases that lead to a resolution. The ultimate question now is, how do you apply all of this—people, essentials, and phases—to managing a problem solving effort over time?

Phases of a Problem Solving Journey

FIG. A.7

	Orientation	Selection	Initiation	Momentum	Breakthrough	Evaluation
Question	*What are the problems and where are they occurring?*	*Which problems will you solve or prevent?*	*What are your goals, plans and how to engage?*	*How to make it happen?*	*How to "break the back" and make it stick?*	*How to learn and improve?*
Activities	Recogntion Identification Location Confirmation Generation	Definition Preparation Prioritization Prevention	Planning Design Sourcing Budgeting	Prototyping Piloting Adaptation	Concentration Consolidation Closure	Assessment Reflection Implications
Objective	Clarity Visibility	Specificity Proactivity	Maximize rewards, minimize cost and risk	Movement Transform	Persistence Control	Learning

Selected Classes of Problems and Opportunities

FIG. A.8

- Company growing
- New product development
- Sales and service
- Turnarounds
- Deals and negotiations
- Improvement projects
- Crises and conflict resolution
- Research and analysis
- Construction
- Deployments and campaigns
- Repair and maintenance projects
- Applied research
- Exploration

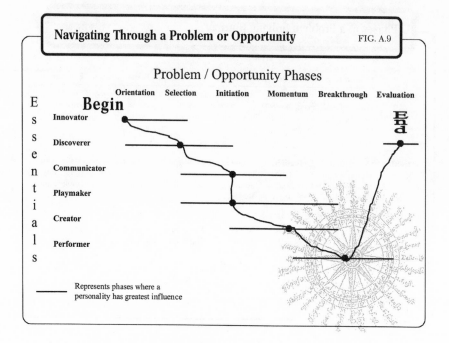

Navigating Through a Problem or Opportunity   FIG. A.9

Problem / Opportunity Phases

Essentials

Managing Personalities and Problems over Time: Navigating Through a Problem

To complete most problem solving journeys successfully, professionals must make hundreds of choices about enablers (e.g., choices about ideas, knowledge, people, plans, solutions, and practices) and apply each enabler to help them define and achieve their goal. The six essentials outlined in this book correspond to these different types of enablers, and learning to apply them enhances your capability of making good problem solving choices and thereby getting results.

A problem solver will, at any particular time in the course of solving a problem, want to emphasize a different personality. (See Figure A.9.) The Innovator and the Discoverer have their greatest influence at the beginning of a problem, in orientation and selection, when the lack of a creative perspective and relevant knowledge can doom an effort from the start. The Playmaker's role is especially vital in the initial stages of planning and goal-setting, and continues through the phases where a great deal of steering may be required. The Creator rises in importance once a problem is fairly well defined and concrete solutions are necessary to initiate resolution. The Performer shines during the phases in which the momentum for change is being built and when the effort is moving past the point of no return, or breakthrough.

The process of solving any problem can be reduced to the pattern of choices made by a particular problem solver as he moves through the phases of a problem. I call this navigating through a problem.

The patterns of movement, or "navigational routes," range from simple and linear (i.e., a cookbook approach) for straightforward problems (e.g., applying for a job) to complex and nonlinear for larger-scale, more difficult problems (e.g., starting a new company). Problem solvers may freely move around and alter their course in solving a problem. This might mean switching rapidly from essential to essential and phase to phase as you attack different aspects of the problem. It might even mean backtracking if necessary to get something absolutely right before proceeding further or as you move to scale.

Just to take a brief example (refer again to Figure A.9), when you're orienting yourself in a situation and taking account of potential problems and opportunities, the unconstrained mindset of the Innovator helps avoid locking in to any preconceived notions about what is or isn't possible.

As you move to select a problem to work on, more knowledge of the territory from the Discoverer is crucial, to determine which problems are real and what their impact on you could be.

By the time you are initiating a problem solving effort, the Communicator's ability to make the case for change and build a core team combines with the Playmaker's ability to set direction and so get things going in the right direction.

To build momentum, in the next phase, requires the leadership of the Creator, working with the Performer, to refine solution design rapidly in a way that takes account of any unforeseen conditions.

In the next phase, breaking through past the point of no return demands the resourcefulness and disciplined focus of the Performer, to help the team persevere in spite of setbacks and negotiate difficult barriers to progress.

Finally, as you come to the completion of a problem, your attention will again be shifting to the Discoverer, digesting what you have learned about the territory, and to relationships, confirming with those important people, your customers and stakeholders, that what you've delivered has been worth the time, cost, and effort.

Assessing Your Overall Problem Solving Ability

Over time, one gains skill in mastering and applying the variations on the six essentials that may be necessary in widely varying problem solving situations. To differentiate between levels of problem solving ability, I assess any individual or organization on a simple scale. This scale takes into account a number of different factors, including whether problems are being identified, whether they are

The Levels of Problem Solving Effectiveness   FIG. A.10

BEST	**Create potential**	Create opportunity	Dramatic success	Able to identify and solve new or tough problems
	Fulfill potential	Master problem solving	Repeatable success	Able to solve wide variety of problems better
	Advance potential	Tackling problems	One-time success	Able to improve ability to solve a problem
	Know potential	Understanding self	Muddle through	Knowing which problems to solve
	Deny potential	Organizing tasks	Chaotic repression	Knowing how to prioritize tasks
	Degrade potential	Taking instructions	Intentional repression	Knowing which instructions to execute
WORST	**Destroy potential**	Repressing spirit	Organized repression	Knowing how to suppress spirit

being solved well, and solved well repeatably, and whether potential is simply being realized or actually created. (See Figure A.10.)

Although I have developed more detailed diagnostics, not included here, using this simple version can help you make your own general assessment and gain some insight into how good you or your organization are at problem solving.

Once you've made an overall assessment, you need to consider what to do to strengthen your performance. There may be one or two essentials that need to be strengthened. You may simply need to find someone else with those abilities to work with you and complement your own skills.

You may need some work on integrating the different pieces so that they work better together.

Or the problems and opportunities you are tackling may be out of proportion to the level of skill you've demonstrated in each of the areas.

To analyze your own situation further, this next chart (Figure A.11, repeated from Figure I.3 in the Introduction) shows at a high level how variations in the six essentials relate to overall levels of capability. It can help you determine whether your issue may lie with one essential in particular, or with how they are being used in concert.

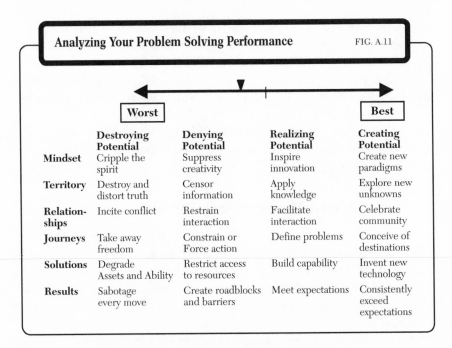

How Fast and How Much Can You Improve?

Everyone's problem solving journey is different. We have all been given the gift of a range of talents. The point is to exploit everything you've been given, to play the hand you've been dealt as best you can. Once you start to think about the six essentials actively in the context of a real problem or opportunity, they are self-implementing. Just start using them.

To set appropriate expectations, imagine learning a language. You've got to use it a lot, immerse yourself, and work at applying new ideas without being afraid of making mistakes:

- Work on actual problems and experiment with the vocabulary.
- Test the principles.
- Diagnose a syndrome.
- Track your progress.
- Cultivate your awareness.
- Keep project logs.
- Have discussions with others.
- Describe what works well and what doesn't.

Take many small steps and soon you'll find you've covered a great distance. At a certain point, your learning rate can change from linear to geometric as you gain a critical mass of vocabulary and experience.

Through practice, your sophistication and capability to get results will increase. Gradually, you will develop a different, powerful method of thinking, communicating, behaving, and perceiving. You'll find that improvement becomes self-sustaining and your problem solving ability will begin to improve more consistently. You will find yourself on a new path where, just ahead, lie destinations you thought you could never reach.

Finding More Knowledge Outside the Book

The Problem Solving Journey is a work in progress. If you would like to know more about problem solving in general or specifically how to apply the six essentials, I would be happy to try and help. You can find me via the company I founded as the primary source for problem solvers: Exolve, Inc. Visit our website at www.exolve.com. Or please e-mail us at thejourney@exolve.com.

On our website, you can investigate problem solving in more depth or learn more about the specific methodology behind this study. There, you can also find

- a select bibliography of the best books on problem solving,
- do a diagnostic to determine what type of problem solver you are and develop a personal action plan,
- a select bibliography of travel and adventure literature,
- a select bibliography of book length problem solving case studies in fields ranging from supercomputing and medicine to aerospace and engineering,
- and a detailed description of my research methodology (i.e., sample selection, state of the practice) and our planned efforts to continue this research in the future.

Description of Methodology

I want to be absolutely clear about what this book is and what it is not from a scientific perspective. It is not offered as proof and does not claim to be definitive. It simply presents two working hypotheses that I hope will generate discussion, debate, and a more formal research agenda: that there is universal problem solving knowledge beyond mere common sense that can be captured and applied to improve human problem solving skills, and that the larger in scale a problem is, the more important this universal knowledge becomes.

I have focused on case study research and my own experience, because this approach offers the best means to formulate new questions and generate hypotheses. My case study research has been conducted using open-ended and focused interviews and documentary analysis. I have incorporated direct observations where I have been involved personally in a problem solving effort. In performing the case studies, I often interviewed selected major participants in a problem solving effort to learn what worked, what didn't, and what might be applicable to problem solving in other areas outside their own field of expertise. Interview information was supplemented with documentary analyses of each organization's existing practices, and reported outcomes. In some cases, because of the scope of the study and limited access to principals, I had only secondary material to base my analysis on.

This book is a milestone on a long journey, not the end of one. I view it as simply one more step on the great adventure of researching and exploring the fundamentals of human problem solving and hope it makes some small contribution to that effort.

SOURCES

Introduction

Shackleton's Trip from S. Georgia Island, December 5, 1914, to May 10, 1916
Sir Ernest Shackleton, *South* (1998), Carroll & Graf; Roland Huntford, *Shackleton* (1985), Carroll & Graf; F. A. Worsley, *Endurance* (1999), Norton; Caroline Alexander, *The Endurance* (1999), Knopf; Alfred Lansing, *Endurance* (1959), Carroll & Graf.

Part 1: "Generate the Mindset"

"Christopher Columbus's First Voyage Across the Atlantic, Aug. 3 to Oct. 11, 1492"
To America and the World: The Logs of Christopher Columbus and Ferdinand Magellan (1990), Branden; Samuel E. Morison, *Admiral of the Ocean Sea* (1970), Little, Brown; Samuel Morison, *Christopher Columbus*, (1983), Meridian; J. M. Cohen, ed. and trans., *Christopher Columbus: The Four Voyages* (1969), Penguin; Oliver Dunn and James Kelley, trans., *The Diario of Christopher Columbus's First Voyage to America 1492–93* (1989), University of Oklahoma.
"Innovators in Action": Dee Hock and Visa International
Author's interviews with Dee Hock, August and October 1999; Dee Hock, "Institutions in the Age of Mindcrafting," Bionomics Annual Conference, San Francisco, Oct. 22, 1994; M. Mitchell Waldrop, "The Trillion Dollar Vision of Dee Hock," *Fast Company*, Oct./Nov. 1996; Dee Hock, *Birth of the Chaordic Age* (2000), Berrett-Koehler; Joseph Nocera, *A Piece of the Action* (1994), Simon & Schuster.
"Turn Problems into Opportunities": Ralph Nader and the Consumer Safety Movement

Author's interview with Ralph Nader, June 1999; "Ralph Nader, Consumer Cru-
sader," Interview Feb. 16, 1991, www.achievement.org; *Multinational Mon-
itor Magazine,* founded by Ralph Nader, various articles; testimony of Ralph
Nader before House Budget Committee, June 30, 1999; Anthony Ramirez,
"Consumer Crusader Feels a Chill in Washington," *New York Times,* Dec.
31, 1995; Connie Koenenn, "Where to from Here?," *Los Angeles Times,*
Nov. 25, 1994; Doubting and Believing game attributed to Peter Elbow,
Writing Without Teachers (1994), Oxford University Press.

"Commit to the Summit": Jeff Bezos and Amazon.com

Kara Swisher, "Why Is Jeff Bezos Still Smiling?" *Washington Post,* April 24,
2000; "Ebay vs. Amazon.com, the Fight You Thought You'd Never See"
Business Week, May 31, 1999; Peter de Jonge, "Riding the Wild, Perilous
Waters of Amazon.com", *New York Times,* March 14, 1999New York
Times,; Chip Bayers, "The Inner Bezos," *Wired,* March 1999; Alex Fryer,
"Inside Seattle's Biggest Online Bookstore", *Seattle Times,* July 26, 1998;
"Booked Solid," *Time Magazine,* Sept. 7, 1998; Jonathan Rabinovitz, "Page
of Progress," *San Jose Mercury News,* Oct. 11, 1998; Gale Research Inc.,
Newsmakers 1998; David Streitfeld, "Hitting the Big Time," *Washington
Post,* Sept. 1, 1999, and "Booking the future," *Washington Post,* Sept. 7,
1999.

"Create Strength out of Vulnerability": Toni Morrison and the Power of Stories

Toni Morrison, *Beloved* (1998), Plume; Gale Research Inc., *Newsmakers 1998;*
Barbara Bigelow, ed., *Contemporary Black Biography* (1997), Volume 15;
Bryan Ryan and Kathleen Wilson, eds., *Major Twentieth Century Writers,*
Second Edition (1998),; *60 Minutes,* Aug. 9, 1998; David Streitfeld, "The
Laureate's Life Song," *Washington Post,* Oct. 8, 1993*Washington Post*;
Claudia Dreifus, "Chloe Wofford Talks about Toni Morrison," *New York
Times Magazine,* Sept. 11, 1994; Christopher Borrelli, "Elusive Beloved,"
Block News Alliance, Oct. 15, 1998; Christine Vidal, "A Look at Nobelist's
Writing Process," *Reporter,* State University of New York at Buffalo, May 1,
1997; Eugene Robinson, "Toni Morrison's Measured Words in Her Nobel
Lecture," *Washington Post,* Dec. 8, 1993.

"Have It Both Ways": Ron Barbaro and Living Death Benefits for AIDS Patients

Author's interview with Ron Barbaro, June 1999; David Bollier, *Aiming Higher*
(1996) The Business Enterprise Trust; Tony Wong, "Meet the Economy
Builders", *Toronto Star,* March 29, 1999.

"Transcend Limits": Charles Krulak and the Formation of U.S. Marines

Author's interview with Charles Krulak, November 1999; Thomas Ricks, *Making
the Corps* (1997), Scribner; David Freedman, *Corps Business: The 30 Management Principles of the U.S. Marines* (2000), Harper Business; Charles
Krulak, "Farewell to the Corps," *Marines Magazine,* May 1999; Jon Katzenbach and Jason Santamaria, "Firing up the Front Line," *Harvard Business*

Review, May/June 1999; David Freedman, "Corps Values," *Inc. Magazine,* April 1998.

Part 2: "Know the Territory"

"The Lewis and Clark Expedition, July 5, 1803–Sept. 23, 1806"

Elliott Coues, ed., *The History of the Lewis & Clark Expedition* (1893), Dover Editions, Volumes I-III; Stephen Ambrose, *Undaunted Courage* (1996), Simon & Schuster; Bernard DeVoto, ed. *The Journals of Lewis & Clark* (1997), Houghton-Mifflin.

"Discoverers in Action": Robert Shapiro and Monsanto Corporation

Author's interview with Robert Shapiro, October 1999; Alicia Hills Moore, "Monsanto's Bet," *Fortune Magazine,* April 14, 1997; John D. Cook, et al., "Food Biotechnology," *McKinsey Quarterly,* 1997, no. 3; Michael Specter, "The Pharmageddon Riddle," *The New Yorker,* April 10, 2000; Robert Shapiro, Remarks before Greenpeace Business Conference, Oct. 6, 1999; David Barboza, "Biotech Companies Take on Critics of Gene-Altered Food," *New York Times,* Nov. 11, 1999; William Claiborne, "Biotech Crops Spur Warning," *Washington Post,* Nov. 24, 1999; Juan Enriquez and Ray Goldberg, "Transforming Life, Transforming Business: The Life Science Revolution," *Harvard Business Review,* March/April 2000; Scott Kilman, "Seeds of Doubt," *Wall Street Journal,* Nov. 19, 1999; Zins Mouhheiber, "A Hail of Silver Bullets," *Forbes,* Jan. 26, 1998.

"Know What and How to Know": The Human Genome Project

Author's interviews with William Haseltine, June 1999, and Craig Venter July 1999; James Schreeve, "The Code Breaker," *Discover,* May 1998; Eliot Marshall, "A High-Stakes Gamble on Genome Sequencing," *Science Magazine,* June 20, 1999; Harvard Business School, "Gene Research, the Mapping of Life and the Global Economy" Case No. N9–599–016, Oct. 19, 1998; "The Future of Medicine," *Time Magazine,* Jan. 11, 1999; "BioTech Century," *Business Week,* March 10, 1997; David Stipp, "The Real BioTech Revolution," *Fortune,* March 31, 1997; Nicholas Wade, "Beyond Sequencing of Human DNA," *New York Times,* May 12, 1998; Linton Weeks, "Mr. Green Genes," *Washington Post,* Feb. 17, 1998; J. P. Donlon, Interview for *CEO Magazine,* June 1999; Lisa Belkin, "DNA Is His Pay Dirt" *New York Times,* August 23, 1998; Tim Beardsley, "An Express Route to the Genome?" *Scientific American,* August 1998; Justin Zivin, "Understanding Clinical Trials," *Scientific American,* April 2000; Lawrence Fisher, "The Race to Cash in on the Genetic Code," *New York Times,* August 20, 1999; Louise Fickel, "Writing the Book of Life," *CIO Magazine,* March 1, 2000. Oliver Wendell Holmes, Jr., Lecture, Harvard University, Feb. 17, 1886.

"Spot the Patterns": NOAA and Weather Prediction

Author's interviews with Ants Leetmaa, June 1999, and D. James Baker, August 1999; Michael King and David Herring "Monitoring Earth's Vital Signs," *Scientific American*, April 2000; Curt Suplee, "This Season's El Niño Forecast to Have No Small Consequences,", *Washington Post*, Dec. 5, 1997; Guy Gugliotta, "Beyond La Niña, A Changing Climate for Research," *Washington Post*, June 14, 1999; Nicole Lewis, "IT Tracks El Niño's Path," *Federal Computer Week*, Oct. 20, 1997; William Stevens, "Climate Expert's New Worry," *New York Times*, May 18, 1999, and "Remember El Niño?" *New York Times*, Jan. 27, 1999; "A Problem as Big as the Planet," *The Economist*, Nov. 5, 1994; graphic adapted from Lynn Steen, ed., *On the Shoulders of Giants* (1990), National Research Council.

"Assess the Players and Stakes": The Barker Foundation and Adoption

Author's interview with Robin Allen, December 1999; Ann Humphrey, "Adoption in the Future," *Washington Parent Magazine*, May 20, 1999; Barbara Mathias-Riegel, "Dating, Identity and the Adolescent Adopted Child," *Washington Post*, March 1, 1999; Carol Demuth, "Courageous Blessing— Adoptive Parents and the Search" (1993) Aries Center; Lincoln Caplan, *An Open Adoption* (1990), Farrar, Straus and Giroux; Arthur Sorosky, et al., *The Adoption Triangle* (1984), Anchor; Jill Krementz *How it Feels to be Adopted* (1988), Knopf; Nancy Verrier, *The Primal Wound* (1997), Gateway Press; David Brodzinsky, et al., *Being Adopted* (1992), Doubleday.

"See the Whole, but Get to the Heart": The NTSB and Aviation Accident Investigation

Author's interviews with Bernard Loeb, November 1999; FAA letter of comment on NTSB Safety Recommendation A–98–88–106; Jonathan Harr, "The Crash Detectives," *The New Yorker*, August 5, 1996; David Josar, "Icing May Have Gone Undetected on Comair," *The Detroit News*, May 22, 1997; "Flights Reported Ice Before Fatal Crash," *The Orlando Sentinel*, Jan. 11, 1997; AP, "Plan Crashes Near Detroit, Killing 29" Jan. 10, 1997; Aircraft Accident Report: "In-flight Icing Encounter and Uncontrolled Collision with Terrain—Comair Flight 3272, Embraer EMB–120RT, N265CA, Jan 9, 1997"; Franklin Main "FAA: Turboprops Need Ice Detector," *The Cincinnati Post*, May 13, 1997; Manny Lopez, "Teams Pore over Twisted Metal to Unlock Flight 3272 Mystery," *The Detroit News*, Jan. 17, 1997; Keith Bradsheer, "All 29 on Commuter Aircraft Die in Crash Outside Detroit," *New York Times*, Jan. 10, 1997; Richard Leiby, "The Fragments of Flight 427," *Washington Post*, May 13, 1999.

"Learn to Learn": Xerox Business Services

Author's interviews with Raymond Lammes and Louis Olmos, January 2000; Alan Webber, "XBS Learns to Grow," *Fast Company*, Oct./Nov. 1996; Ellen Langer, *The Power of Mindful Learning* (1997), Addison-Wesley; Charles

Gallistei, *The Organization of Learning* (1990), MIT Press; Howard Gardner, *The Disciplined Mind* (1999), Simon & Schuster.

Part 3: "Build the Relationships"

"The Long March of the Chinese Revolutionaries, Oct. 16, 1934, to Oct. 19, 1935"

Jonathan Spence, *Mao Zedong* (1999), Lipper/Viking; Dick Wilson, *The Long March* (1971), Viking Press; Jean Fritz, *China's Long March* (1988), Putnam's; Harrison Salisbury, *The Long March* (1985), Harper & Row.

"Communicators in Action": Orpheus Chamber Orchestra

Author's interviews with Harvey Seifert, Nardo Poy, Ronnie Bauch, and Eric Wyrick, November 1999; Allan Kozinn, "Seeking Harmony in Discord: The Orpheus Ensemble Reconsiders the Way It Makes Music" *New York Times*, Oct. 27, 1999; James Traub, "Passing the Baton: What CEO's could learn from the Orpheus Chamber Orchestra," *The New Yorker*, August 26 and Sept. 2, 1996; Jared Burden, "The Chamber Orchestra Orpheus Wants No Conductor," *Connoisseur*, Feb. 1988; James Oestreich, "An Orchestra Navigates by the Stars," *New York Times*, Sept. 30, 1999; Raphael Mostel, "Sounds Like Chamber Music," *Chamber Music*; John Lubans, "Orchestrating Success," *Hemispheres Magazine*, Jan. 1999; "Case Study in C-Sharp Minor," *Training Magazine*, Oct. 1998.

"Conversation Is King": Franklin D. Roosevelt and His Fireside Chats

B. D. Zevin, ed. *Nothing to Fear, The Selected Addresses of FDR* (1946), Houghton Mifflin; James MacGregor Burns, *Roosevelt: The Lion and the Fox*, Vol. 1; David Brinkley, *Washington Goes to War* (1988), Ballantine; Liza Mundy, "What They Talk About When They Talk About Talk," *Washington Post Magazine*, Feb. 4, 1996.

"Give and Take": The United Space Alliance and Software Development for the Space Shuttle

Author's interview with Tom Peterson and Jim Orr, November 1999; Charles Fishman, "They Write the Right Stuff," *Fast Company Magazine*, Dec./Jan. 1997; "How Management Teams Can Have a Good Fight," *Harvard Business Review*, July/August 1997; Frederick Brooks, *The Mythical Man-Month* (1995), Addison-Wesley; Terry Winograd, *Bringing Design to Software* (1996), Addison-Wesley; Jim McCarthy, *Dynamics of Software Development* (1995), Microsoft Press.

"Develop Yourself Through Others": John Thompson and Georgetown Basketball

Michael Wilbon, "The Class of Style and Substance," *Washington Post*, Feb. 1, 1991; Colman McCarthy, "Mentoring Matters," *Washington Post*, March 29, 1996; Bill Bradley, *Values of the Game* (1999) Broadway Books; William

Gildea, "Thompson Resigns Citing Personal Reasons," *Washington Post*, Jan. 9, 1999; Tony Kornheiser, "To the Contrary, and Loving It," *Washington Post*, Jan. 9, 1999; Thomas Boswell, "There's No Denying, His Aim is True," *Washington Post*, Jan 9, 1999; Michael Wilbon, "Thompson's Long Shadow Comforts Prized Pupil", *Washington Post*, June 5, 1994; Thomas Boswell, "Thompson Stood for Something," *Washington Post*, June 25, 1999; Michael Wilbon, "A Coach with the Courage to Make America Think" *Washington Post*, Jan. 9, 1999. Herminia Ibarra, "Making Partner: A Mentor's Guide to the Psychological Journey," *Harvard Business Review*, March/April 2000; Randy Komisar, "Goodbye Career, Hello Success," *Harvard Business Review*, March/April 2000;

"Cultivate a Network": Bill Shore and Share Our Strength
Author's interview with Bill Shore, June 1999; Bill Shore, *The Cathedral Within* (1999), Random House; Steven Pearlstein "The New Prophet of Non-Profits," *Fast Company*, April/May 1996; Elizabeth Kastor, "From Rat Race to the Human Race," *Washington Post*, Feb. 2, 1993; Bill Shore, "It's Not How Much You Give, It's How You Give It," *New York Times*, Sept. 27, 1997; Marlon Millner, "Nonprofits Open Up Shop," *Washington Business Journal*, April 10, 1998; "The Business of Doing Good," *Worth Magazine,* March 1996; Bill Shore, "Charities Change Role by Turning a Profit," *USA Today,* March 26, 1996.

"All for One and One for All": McKinsey & Company
The author was a consultant with McKinsey & Co. from 1987 to 1991.

Part 4: "Manage the Journeys"

"The United States of America's Journey to the Moon, July 16–20, 1969."
James Schefter, *The Race: The Uncensored Story of How America Beat Russia to the Moon* (1999), Doubleday; Eldon Hall *Journey to the Moon* (1996), American Institute of Aeronautics and Astronautics; Jim Lovell and Jeffrey Kluger, *Lost Moon* (1994), Houghton Mifflin; Alan Shephard and Deke Slayton, *Moon Shot: The Inside Story of America's Race to the Moon* (1994), Turner Publishing.

"Playmakers in Action: Kleiner, Perkins Venture Capital, and the Technology Industry"
David Kaplan, *The Silicon Boys* (1999), William Morrow; Laura Holson, "A Capitalist Venturing in the World of Computers and Religion," *New York Times*, Jan. 3, 2000; Michael Malone, "John Doerr's Startup Manual," *Fast Company*, Feb./March 1997; John Heileman, "The Networker," *The New Yorker*, August 11, 1997; Melanie Warner, "The Silicon Valley Machine," *Fortune*, Oct. 26, 1998; Elizabeth Corcoran, "Mother Hen to an Industry," *Washington Post*, Sept. 13, 1996; Anthony Perkins, "The Angler: The Se-

crets of Kleiner Perkin's Success," *Red Herring,* Nov. 1, 1999; Roger Taylor, "New Economy's Capitalists See Glowing Future Fueled by Ideas," *Financial Times,* August 8, 1999; Michael Peltz "High Tech's Premier Venture Capitalist," *Institutional Investor,* June 1996; Zina Moukheiber, "Kleiner's Web," *Forbes,* March 25, 1996; Jerry Kaplan, *Startup* (1994), Penguin Books; Charles *Ferguson High Stakes, No Prisoners* (1999), Random House.

"Solve the Right Problems at the Right Time": Johns Hopkins Emergency Room
Author's interview with Dr. David Nicolaou, August 1999; Valerie Grossman, *Quick Reference to Triage* (1999), Lippincott-Raven; Gail Handysides, *Triage in Emergency Practice* (1995), Mosby Saunders; Mackway Jones, *Emergency Triage* (1996), BMJ Publishing; Michael Allen, *Business Portfolio Management* (2000), Wiley & Sons; P. Bernstein, *Streetwise: The Best of the Journal of Portfolio Management* (1998), Princeton University Press; Robert Cooper, *Portfolio Management for New Products* (1998), Harper Collins; Frank Fabozzi, *Handbook of Portfolio Management* (1998), McGraw-Hill.

"Choose Where to Go and How to Get There": IDEO and Designing Business Strategy
Author's interview with Aura Oslapas, November 1999; Diane Calmenson, "Reinventing the Wheel," *IS Magazine,* Sept. 1997; Christina Bicchieri, ed., *The Logic of Strategy* (1998), Oxford University Press; Kathleen Eisenhardt, *Competing on the Edge* (1998), Harvard Business School Press; Stephen Cimbala, *Coercive Military Strategy* (1998), Texas A&M Press; Thomas Clear, ed., *Book of Leadership and Strategy: Lessons from Chinese Masters* (1996), Random House; Mary Cronin, *Internet Strategy Handbook* (1996), Harvard Business School Press; *Harvard Business Review on Corporate Strategy* (1999), HBS Press; Mikhail Shereshevsky, *Endgame Strategy* (1994), MacMillan.

"Define Success": Nelson Mandela and the Freeing of South Africa
Author's interview with Prof. Jeffrey Herbst, Princeton University, October 1999; Nelson Mandela, *Long Walk to Freedom* (1994), Little, Brown; Gilbert Hewthwaite, "Mandela's Long Walk Continues At a New Pace," *The Age,* March 28, 1999; Alice Howard and Joan Magretta, "Surviving Success," *McKinsey Quarterly,* 1995, No. 4; Derek Slater, "Is Benchmarking Worth the Bother?" *CIO Magazine,* Nov. 15, 1997; Robert Kaplan and David Norton, "The Balanced Scorecard," *Harvard Business Review,* Jan./Feb. 1992; Arie Halachmi and Geert Bouckaert, *Organizational Performance Measurement* (1996), Greenwood Press; Jerry Harbour, *Basics of Performance Measurement* (1997), Quality Resources; Harry Hatry, *Performance Measurement, Getting Results* (1999), Urban Institute Press; The Conference Board, "New Corporate Performance Measures", July 1995.

"Plan for Chance": American Airlines and Sabre's Integrated Forecasting System

Author's participation in case study of Sabre IFS; John Foley, "Sabre's Challenge" *Information Week,* August 18, 1997; M. Allison, *Strategic Planning for Nonprofit Organizations* (1997), Wiley & Sons; John Bryson, *Strategic Planning* (1995) Jossey-Bass; Alvin Gunneson, *Transitioning Agility: Creating Twenty-First Century Enterprise Strategic Planning* (1996), Addison-Wesley.

"Lead the Way": Colin Powell and America's Promise

Author's interview with Harris Wofford and Leslie Hortum, August 1999; Colin Powell, *My American Journey* (1995), Ballantine; America's Promise, *Report to the Nation for 1999;* Reed Abelson, "Charity Led By Gen. Powell Comes Under Heavy Fire: Organization Accused of Inflating Results," *New York Times,* Oct. 8, 1999; Kevin Merida, "Enjoying Private Life: Powell Stays in Public Eye" *Washington Post,* April 26, 1997; David Gergen, "Keeping Faith in Kids," *U.S. News & World Report,* May 31, 1999; Margaret Carlson, "Once Again on the March," *Nation,* May 24, 1999; Warren Bennis, *Managing the Dream: Reflections on Leadership and Change* (2000), Login Publishers; Dan Ciampa and Michael Watkins, *Right from the Start* (1999), Harvard Business School Press; William Cohen, *Stuff of Heroes: Eight Universal Laws of Leadership* (1998), Andrews & McMeel; Max Depree, *Leadership is an Art* (1989), Doubleday; Gilbert Fairholm, *Perspectives on Leadership* (1998), Greenwood; Howard Gardner, *Leading Minds* (1996), Harper Collins; Frances Hesselbein, ed., *Leader to Leader* (1999), Jossey-Bass.

Part 5: "Create the Solutions"

"The Allied Landing at Normandy, June 5–6, 1944"

Stephen Ambrose, *D-Day* (1994), Simon & Schuster; Ed Cray, *General of the Army: George C. Marshall, Soldier and Statesman* (1990), Simon & Schuster.

"Creators in Action: Academic Systems Corporation and Education in the Knowledge Age"

Author's interviews with founders Bernie Gifford and Edward Landesmann, and CEO John Brandon, December 1999; Edward Landesman, "Visual Technology in the Teaching and Learning of Mathematics," *Syllabus Magazine,* May 1999; Thomas Deloughry, "A California Company Finds Success with Computerized Mathematics Courses," *The Chronicle of Higher Education,* Oct. 25, 1996.

"Find the Right People for the Right Work": Microsoft Corporation

Author's interviews over several years with prospective and current Microsoft executives; Michael Cusumano and Richard Selby, *Microsoft Secrets* (1995),

Free Press; Microsoft Corporation, "Solutions Framework," business document; Julie Bick, *The Microsoft Edge* (1999), Pocket Books; Tom Davenport, "The Skills that Thrill," *CIO magazine*, Jan. 15, 1997; Alan Webber, "He Breeds Dodger Blue," *Fast Company*, April/May 1997; Nina Munk, "Organization Man," *Fortune*, Mar. 16, 1998; Thomas Stewart, "In Search of Elusive Tech Workers," Feb. 16, 1998; Jon Katzenbach and Doug Smith, *The Wisdom of Teams* (1993), HBS Press; David Thielen, *The 12 Simple Secrets of Microsoft Management* (1999), McGraw-Hill.

"Design the Tools to Do the Job": NASA and the Mars Pathfinder Expedition

Author's interviews with NASA Executives, November 1999; Brian Muirhead and Price Pritchett, *The Mars Pathfinder Approach to Faster-Better-Cheaper* (1998), Pritchett & Assoc.; Brian Muirhead, *High Velocity Leadership* (1999), Harper Business; Susi Trautman Wunsch, *The Adventures of Sojourner* (1998), Mikaya Press; George Musser and Mark Alpert, "How to Go to Mars," *Scientific American*, March 2000; Kathy Sawyer, "Another Avoidable Mistake for NASA," *Washington Post*, March 29, 2000.

"Target and Conserve Scarce Resources": John Sawhill and The Nature Conservancy

Author's interview with John Sawhill, November 1999; "Surviving Success: An Interview with John Sawhill," *Harvard Business Review*, Sept./Oct. 1995; "The Perfect President Discovered," *George Magazine*, Nov. 1996; Bill Birchard, "A Pragmatic Activist," *Tomorrow Magazine*, July/August 1999.

"Get the Right Information to the Right People": The CDC and Tuberculosis

Author's interview with Kenneth Castro, November 1999; Ed Regis, *Virus Ground Zero: Stalking the Killer Viruses with the CDC* (1996), Pocket Books; Elizabeth Etheridge, *Sentinel for Health: A History of the CDC* (1992), University of California Press; Richard Preston, *The Hot Zone* (1994), Random House; Gina Kolata, *Flu* (2000), Farrar Straus Giroux; Judith Miller, "Study Says New TB Strains Need an Intensive Strategy," *New York Times*, Oct. 28, 1999; Peter Radetsky, "Last Days of the Wonder Drugs," *Discover*, Nov. 1998; Michael Waldholz, "As Bacteria Outsmart Old Antibiotics, Drug Makers Ready New Arsenal" *Wall Street Journal*, Sept. 27, 1999; Susan Okie, "TB fights Back," *Washington Post*, August 17, 1999, and "The Frontiers of Medicine: Science Races to Stem TB's Threat," *Washington Post*, August 10, 1999; Daniel Williams, "Siberian Sick Bay: Prisons Are Incubators for TB" *Washington Post*, March 14, 1999; Steven Levy, *Insanely Great* (2000), Penguin.

"Design Solutions that Evolve": Dr. Eric Wieschaus and the Growth of Embryos

Author's interview with Dr. Eric Wieschaus, September 1999; Sharon B. McGrayne, *Nobel Prize Women in Science* (1998), Birch Land Press; Eric Wieschaus and Christiane Nusslein-Volhard, "Mutations Affecting Segment Number and Polarity in Drosophila," *Nature*, Oct. 30, 1980; David Brown,

"Two Americans, German Share Nobel Prize for Genetics Research," *Washington Post*, Sept. 10, 1995; Jennifer Ackerman, "Journey to the Center of the Egg," *New York Times,* Oct. 12, 1997; Natalie Anger, "Scientist at Work," *New York Times,* Dec. 5, 1995.

"Shift the Balance of Power": Microsoft and the Department of Justice Antitrust Case

Author's interview with attorney George Cary, October 1999; Ken Auletta, "Hard Core" *The New Yorker,* August 16, 1999; James Grimaldi, "The Man Going After Microsoft," *Seattle Times,* Feb. 12, 1998; "Bill and Warren" Fortune, July 20, 1998; Rajiv Chandrasekaran, "Microsoft Trial Ends with Firm Chastened," *Washington Post*, June 25, 1999; Joel Brinkley, "U.S. Judge Declares Microsoft a Market-Stifling Monopoly," *New York Times,* Nov. 6, 1999; Rajiv Chandrasekaran, "Judge Says Microsoft Wields Monopoly Power over Rivals," *Washington Post*, Nov. 6, 1999; John Markoff, with Steve Lohr, "Silicon Valley Cites Concern amid Glee on Microsoft Case," *New York Times,* Nov. 8, 1999; Steve Lohr, "Microsoft's Horizon," *New York Times,* Nov. 7, 1999; William Shakespeare, *Measure for Measure.*

Part 6: "Deliver the Results"

"Reinhold Messner's Solo Ascent of Mount Everest, August 15–20, 1980"

Reinhold Messner, *The Crystal Horizon: Everest, the First Solo Ascent* (1989), The Mountaineers; Reinhold Messner, *Everest: Expedition to the Ultimate* (1999), The Mountaineers; Reinhold Messner, *The Big Walls* (1977), Kaye & Ward:

"Performers in Action: Isabelle Autissier and Sailing Solo Around the World"

Derek Lundy, *Godforsaken Seas* (1999), Algonquin Books; Sheila Norman, "She May Have Lost Her Dream, But She Escaped with Her Life," interview with Isabelle Autissier, *Los Angeles Times,* Jan. 29, 1995; Deborah Bennett, "Alone But Not a Loner," *Cruising World,* July 1, 1994; Herb McCormick "The Unluckiest (and Luckiest) Day of Isabelle's Life," *Cruising World,* April 1, 1999; Dana Thomas, "Solo Survivor," *Women's Sport and Fitness,* Nov./Dec. 1999; Herb McCormick, "Alone No Longer," *Sailing World,* May 1999; Ivor Wilkins, "Isabelle Autissier: A Singular Woman," *Sunday Star-Times,* Feb. 21, 1999; Claudio Aspesi and Dev Vardhan, "Brilliant Strategy, but Can You Execute?" *McKinsey Quarterly,* 1999, no. 1.

"Simplify and Specify": Ron Ponder and Federal Express Package Tracking

Author's interviews with Ron Ponder, January 1998 and June 2000; Carl Nehls, "Custodial Package Tracking at Federal Express," in Bruce Guile and James Quinn, ed., *Managing Innovation: Cases from the Service Industries* (1988). National Academy Press; "Fedex Wins Award for Its Excellence in Technology," *Information Week,* June 16, 1986; IMD Case Study 392–001–1, "Federal Express Quality Improvement Program" (1990); Laton McCartney, "AT&T Calling," *Information Week,* March 31, 1997; Speech by Ponder to IBM Transportation Conference, Palm Springs, April 8, 1991; Walter Carlson, "Transforming an Industry Through Technology," *IEEE Annals of the History of Computing,* Vol. 15, No. 1, 1993; Kathy Chin, "The Two Who Absolutely, Positively Run Fed Ex's Networks," *Communications Week,* Dec. 22, 1986.

"Set the Pace and Pilot a Course": Lou Gerstner and IBM

Robert Slater, *Saving Big Blue* (1999), McGraw-Hill; Amy Cortese and Ira Sager, "Gerstner at the Gates," *Business Week,* June 19, 1995; Ira Sager, "The View from IBM," *Business Week,* Oct. 30, 1995; Geoffrey Brewer, "Lou Gerstner Has His Hands Full," *Sales & Marketing Management,* May 1998; "Blue is the Colour," *Economist,* June 6, 1998; Michael Verespej, "Gerstner Looked Before Leaping," *Industry Week,* Jan. 23, 1995; George Febish, "Not Bad, Mr. Gerstner," *Datamation,* Nov. 1996; David Ignatius, "Back from the Brink of Extinction," *Washington Post,* May 3, 1999; D. Quinn Mills, "The Decline and Rise of IBM," *Sloan Management Review,* June 22, 1996; Barbara DePompa, "IBM's Comeback Team," *Information Week,* Jan. 9, 1995; Betsy Morris, "He's Smart, He's Not Nice. He's Saving Big Blue," *Fortune,* April 14, 1997; Lou Gerstner, Remarks to 1999 IBM Annual Meeting of Stockholders, Miami, Florida, April 27, 1999.

"Make the Right Decisions at the Right Time": Kathleen Sullivan and Waikiki Beach

Author's interview with Kathleen Sullivan, September 1999; John Hammond, Ralph Keeney, and Howard Raiffa, *Smart Choices: A Practical Guide to Making Better Decisions* (1998), Harvard Business School Press; Charalambos Aliprantis, *Games and Decision Making* (1999), Oxford University Press; C. Clayton, *Supreme Court Decision Making* (1998), University of Chicago Press; Terry Connolly, ed., *Judgment and Decision Making: An Interdisciplinary Reader* (1999), Cambridge University Press; Harry Greene, *Decision Making in Medicine* (1998), Harcourt Health; Reid Hastie, ed., *Inside the Juror: The Psychology of Juror Decision Making* (1994), Cambridge University Press; P. N. Johnson-Laird, *Reasoning and Decision Making* (1994), Basil Blackwell.

"Optimize Risk and Return": Jeff Skilling and Enron Corporation

Author's interview with Jeffrey Skilling, December 1999; Daniel Southerland, "You've Heard of Big Oil, This Is the Story of Big Gas . . . and It Begins with Enron Corp, Which Wants to Be No. 1 in the World." *Washington Post,* Feb. 4, 1996; Sharon Walsh, "A Hot and Cold New Investment Opportunity" *Washington Post,* July 4, 1998; Agis Salpukas, "A Culture of Trial, Despite Error," and "Firing Up an Idea Machine," *New York Times,* June 27, 1999; Carol Alexander, *Risk Management and Analysis* (1998), Wiley &

Sons; M. Doherty, *Integrated Risk Management* (2000), McGraw Hill; Ku-
latila Amram, *Real Options* (1998), Harvard Business School Press; Lenos
Trigeorgis, *Real Options: Managerial Flexibility and Strategy in Resource
Allocation* (1995), MIT Press.

"Fail Small and Early to Win Big Later": Dominic Fonti and Worldwide Plaza

Author's interview with Dominic Fonti, October 1999; Karl Sabbagh, *Sky-
scraper, The Making of a Building* (1989), Penguin Books. Barry Boehm, "A
Spiral Model of Software Development and Enhancement," *IEEE Com-
puter,* May 1988; Steven. S. Ross, *Construction Disasters* (1984), McGraw-
Hill; Lowell Arthur, *Rapid Evolutionary Development* (1992), Wiley &
Sons; Derek Dean and Robert Dvorak, "Do It, then Fix It: The Power of
Prototyping," *McKinsey Quarterly,* 1995, no. 4; Gene Bylinsky, "Industry's
Amazing Instant Prototypes," *Fortune,* Jan. 12, 1998; Rochelle Sharpe,
"How a Drug Approved by the FDA turned into a lethal failure," *Wall
Street Journal,* Sept. 30, 1998;

"Maintain an Edge": Paul Kaminski and the Stealth Program

Author's interview with Paul Kaminski, July 1999; George Wilson and Peter
Carlson, "Stealth Albatross," *Washington Post,* Oct. 29, 1995; Allan Afuah,
Innovation Management Strategies (1998), Oxford University Press; David
Audretsch, *Innovation and Industry Evolution* (1995), MIT Press; Freder-
ick Betz, *Managing Technical Innovation* (1997), Wiley & Sons; R. Kanter,
Innovation (1997), Harper Collins; Richard Rosenbloom, ed., *Engines of
Innovation* (1996), Harvard Business School Press; John Seely Brown, "Re-
search That Reinvents the Corporation," *McKinsey Quarterly,* 1992, no. 2;
Richard Foster, *Innovation* (1986), Summit Books; Don Kash, *Perpetual Innovation* (1989), Basic Books; Eric Von Hippel, *The Sources of Innovation*
(1988), Oxford University Press.

LIST OF FIGURES

Part V–Create the Solutions

Part VI–Deliver the Results

Guide to the Guide

INDEX